Reducing Stress in Schools

Reducing Stress in Schools

Restoring Connection and Community

MATHEW PORTELL
INGRID L. COCKHREN
TYISHA J. NOISE
JULIE KURTZ
JULIE NICHOLSON

HARVARD EDUCATION PRESS
CAMBRIDGE, MASSACHUSETTS

Copyright © 2025 by the President and Fellows of Harvard College

All rights reserved. No part of this publication may be reproduced or transmitted in any form or by any means, electronic or mechanical, including photocopy, recording, or any information storage and retrieval systems, without permission in writing from the publisher.

Paperback ISBN 9781682539552

Library of Congress Cataloging-in-Publication Data is on file.

Published by Harvard Education Press,
an imprint of the Harvard Education Publishing Group

Harvard Education Press
8 Story Street
Cambridge, MA 02138

Cover Design: Patrick Ciano
Cover Image: phokin via iStock

The typefaces in this book are Adobe Garamond Pro and Myriad Pro.

To my beloved family, whose unwavering support has been my anchor throughout my life. To the resilient students, dedicated staff, caring families, and vibrant community of Fall-Hamilton Elementary, whose stories have woven themselves into the fabric of this book. And to Dr. Taylor Fife, whose wisdom and guidance opened my eyes to the profound impact of trauma and inspired the journey that led to these pages. This book is a testament to our shared experiences, challenges, and triumphs. Thank you for being my inspiration and driving force.

—M. P.

My contributions to this work are dedicated to Yves, Zheke, and Savvy. I hope your school experiences are filled with love, support, connection, community, and learning. I hope the adults in your schools see YOU. I hope they see your full humanity, potential, and genius.

—I. C.

I would like to extend my gratitude to my first mentors, Jacob Edwards and Dr. Jamaal Williams, and Professor Raul Alarcon for seeing what I was capable of, opening doors and setting me free with support to always pursue what I do best. I would like to thank my family for always fanning my flames! And finally I would like to thank my two moms, Pastor Beverly, for raising me with a faith that gave me purpose; and Mom Flo, who put me back together again every time the call to this work broke me and never letting me forget what I was made to do.

—T. N.

I dedicate this to my entire family, especially my husband for lifelong grounding and support, and finally my mentor, Dr. Julie Nicholson, who saw something in me that I did not see that helped me shine brighter to do this important work.

—J. K.

To my students, whose provocative and courageous questions inspire me and compel us to build a world with more kindness and justice.

—J. N.

Finally, we dedicate this book to educators all over the world. We have immense gratitude for your tireless efforts. We recognize the power of one adult in the life a child to promote not just knowledge, but resilience, empathy, and hope. Your commitment is the beacon lighting the path to a world where all children can have a foundation of social and emotional health, with a promise of a more humane planet.

—Julie, Mathew, Tyisha, Ingrid, and Julie

Contents

	Foreword	ix
	Preface	xiii
INTRODUCTION		1
CHAPTER 1	The Neurobiology of Stress and Regulation of the Nervous System	25
CHAPTER 2	The Impact of Stress on Behavior	49
CASE STUDY 1	The System Is Ill Prepared for the Real Lives of Young People Who Walk Through the Door	81
CHAPTER 3	Creating School Environments That Strengthen Adults' Nervous System Regulation	89
CASE STUDY 2	"Either You're Going to Let Me Take You Off Work, or Your Body's Going to Take You Off of Work"	119
CHAPTER 4	Creating School Environments That Reduce Stress and Strengthen Students' Nervous System Regulation	125
CASE STUDY 3	"My Daddy Was Killed by the Cops": The Importance of Listening, Observation, and Flexibility in Reducing Children's Stress	167
CHAPTER 5	Rethinking Discipline and Classroom Management	177
CASE STUDY 4	"I Know Byron's Life Is Better Because We Decided to Love Him Instead of Expel Him"	203

CONCLUSION 211

Notes 215
Acknowledgments 227
About the Authors 229
Index 233

Foreword

As I sit down to write this foreword for *Reducing Stress in Schools: Restoring Connection and Community*, I am transported back to my thirty-three years as an educator, most notably to my tenure as the principal of Lincoln High School in Walla Walla, Washington. At Lincoln High, we enrolled students who were expelled from our traditional high school and those students who were failing and floundering in a large high school environment. Many of these students experienced emotional, physical, or sexual abuse. Upon my arrival, there was a palpable disdain for authority figures and a prevailing school culture where neither students nor educators felt safe.

My staff and I came together as we embarked on a profound journey to transform our school into a trauma-responsive environment, which garnered national attention due to a dramatic decrease in out-of-school suspensions, increased graduation rates, and more students advancing to postsecondary education. Once an old-school disciplinarian, a pivotal change occurred when I attended a conference on adverse childhood experiences (ACEs). There, Dr. John Medina, an affiliate associate professor in the University of Washington's bioengineering department, spoke about the effects of toxic stress on brain development. His insights deeply influenced my understanding of the trauma impacting our students, highlighting the urgent need for a more empathetic and trauma-informed approach in schools.

I came up with the "Power of One" as I connected the power of one caring adult in the life of a student. The research was clear: as educators, we needed a new approach in our schools. Our educational methods needed to evolve to better support our struggling students. This epiphany was a turning point in my leadership.

I had always believed that behavior was a choice and that it was my job to hold students accountable. However, this new knowledge led to a profound mindset shift. As the school leader, I was adamant that we were going to embark on a new direction supported by the research evidence. I told my staff, "We have to make big changes." They rallied behind me, and we started to build the plane as we were flying it.

The first and most significant change we implemented was recognizing the power of relationships for our students. In classrooms, teachers moved around, constantly checking in on kids—they taught from their feet, not from their seats. Staff seized every opportunity to connect positively with students walking in the halls. Comments like, "I love your pink hair; I wish I could have mine that way" became commonplace. I sought to create as many positive interactions with kids as possible each day. Upon arrival, we warmly greeted our students, wishing them a great day. I paid special attention to students like Aaron, who didn't want to be bothered by anybody. Every morning, I walked by him and said, "Good morning, Aaron—it's so good to have you here." It took weeks before I even got a grunt in response. But over time, he thrived, feeling loved and cared for at school.

We also changed our language to reflect our commitment to students, saying things like, "We will be like a dog on a bone with attendance because we love you that much." We taught students about their brains to help them understand what happens when they are stressed and their nervous systems are activated. They learned that it is impossible for anyone to problem-solve or absorb new knowledge when highly stressed. We advised them that if they felt like they were going to blow, they could come to my office and say, "I need a time out."

We began holding "student concerns" meetings twice a month, where we shifted the focus from disciplining "problem" kids to discussing those who needed additional support and creating action plans for them. These meetings proved to be incredibly impactful, the most significant of all our new practices, followed closely by ensuring that adults were highly visible and interactive with students.

We transformed our approach to school discipline. We shifted our focus to creating opportunities for positive interactions, connecting with students, and addressing the underlying causes of their challenging behaviors instead of resorting to suspensions and expulsions. When a student became disruptive, teachers were quick to intervene offering alternatives like, "Class isn't working today—how about taking a time out with Shelly to help you calm down?" or "You seem really upset. Would you like to speak to someone in the Health Center?" We realized as a staff that when students lash out, it's not personal; there is always an underlying story driving their behavior.

One memory particularly embodies our shift in disciplinary approach. One day, John, a student, was sent to me after blowing up at a teacher and dropping the F-bomb. Typically, the response at Lincoln High School—and, safe to say, at most high schools in this country—is automatic suspension. However, I chose not to take that road. Instead, I calmly told him, "I'm not going to talk to you until you calm down. I care too much about you to try to problem-solve with you while your brain is overwhelmed." It took about ten minutes, but once he was calm, I asked him, "What do you think caused you to tell your teacher to F off?" His reply was difficult to hear: "My dad's an alcoholic. He's broken promises my whole life. It's my sixteenth birthday today, and he didn't show up. Again." After he calmed down and shared his story, he realized, "I shouldn't have exploded at the teacher. I need to apologize."

At the end of our conversation, John expressed a desire to make things right. We agreed that he wouldn't be sent home but would apologize to his teacher and then have in-school suspension in a quiet, comforting room where he could talk about anything with the attending teacher, catch up on his homework, or just sit and think about how he might handle things differently in the future. As John left my office, he turned and said, "Thanks for talking with me." Although it wasn't an actual conversation, what mattered most was that I listened, asked him a meaningful question, and validated his feelings instead of reacting with punitive measures. With that approach, we connected and strengthened our relationship.

Since I created a safe and supportive environment for John to express his emotions and receive guidance, he experienced a transformative moment of connection and healing. John's willingness to address his emotions and offer a sincere apology highlighted the impact of building relationships based on trust and empathy. This experience, along with many others during my time at Lincoln High, reinforced the importance of emotional intelligence, self-reflection, and compassion in education. It demonstrated the effectiveness of adopting a trauma-responsive approach and prioritizing the well-being of both students and educators. This new disciplinary approach was so successful that I never again equated discipline with punishment or control. In my last two years at Lincoln High, we observed a significant improvement in students' emotional regulation and a substantial decrease in emotional explosions and outbursts.

Implementing these changes requires substantial energy, but it pays big dividends and the rewards will definitely come. When an entire staff wraps themselves around kids with circles of support, hope is developed through relationships. Accountability looks different because the focus is on teaching, not punishing, children. Adults teach children about emotional regulation and their responses to stress and their options when their nervous systems are activated. The approach profoundly affects school culture. Change takes time and collective effort; we cannot afford to cling to outdated mindsets. The research is clear, and it directs us away from traditional methods and toward practices that genuinely heal our students.

Reducing Stress in Schools: Restoring Connection and Community is a groundbreaking book that will be an invaluable resource for preK–12 teachers, administrators, paraprofessionals, and other school personnel aiming to transform their school cultures into school environments that promote connection, community, and regulation. Having witnessed the transformative effects of tackling educational challenges with compassion, I can attest to the profound impact of the strategies shared in this book. They skillfully address the effects of stress on the nervous system, behavior, and overall well-being, providing a deep dive into the neurobiology of stress and its regulation. They advocate for trauma-responsive education and call for a fundamental shift in our approach to discipline and classroom management. By emphasizing social-emotional learning, self-regulation, and student well-being, they guide readers to understand how to create nurturing environments that transform schools from sources of stress to sanctuaries of healing.

Reducing stress in schools requires a collective effort from teachers, administrators, policy makers, and stakeholders. Let's work together to build a brighter future for our students and educators, one that prioritizes their social-emotional health, well-being, and resilience to provide hope for the future. It's time to restore connection and community in our schools and create a safe haven for all. Use this wonderful book as a resource to accomplish your goals and to be the "Power of One."

—Jim Sporleder
National expert on trauma-informed education in schools
Former principal, Lincoln High School, location of the documentary
Paper Tigers
Coauthor of *The Trauma-Informed School: A Step-by-Step Implementation Guide for Administrators and School Personnel* (2016)

Preface

In the bustling world of education, everyone plays a pivotal role in shaping the future of our society. Educators (paraprofessionals, teachers, principals, administrators, and others) are the architects of knowledge, compassion, and inspiration, supporting students' development with unwavering dedication. Yet behind our cheerful smiles and contagious enthusiasm lies a profound challenge that often goes unnoticed—educator stress, compassion fatigue, and even direct or vicarious trauma. This book delves deep into the realms of these critical issues, shedding light on their causes, both systematic and historical; describing the consequences; and, most important, offering practical strategies to mitigate them.

Educators, without a doubt, are the heartbeat of any educational institution. Our passion for teaching and learning and our commitment to our students are unmatched, but the pressures that we face are equally unparalleled. The modern educational landscape is rife with relentless demands—juggling teaching responsibilities, administrative tasks, assessments, and constant evaluations. On top of that, the complexities brought by the increase in school shootings, active shooter drills, the COVID-19 pandemic, and many other factors.

Despite our unwavering dedication, many educators silently suffer from the overwhelming weight of their responsibilities, leading to stress that seeps into their personal lives. Educator stress is not merely a personal concern; it reverberates through the classroom and affects students' learning experiences, school environments, and so much more. Stressed educators and students need systems that support strong, stable, and nurturing learning environments that allow all of them to meet their fullest potential as leaders and learners.

This book is an earnest attempt to bring student and educator stress into the spotlight and to offer viable solutions to alleviate its impact. It recognizes that addressing this issue goes beyond individual coping mechanisms—it requires a systemic approach. We will explore the multifaceted nature of educator stress, encompassing external factors such as administrative policies, workloads, and societal expectations. Equally important, we will also examine internal factors such as systemic self and collective care, emotional resilience, and professional learning, as well as how each directly affects the student educational experience.

Through meticulously researched insights, interviews with experienced educators, and evidence-based practices, this book aims to empower teachers, school administrators, policy makers, and stakeholders with the knowledge and tools to support the well-being of our educators and students. The ultimate goal is to foster an environment where educators, students, parents, and the community can thrive and continue to inspire the generations that they shape.

Addressing school stress is a collective effort, requiring collaboration among all stakeholders. Teachers and school staff play a significant role in mitigating and eliminating toxic stress in classrooms through the practices that they teach and utilize with students. School administrators must recognize the importance of teacher well-being and serve to create nurturing environments that promote a healthy work-life balance. Policy makers must recognize the significance of investing in teacher support systems and professional learning. Parents and the community must appreciate the profound impact of their role and the influence that all educators have on their children's lives, offering them the understanding and support that they deserve.

As you embark on this journey through the pages of this book, I encourage you to approach it with an open mind and a compassionate heart. May the insights shared within these words ignite a flame of change, paving the way for a brighter, more sustainable future for our educators and, by extension, for the generations they nurture—our students.

In closing, I extend my heartfelt gratitude to all educators for their selfless dedication and unwavering commitment. Your tireless efforts to shape minds and hearts inspire us to strive for a better tomorrow. Together, let us embark on the path to understanding and addressing teacher stress, for the future of education and society depends on it.

—Mathew Portell

INTRODUCTION

At the very beginning of my principal career, I walked down the hall with a puffed-up chest. I sent kids home when they misbehaved, and we restrained kids almost weekly. This is what I thought principals should do. It's what I was taught to do. Then I attended a lecture on adverse childhood experiences, neuroscience, and their connection to students' behavior. I remember the feeling, the tightness in my chest, and what I was thinking: "This is it. This is what I experience every day. This is what I see with kids." I could feel my heart just exploding. And I broke. I broke as an educator. I broke as a principal. I broke as a human being because I realized that not only was I not doing what was right for kids, I was actually hurting kids. I learned that what we were doing was about compliance and based on a lack of our understanding and preparation to meet kids where they were. What we were doing to kids wasn't about what we should be doing for kids. Writing an office referral wasn't an intervention; it wasn't a relationship builder. Sending a child home was taking a child that already felt disconnected and creating even more stress and isolation for them. We come to a crossroads in our careers where we are given new information and we have two options: we can act upon it and do something different, or we can continue forward on the path we are already on. I knew I had to do better as an educator and as a principal. As Maya Angelou states, "Do the best you can until you know better. Then, when you know better, do better." If I continued forward with the way I was trained, it would be malpractice. If we know what we're doing isn't in the best interest of the kids, not just in the moment, but in the long term, then we have to change what we're doing. We just have to. So that is how I began my journey toward a new way of practicing leadership—a journey rooted in empathy and understanding.
—Mathew Portell (M. P.), principal, Fall-Hamilton Elementary

Despite decades of research demonstrating the negative impacts of punitive and stress- and trauma-inducing school environments, authoritarian control, use of reward charts, and harsh punishment of students, these practices persist in many schools today.[1] As recounted in the opening quote, suspending and restraining children are what so many principals are taught they are "supposed to do." Yet the need to disrupt these traditional approaches to schooling has never been more pressing.

Toxic stress and trauma among students, families, and school staff have reached crisis levels. Rates of anxiety, depression, and school violence continue to increase, while teacher and administrator burnout rates are near 50 percent nationally.[2] There is an urgent need to reduce stress in schools and to create educational environments that foster a sense of belonging and help educators, students, and families to feel safe.

Fortunately, advances in neuroscience have shed light on the interdependent relationship between stress and its impact on learning, teaching, and educational environments.[3] These insights offer a pathway for reimagining school environments to be more humanizing for both students and educators. This includes guidance to create the healthy conditions that students need to learn in the company of caring adults and that educators need to be effective with students who are entering schools with historically high levels of stress, trauma, and mental health and behavioral challenges.

The future of our children and the strength and retention of our public-school workforce hinge upon our capacity to adapt to a new paradigm in schools, where we create educational environments that prioritize holistic learning, stress reduction, and well-being. Understanding and applying the science of stress, trauma, and resilience in schools can help educators "do better."

URGENT NEED TO REDUCE STRESS IN SCHOOLS

Historic levels of stress and trauma are affecting children, youth, adults, and communities across the United States. The last few years have seen the levels of individual and collective trauma in society increase. The COVID-19 pandemic has been described as the most collective trauma of our lifetime.[4] A recent American Psychological Association survey found nearly two-thirds of respondents reporting that their lives had been permanently changed by the pandemic, and a large proportion of the country has been living in "sustained survival mode."[5] A conservative estimate of the current death toll in the United States is over a million lives lost to date from COVID, and more than 204,000 US children under eighteen have lost a primary or secondary caregiver, with even more lives affected by debilitating medical complications and economic instability.[6]

Exacerbating these hardships, racial hate crimes and assaults on the LGBTQIA+ community have reached alarming levels and both housing insecurity and hunger/food insecurity are at record levels.[7] Further, 2022–2023 had a record high number of school shootings and 40 percent of educators say that they have fears of a mass homicide event taking place at their schools.[8] Add to these factors distress related to immigration, migration, and/or deportation, overdose deaths from opioids and fentanyl, extreme political polarization, catastrophic environmental disasters, and ongoing economic concerns.[9] Our nation and schools are at a breaking point. It is up to us to advocate for the change necessary to re-create and reform our schools and revitalize those who serve in them.

All this increased stress and trauma is entering the doors of our preK–12 school classrooms on a daily basis. A 2021 nationally representative RAND survey of 2,360 teachers and 1,540 principals found that both teachers and principals are more stressed, burned out, and depressed than other working adults, and many have either already left the profession or report that they plan to exit within the next few years.[10] Almost 75 percent of teachers and 85 percent of principals report having frequent job-related stress, compared to just one-third of working adults. Further, 59 percent of teachers and 48 percent of principals say that they're burned out, compared to 44 percent of other workers.[11] It is not surprising, given these conditions, that educator job satisfaction is at an all-time low.[12]

Closely connected to educators' concerns are the negative impacts that the pandemic has had on students' development, learning, and well-being. Recent data show that 80 percent of US public schools report that the pandemic negatively affected student behavior and socioemotional development, that students' behavioral challenges have increased and students' mental health has declined.[13] In fact, the majority of public schools (70 percent) report that the number of students who sought or required mental health services increased as a result of the pandemic.[14]

Advocating for stricter, authoritarian control and harsher punishment in schools will only worsen student behavior issues. Harsh discipline makes students feel unsafe and threatened, heightening their stress, which often manifests in escalating behavior challenges. Moreover, due to relational contagion, individuals absorb and reflect the emotional states of others around them.[15] When students and teachers are dysregulated and stressed, it amplifies stress schoolwide via this contagion effect. Reactive punitive practices will fuel a self-perpetuating cycle that undermines learning and well-being.

The only way to stop this spiraling multiplier effect is to reduce the level of stress—individually and collectively—in schools. Rather than suppression through force, students need environments where they feel both safe and supported. This is the only way to reduce the activation of their stress response systems and the display of survival behaviors (fight, flight, freeze, and fawn). As Bruce Perry, renowned neuroscientist and trauma expert, states, for students to learn effectively—especially those living with high levels of stress—they need to be in the presence of calm, regulated adults in calm and regulated environments intentionally designed to reinforce safety and to provide opportunities to engage in nervous-system *regulating* activities throughout the school day.[16] This is why the solutions needed to shore up learning loss, reduce students' challenging behaviors, and create positive learning and working environments for both students and educators share one underlying requirement: the need to substantially *reduce the level of stress in our schools*.

Educators Are the Emergency Responders of Many, Many Children's Lives

One of the coauthors, Dr. Tyisha Noise, invites educators to recognize their important role as the first responders in many students' lives. She explains:

> We must care for educators the way we care for our other first responders. This is not a broken leg or resuscitation from a heart attack. This is our children's lives. Their health, their support, every day. We are shaping the next generation who will lead the country and the world that we live in.
>
> In medicine, people specialize for a reason. When we talk about serving in highly impacted communities, we also need to talk about specialized training for educators who are going to go into those environments because of what we are asking people to carry. When people train to be a therapist or a psychologist, the first thing they tell you is: every therapist needs a therapist. Every psychologist needs their own therapist. Because when you become the receptacle for so much stress and trauma, educators need to have a safe place to direct it.
>
> What we are seeing with the constant flight of teachers—coming in with enthusiasm and then leaving after two or three years—is that they are

burned out. It's not because they are not committed; it is not because they don't love their work. It is not because they don't love children. *It's because there is no system of support.* Asking somebody to walk in and teach the ABCs or literature or history is one thing, but asking somebody to carry this level of stress and trauma is another.

We can't ask teachers to pour into children things that we do not pour into the teachers. We can't ask administrators to pour into teachers things that we do not pour into the administrators. Because if we do—which is what we're doing now—we run the constant risk of asking many people to pour from an empty cup and giving them no place to go where they can get those cups refilled. And then what inevitably happens is that they leave the profession.

THE NEED FOR A PARADIGM SHIFT: UNAPOLOGETICALLY DISRUPTING EDUCATIONAL SYSTEMS

Historically, our education system has been strongly shaped by behaviorist approaches to classroom management, with a belief that bribes, rewards, and punishments including reprimands, loss of privileges, detention, suspensions, and expulsions can be effective techniques for decreasing undesirable student behavior. By punishing unwanted behavior, the assumption is that students can be conditioned to avoid these behaviors in the future. Threats and punishments, when combined with positive reinforcements for desired behaviors, are historically assumed to be the most effective approaches to shaping student conduct in schools. In reality, the research evidence is clear: there are adverse consequences associated with a traditional behaviorist approach to classroom management and school discipline. *Punishment exacerbates stress and trauma, which exacerbates stress-related behaviors in students.*

Effective learning and accountability (academically and behaviorally) increase with a foundation of safety, positive relationships, affirming and supportive learning environments, and a commitment to teach social and emotional skills. Adopting a commitment to reduce stress in your school does not mean that students are free to behave however they please, with no accountability. It does mean that if students are having a rough day, their need for regulation and connection will be met first so they have the capacity to think, reason, and problem-solve. Further, in schools committed to reducing stress for students and staff, instead of punishing students, educators *teach them strategies to calm their nervous systems*. Students are taught to understand how stress affects their thinking and behavior and how they can use various deescalation strategies to help them navigate overwhelming feelings and challenging situations.

Consider that in schools, we have emergency earthquake, tornado, fire, and active shooter safety drills. We also need to do emotional emergency drills where we help educators and students to prepare for stressful physiological reactions or emotional emergencies. This can be done only through intentionally teaching and practicing such skills as self-awareness, self-regulation strategies, and healthy problem-solving skills. Unless students and adults practice these skills over and over when their nervous systems are calm, they will not be equipped to handle challenging situations in optimally healthy ways. As a result, schools committed to reducing stress make time for teaching self-awareness and practicing skills for regulating the nervous system on a regular basis. Schools that prioritize reducing stress for students will ultimately see fewer dysregulated behaviors and will increase students' capacity to learn academics and social emotional skills, as well as reflecting more readily on the consequences of their choices and behaviors.

Students' Invisible Backpacks

Students enter schools each day wearing an "invisible backpack" filled with unseen stressors, traumas, and cumulative risk factors that affect their brains, behaviors, and capacity for regulation.[17]

- Some students walk to school through unsafe neighborhoods.
- Some live in public housing or in very poor rural areas where there is very little safe ground between their homes and the school door.
- Some attend schools with high gang activity, and for them, walking down the hallway between classes is not safe and a trip to the bathroom at the wrong time of day is dangerous.
- Some students arrive having slept in a car for three nights; they are hungry and feel sick.

> Our students are affected by the interplay of a thousand things that we cannot always see. Poverty, homelessness, hunger, lack of safety, racialized experiences, discrimination based on having an accent, living with someone with (diagnosed or undiagnosed) mental illness, missing incarcerated loved ones, and managing grief and the loss of loved ones, especially since COVID. These are just some of the stressors that students carry in their invisible backpacks every single day. Too often, we ask them to leave these stressors at the door and behave. But this is impossible. So those of us who have chosen to serve children and families must recognize the needs in front of us and intervene in ways that can nurture, support, and uplift our communities instead of asking stressed, hurting, and dysregulated students to comply and behave or be punished or expelled.

Recognizing the invisible stressors that students carry is important for cultivating empathy first and then intentionally creating a culture that prioritizes stress-reducing and trauma-informed schools. This acknowledgment enables educators to respond with empathy rather than harsh discipline, which only exacerbates stress levels. Understanding that dysregulated behavior often signals an underlying distress within the nervous system empowers schools to provide support and implement strategies to alleviate student stress. By doing so, students can more effectively engage in school, both socially and academically, and they acquire the capacity to gain perspective about the consequences of their behavior, as well as to make alternative, healthier choices.

INTERACTING LAYERS OF STRESS, TRAUMA, RESILIENCE, AND HEALING

Most books on reducing stress in schools do not acknowledge the impacts and complex layers of historical trauma in communities. To holistically examine the complex web of interconnected layers of historical and contemporary stress and trauma in our school systems, as well as imagining how we can promote resilience, healing, and well-being for students and educators, we draw from a conceptual model—Interacting Layers of Trauma and Healing—developed by the RYSE Center, a youth voice institution in Richmond, California. This model builds upon Urie Bronfenbrenner's bioecological model, which highlights that human development and daily experiences are shaped not only by individual factors, but also by broader societal systems, structures, and values and the inequitable distribution of power.[18]

The RYSE model analyzes trauma and healing across four distinct levels, each affecting students and schools in different ways.[19] We have adapted the original model for application in preK–12 education settings (see figure I.1). The nested circles communicate that many factors represented across different layers of influence intersect in a dynamic manner over time to contribute to students' and educators' experiences of stress and trauma in schools on a daily basis.

We briefly introduce each of the four levels included in the RYSE model—(1) Individual and Interpersonal, (2) School and Community, (3) Systems, and (4) History and Structures—below and describe how each relates to the project of reducing stress in schools.

FIGURE INTRO.1 Adapted RYSE model: Interacting layers of stress, trauma, resilience, and healing

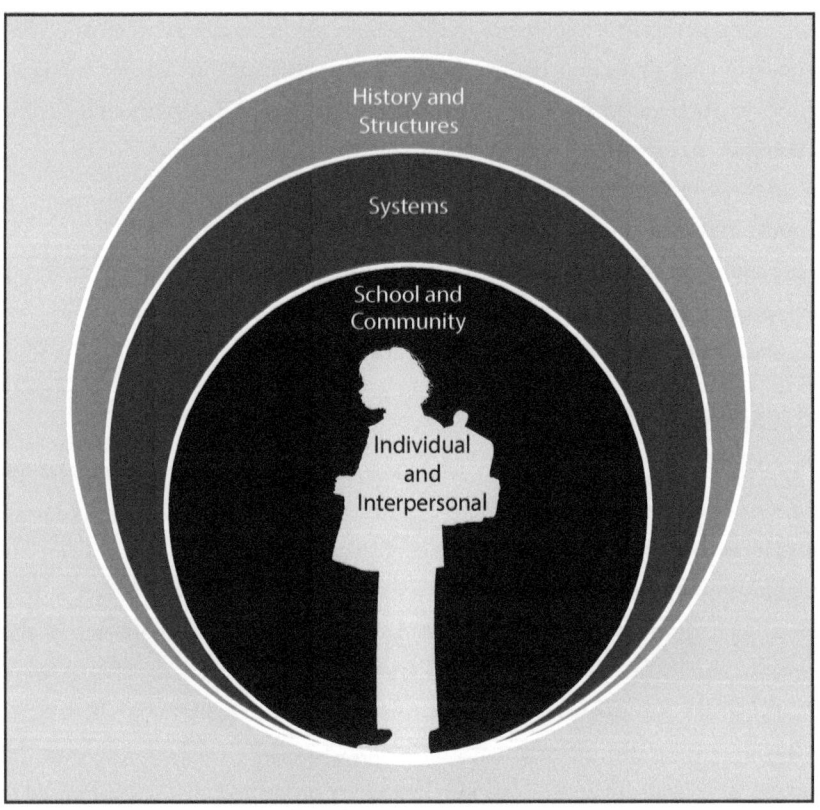

Individual and Interpersonal Factors **That Contribute to Stress in Schools or Strengthen Students' and Educators' Well-Being**

- **Toxic stress and trauma.** At this level, adverse childhood experiences (ACEs) such as substance abuse, parental mental illness, racism, poverty, domestic violence, and abuse in the home can shape an individual's beliefs, behaviors, and identity. These experiences can also affect future generations through the transgenerational transmission of trauma, which may be evidenced in epigenetic changes—heritable changes in gene expression not associated with alterations in deoxyribonucleic acid (DNA) sequences (see the box titled "Social Epigenetics"). Societal discussions about trauma often do not move beyond the individual level. Yet personal trauma does not occur in isolation. Most interventions for trauma in schools concentrate on these individual manifestations and expressions of distress, aiming to address students' challenging behaviors. Although this approach is essential, interventions that solely focus on individual behaviors are incomplete. They do not address the other layers of influence represented in this model.
- **Reducing stress, fostering resilience, and promoting healing and well-being.** Reducing stress and healing trauma are grounded in nurturing connections. Educators, staff, peers, and communities play a pivotal role in providing a web of supportive relationships that can foster resilience for students and adults, creating a sense of hope and joy and promoting the skills and capacities that they need to overcome adversity.

Social Epigenetics

Social epigenetics examines how physical, built, and social environments influence gene expression and health outcomes at the individual and community levels.[20] This emerging field helps us understand how stressors and buffers literally "get under our skin" and create health disparities across lifespans and generations.[21] The process of stress and buffers affecting genetic expression is explained as follows:

> During development, the DNA that makes up our genes accumulates chemical marks that determine how much or little of the genes is expressed. This collection of chemical marks is known as the "epigenome." The different

experiences children have rearrange those chemical marks. . . . The epigenome can be affected by positive experiences, such as supportive relationships and opportunities for learning . . . or negative influences, such as stressful life circumstances . . . leave a unique epigenetic "signature" on the genes. These signatures can be temporary or permanent and both types affect how easily the genes are switched on or off.[22]

Researchers have proposed various mechanisms for how experiences influence genetic expression. Hicken, Keene, and Bound, along with Geronimus, have hypothesized that chronic stress becomes embodied and impairs health and well-being over time.[23] This stress alters the physiology of the stress response system—biological changes linked to negative health outcomes.[24]

Recent research suggests that there may be the potential to modify or even reverse the negative impacts of early adversity, leading to epigenetic adaptation. Although there is a need for more definitive research, some studies suggest that supportive therapeutic caregiving and nurturing environments may play an important role in reprogramming epigenetic adaptations.[25] More research is needed to establish causal evidence regarding these hypothesized relationships.

The emerging field of social epigenetics has profound implications for how educators approach supporting students experiencing adversity. While early environments shape genetic expression, research shows that nurturing schools and caring teachers can help rewrite biological scripts. Educators' consistent support may likely affect the chemical markers that will help students cultivate coping skills and resilience. By providing stability and fostering a sense of belonging, educators can buffer stress and counteract the epigenetic risk factors for students. Evidence is mounting that caring relationships and stress-reducing environments have the power to biologically reprogram harmful epigenetic changes that result from early adversity.

School and Community Factors **That Contribute to Stress in Schools or Strengthen Students' and Educators' Well-Being**

- **Toxic stress and trauma.** Community-level trauma arises from chronic stressors within schools and the broader community that adversely affect children and adults. In schools, toxic stress results from such experiences as bullying, teacher/administrator bias, microaggressions, racism and/or racialized experiences, school shootings and gun violence, unprofessional or harmful behaviors from teachers or administrators (e.g., exclusionary discipline practices, corporal punishment). Within the larger community, exposure to interpersonal, domestic, and community violence creates an atmosphere of constant threat for some students, contributing to lifelong health risks.[26] Community-level distress disproportionately burdens communities of color and neighborhoods facing generational poverty, as they endure higher levels of violent crime, underfunded schools, scarce green spaces, and heavy police presence—forces that create unsafe conditions and deny resources and opportunities.

- **Reducing stress, fostering resilience, and promoting healing and well-being.** Addressing the impact of harm-inducing environments on mental health necessitates a school culture that builds resilience and promotes healing.[27] This includes empowering students to understand and challenge racism, nurturing strong racial identities and cultural awareness through curricula that celebrate and affirm students' diverse cultures and histories, actively working to reduce feelings of internalized oppression and self-doubt from developing, and ensuring that all students have a voice in decision-making in school processes that affect them.

Systemic Factors **That Contribute to Stress in Schools or Strengthen Students' and Educators' Well-Being**

- **Toxic stress and trauma.** Systemic racism inflicts trauma through historically inequitable systems and policies that continue to harm marginalized communities of color. From slavery to sharecropping, Jim Crow laws to redlining, the war on drugs to anti-immigrant policies, institutions continue to disproportionately harm Black and Indigenous people, as well as people of color. Unequal education remains a profound manifestation of systemic racism. Redlining and funding formulas rooted in property taxes consign many schools in marginalized neighborhoods to be underresourced. Biased testing and harsh discipline drive the school-to-prison pipeline. Eurocentric curricula erase diverse cultures' histories. In addition, free or reduced lunch policies that shame economically disadvantaged children, zero tolerance policies, bias in gifted education placement, and punitive

Black hair policies are examples of discriminatory policies that constrain opportunities for students of color and perpetuate systemic racism in our schools.
- **Reducing stress, fostering resilience, and promoting healing and well-being.** Implementing healing-centered and restorative policies and practices is key to reducing stress in educational settings. Policies and practices that are adaptable and cocreated with student and community input can create a safer and more equitable environment for learning. When policies are inclusive and crafted with direct input from those that they affect, they are more likely to act in the best interests of students and the communities served by the school without perpetuating historical biases. Reducing stress in schools requires increasing collective care processes in schools and educational systems.

Policies that mandate trauma-informed care, peer support, and peer learning can facilitate collective care and well-being in schools. This is also the case for policies that ensure realistic workloads for students and school personnel. In addition, diversity, equity, and inclusion (DEI), antibullying, and identity-affirming policies directly affect students' sense of safety and belonging. Policies that support community partnerships and family involvement facilitate collective care and well-being by creating a sense of connection with the larger community.

Historical and Structural Factors That Contribute to Stress in Schools or Strengthen Students' and Educators' Well-Being

- **Toxic stress and trauma.** The very building of the United States rests on oppression—from genocide and colonization to slavery and resource extraction. The intergenerational trauma of this nation-building has historically affected, and continues to affect, society and our schools in many ways. For example, scientific racism (a body of research asserting that a racial hierarchy existed within the human species), which spread throughout the eighteenth and nineteenth centuries, is perpetuated in our schools today through deficit views of students, families, and communities of color in education research, interventions, and persistent achievement and opportunity gaps between children of color and their white counterparts.[28] These gaps in achievement and opportunity are related to scientific racism because, throughout history, this body of research has

been used to justify oppression, enslavement, segregation, antiliteracy efforts, wage theft, and other harms perpetrated upon people of color.
- **Reducing stress, fostering resilience, and promoting healing and well-being.** Healing at this level involves addressing the historical and structural causes of trauma, the legacies of oppression, and the need for system change through the provision of reparations, redistribution of resources, and strengthening multiracial solidarity.

We employ the RYSE model as a lens to envision schools that are committed to intentionally reducing stress, breaking cycles of historical trauma and oppression, and creating environments where students and educators—particularly those from historically marginalized groups—feel affirmed, safe, and supported to succeed. In this book, we analyze four case studies—three drawn from the firsthand experiences of Noise—using the RYSE framework to demonstrate its application in diverse educational settings.

POSITIVE CHILDHOOD EXPERIENCES

The paradigm shift that we champion here is also about intentionally supporting students to have positive childhood experiences (PCEs) while they are at school.[29] Research is expanding on the impact of PCEs, and their important influence on children's development and their well-being across the lifespan. Preliminary findings suggest that PCEs may serve to reduce or even prevent long-term harm from ACEs.[30] Emerging research examining PCEs has documented the following:

- Having positive experiences in school and in one's neighborhood—as well as feeling safe—can significantly improve an individual's mental and physical health outcomes throughout their lifespan, regardless of their history of adversity.
- Having experiences of positive relationships and feelings of belonging in childhood is a protective factor that reduces the risk of emotional distress, suicidal ideation, and substance use in adulthood.
- Improving safety in schools and neighborhoods is an important way to enhance mental and physical health outcomes throughout the lifespan.

The goal of our book is not only to mitigate stress in schools, but also to be intentional about helping children to have positive experiences. There are several specific PCEs that can be supported in school environments, which are described next.

Having at Least Two Nonparent Adults Who Genuinely Care

Having genuine connections with nonparent adults, such as teachers and administrators, can be invaluable in the following ways:

- Teachers, administrators, and other school personnel in a child's life can provide essential advice, knowledge, and context during the sensitive periods of social and emotional development that occur during the school-age years.[31]
- Schools can provide an environment where school personnel can support students to see failures and setbacks as growth opportunities.
- Teachers, administrators, and other school personnel can play a significant role for students by offering emotional support and empathy, engaging in coregulation, and modeling resilience for students.

Being Supported by Friends

Resilience in children is fostered by nurturing relationships with family, nonfamily adults, and peers, as follows:[32]

- When it comes to peer relationships, teachers and administrators can play a role by assisting students in gaining interpersonal and other skills needed to improve and maintain relationships, such as conflict resolution, negotiation, and teamwork.
- Systemically, schools can accomplish this by operationalizing peer-to-peer learning, establishing student clubs and councils, creating an identity-affirming student environment, and fostering an overall environment of support among students.

Feelings of Belonging in School

Inclusion, belonging, and feeling valued are important for all students in school. And PCE science documents that adolescence is a particularly sensitive period of social, emotional, and physical development.[33] Safe, stable, and nurturing high school environments that are responsive to the needs of students at this critical stage of development can play a significant role in students experiencing a sense of belonging.

- Schools can accomplish this by creating an environment where student voices are heard and their experiences are validated. In school settings, this can be accomplished by surveying students, engaging in student listening sessions, and affirming the various identities (Black, Indigenous, and other people of color [BIPOC], LGBTQIA+, etc.) within the student body.
- Schoolwide connectedness can be cultivated when schools provide a variety of opportunities for students and school personnel to have conversations, share experiences and perspectives, and learn about others' cultures and backgrounds.
- School personnel can actively address bullying and microaggressions.

Feeling Safe and Protected by an Adult at Home

Although this particular PCE happens within the home and neighborhood settings, school personnel are positioned to ensure that the community is accountable for a child's safety and well-being, as follows:

- If a child is experiencing a lack of physical, emotional, or psychological safety at home, school personnel are often the first to recognize it, and schools have clear policies and procedures to begin the process of connecting families with resources or assistance.
- Educators can promote programs and activities that involve parents and caregivers, fostering stronger bonds and reinforcing positive, protective relationships at home. Examples include family engagement nights, parenting workshops, or providing resources on effective communication and conflict resolution strategies.

The Ability to Feel Supported by and Talk to Family Members or Caregivers about Feelings

Emotional safety within families is essential to healthy child development. Personal relationships are a significant source of resilience and healing, and children who feel safe discussing their feelings with family members are set up for success in their relationships across the lifespan.[34] However, not all children experience this opportunity outside of school. As a result, the following is the case:

- School personnel can encourage students to share their feelings and confer with families and caregivers to ensure their receptiveness. For example, teachers, administrators, and other school personnel can facilitate a child's ability to discuss sensitive issues, such as school performance and bullying, with their family and caregivers.
- School counselors and therapists, when available to students and their families, can play a significant role in creating a sense of safety between students and their families.
- If a lack of familial support is apparent, school counselors and therapists can either assist families in fostering a supportive home environment or refer families to needed support within the community.

Participating in Community Traditions

Schools are embedded within the larger community and host many common community traditions like sporting events, school dances, graduations, and extracurricular activities. These experiences are likely to become autobiographical memories for students that hold great emotional value and have the capacity to shape their identity.[35]

- Due to the importance of these types of events and experiences, it is essential that schools engage in these types of events in a culturally responsive manner. This can be accomplished by implementing student feedback concerning events and by utilizing interpreters/translators and highlighting students' backgrounds and cultural traditions at the events. These practices can ensure that students feel included and represented in school community traditions.
- Invite local community leaders, elders, and cultural representatives to participate in school events and share their traditions, stories, and cultural practices. This involvement not only enriches the events with diverse perspectives but also helps students build connections with their broader community, reinforcing a sense of belonging and cultural pride.

Schools that intentionally promote positive experiences for students provide them with buffers to their stress and trauma while reducing the potential of longer-term adverse outcomes. PCEs also bring more regulated nervous systems. Students who are more regulated are better able to engage with and learn in school and have fewer dysregulated behaviors.

> **Advice for Educators Who Want to Get Started with Reducing Stress in Their Schools**
>
> Taking an intentional step to reduce stress in your school requires time, intention, and a growth mindset. District leaders, school administrators, teachers, and staff must persist over time and remember that there will be leaps forward and steps backward on the journey to changing your school culture. There are many starting points to begin this work, and each school will carve its own pathway to reducing stress and strengthening regulation. The following are the steps that one school, Fall-Hamilton Elementary in Nashville, Tennessee, took as it aimed to create a school that was more humanizing, joyful, and safe for students and staff:
>
> - **Know the "why."** The initial step was building a collective understanding about why this shift in school culture was so important. Surfacing this rationale—the "why"—led the staff to write a set of core beliefs that defined what they stood for as a school (see figure I.2). These beliefs were essential to guide their discussions, including some difficult decisions that they had to make as a staff (e.g., "This is what we value, but our actions don't align. What support does everyone need to succeed?"). The core beliefs also guided the school's hiring processes, as all applicants for open positions received a letter from the principal that outlined the school's core beliefs (e.g., "We don't send children home, and here is why . . ."). The staff agreed that specific skills and teaching strategies could be taught to new staff, but shifting their values and mindsets would be much harder.
> - **Learn the neuroscience.** The principal, coauthor Mathew Portell, ensured that the entire staff learned about the science of stress, trauma, and resilience so there would be a shared vocabulary and collective understanding about the impact of stress on students' and adults' behaviors. They all learned what stress-related behaviors (fight, flight,

freeze, and fawn) look like in schools and classrooms and the different strategies that are effective for calming the nervous system.

- **Support the staff (not just the students).** A commitment was made to intentionally support the adults—teachers and staff—to ensure that they had opportunities to express their ideas, feedback, concerns, and lessons throughout the process of shifting the school culture.
- **Be forgiving.** A mantra described as "preforgiveness" was embraced. This meant that the principal and other school administrators assumed that staff were doing their best in challenging conditions. They would extend preforgiveness whenever teachers or staff would make mistakes (e.g., "I believe that you are operating at your capacity. No matter what the situation, you are 'preforgiven' if you are upset, irritated, frustrated, or not otherwise at your best. You made a mistake. That's OK. Just come and tell me, and we can figure out how to fix it. I'm not going to write you up."). This approach alleviated pressure and fostered trust and collective learning.
- **Teach skills.** As they strengthened their understanding of how stress affects students' nervous systems and behavior, the staff began to shift from a focus on rewards and punishments to explicitly teaching self-awareness and self-regulation skills. They committed to helping students understand that stress-related behavior is a natural human response to stress. In addition, they began to teach students and families about what happens in their brains and bodies when they were experiencing stress and a range of coping and deescalation/regulation skills that they could develop.
- **Recognize that it's a learning journey.** The staff reinforced the important idea that what they were learning to implement was not a specific curriculum or program, with checklists and pacing guides, but instead was a shift in mindset and philosophy that was in many ways a paradigm shift from traditional approaches to public education. Like all transformative learning, it would take time and should be understood as an ongoing learning process that involved taking risks, making progress, and experiencing wins, mistakes, and failures. Yet the goal is to strive to do what's best for kids in a way that is informed by neuroscience.

FIGURE INTRO.2 The Fall-Hamilton core beliefs

LEADERS
THE FALL-HAMILTON CORE BELIEFS
We are a family of educators, students, families, and community members who collaborate to support one another in the following shared beliefs:

L	E	A	D	E	R	S
Leaders Who Learn	Equitable, Safe Learning Community	Advocate and Act	Diversity and Genius	Empathy and Respect	Relationships	Shared Accountability
We are a community of resilient, responsible, and engaged learners.	We ensure a safe and equitable learning community built upon clear communication.	We foster opportunities to help one another discover our passions and use our voices to advocate for ourselves and others.	We value and honor the innate genius and the unique differences in each of us.	We show empathy and respect by valuing each individual's inherent dignity and worth.	We build strong, stable, and nurturing relationships as the foundation for social, emotional, and academic growth.	We partner with one another to invest in the future of our students.

Fall-Hamilton Mission: At FHE, we will grow as a learning community by working together to discover our passions so everyone can meet their fullest potential as LEADERS!

Reflection/Discussion Question

- Reading about Fall-Hamilton's process for getting started, what do you think your strengths and learning edges are for you as an individual? For your school? For your district?

EVIDENCE BASE INFORMING THIS BOOK

We draw from several bodies of research to inform our discussion of the paradigm that we need to work for collectively to reduce stress significantly in schools.

Trauma-Informed Practice

We pull from professional literature on trauma-informed practice, integrating findings from empirical research across multiple disciplines—including neuroscience, education, psychology, and behavioral health—with effective clinical practices in mental health. Drawing from our collective expertise and the most influential frameworks for trauma-informed care for children and adults, we distilled several core principles of trauma-responsive practice.[36] These principles, which are interwoven throughout the text, lay the groundwork for reducing stress and enhancing nervous system regulation, thereby creating an optimal environment for learning.

Humanizing Education

Humanizing education is a pedagogical approach that emphasizes creating learning environments where students feel safe, respected, and valued at school. Dehumanization is a significant driver of poor mental health outcomes, and humanizing learning environments can be a powerful preventative tool to protect the mental health of children in our nation's schools.[37] Humanizing education aims for students to see learning as relevant to their lives and daily experiences. There is an emphasis on creativity and critical thinking, child and youth empowerment, and policies and practices that do no harm.[38]

Whole Child Education

Whole child education is based on a recognition that students' cognitive, social, emotional, and physical well-being are deeply interconnected, as reflected in neuroscience research and the science of learning.[39] This approach is grounded in decades of empirical evidence on the types of nurturing environments and experiences that children need to thrive. Whole child education fosters strong adult-student relationships, culturally responsive curricula, restorative practices instead of exclusionary discipline, integrated support systems that are responsive to students' needs (e.g., mental health, counseling, and health care), and high-quality extended learning opportunities. The whole child philosophy moves beyond a narrow focus on academic skills to focus on the more comprehensive developmental needs of children, including the need to reduce their stress and increase their feelings of safety in school.

Racial Justice Education

In environments that aim to reduce students' and educators' stress, there is a clear recognition of both historical and cultural traumas. Addressing the enduring effects of such traumas within educational systems is essential to creating schools that are both trauma-responsive and humanizing. This process requires a deliberate focus on improving racial justice. As Benson and Fiarman observe, schools are inherently racialized spaces where racism itself must be acknowledged as a form of trauma.[40] The interactions between teachers and students are often influenced by race and gender, necessitating an educational approach that not only prioritizes humanization and healing, but also actively confronts racism and bias.

Healing-Centered Engagement

We also draw from Dr. Shawn Ginwright's work on healing centered engagement. His approach shifts the focus from a treatment-based model that views toxic stress, trauma, and harm as isolated experiences to an engagement model that is strengths-based, emphasizes a collective view of stress-reduction and healing, and recenters culture as a central aspect of well-being.[41] A healing-centered approach acknowledges that well-being comes from participating in transforming the underlying causes of stress and trauma within our societal structures and institutions, including our schools. This approach prioritizes empathy and care, culturally responsive pedagogy, and taking what Dr. Ginwright calls "loving actions" that reflect students' voice and agency to cocreate inclusive and humanizing learning environments to strengthen health and well-being for educators and students.

WHO SHOULD READ THIS BOOK

This book provides a research-informed, accessible resource for educators working to improve the conditions in preK–12 classrooms and schools. Teachers working directly with students in preK–12 classrooms, the administrators and school leaders responsible for cultivating school environments, support staff (counselors, psychologists, family engagement specialists, etc.), teacher educators working in institutions of higher education and professional development, and specialists and coaches supporting the development of the future and current workforce will all find the content in this book to be valuable. Advocates will also find helpful information that they can use to inform their work with decision-makers who influence policies and practices.

UNIQUE ASPECTS OF THIS BOOK

Today's educators are urgently seeking resources that not only recognize but effectively address the unprecedented levels of stress and trauma affecting students, teachers, administrators, and educational environments. Despite the critical need, there remains a stark lack of publications dedicated to managing stress specifically for educators—a gap that our book aims to fill. We provide accessible, evidence-based strategies, as well as teacher-friendly tools that are both practical and principled. Readers will see the realities of their daily lived experiences reflected throughout this book. As learning happens only in environments where children and adults feel safe and have support to keep their nervous systems calm instead of a state of perpetual activation, they will see many ideas that they can use to support children and youth, especially students affected by high levels of stress and trauma.

Readers will notice that educator well-being is prioritized from beginning to end in the pages of this book. We describe a wide range of interventions to enhance teachers' well-being and the range of supports that they need to prevent burnout and increase their ability to be effective in their work. We share authentic vignettes and case studies throughout the book, inspired by schools and teachers from across the country, as well as the experiences of our veteran coauthor team. Every chapter, including this introduction, starts with a story from the lead author, Mathew Portell, who shares his firsthand experience shifting the paradigm at his elementary school to reduce stress and strengthen resilience for students *and* educators and other adults.

COAUTHOR TEAM

As a coauthor team, we bring a unique combination of positionalities, lived experiences, and professional areas of expertise. Our diverse group includes two African American authors and three white authors; four of us identify as female and one as male. We are teachers, trainers, coaches, administrators, and mental health practitioners who regularly work with students, families, and public-school systems (preK–12) in diverse states and geographical, cultural, linguistic, and political contexts. This provides us with opportunities to learn about the real-time needs and innovations emerging in classrooms and schools across the United States. Individually and collectively, we bring many years of experience in the work of striving to transform traditional school policies and practices to be trauma-sensitive. We understand educators' current pain points, the forms of support that they report they need and want, as well as an understanding of what happens when they try to implement trauma-informed practices into schools and systems that vary in levels of receptiveness and rigidity to change. Here are the team members:

- **Mathew Portell, MEd (he/him),** is an elementary school principal in Nashville, Tennessee, as well as an international keynote speaker. He leads the Trauma Informed Educators Network, a global community of over 33,000 practitioners, which he supports through a biweekly podcast and an annual conference. In 2021, he was Elementary Principal of the Year for Metro Nashville Public Schools.

- **Ingrid L. Cockhren, MEd (she/her),** is the former CEO of PACEs Connection, an international social network dedicated to raising awareness of trauma and resilience, and now a consultant providing executive coaching and training to educators working from early childhood through higher education on trauma-informed and healing-centered community, collective and historical trauma, and antiracist approaches to systems change.
- **Tyisha J. Noise, EdD (she/her),** has over twenty years of experience supporting underserved populations in New York and California in both nonprofit and educational settings. She is a former teacher in grades K–12 and early college and has extensive expertise in special education. She is also an experienced middle and high school administrator and currently leads equity work for over eighty school districts in California.
- **Julie Kurtz, MS, LMFT (she/her),** is an author and national speaker specializing in trauma and resilience, particularly within educational settings spanning from early childhood to twelfth grade. As the founder and executive director of the Center for Optimal Brain Integration, she trains and coaches administrators, educators, mental health specialists, social workers, and parents on trauma and the hope of healing and resilience. She is also a practicing clinician, providing therapy and crisis intervention services in California for children, youth, adults, and families.
- **Julie Nicholson, PhD, MBA (she/her),** is an expert in early childhood education who trains teachers and administrators across the country on bridging early childhood with public education. Her most recent book is titled *Principals as Early Learning Leaders: Effectively Supporting Our Youngest Learners* (Teachers College Press, 2022). As a professor of practice at Mills College in Oakland for seventeen years, she directed the Leadership Program in Early Childhood, the Center for Global Play Research, and was research director for the Mills Teacher Scholars (now Lead by Learning).

Our goal is that all readers will find that this book affirms many aspects of what they are already doing in their classrooms, schools, and districts. We invite all of you to keep learning, taking risks, and improving your commitment to ensure that all students feel safe, engaged, and supported to learn in school.[*]

---

[*] As you read through this book, you may find that this content brings up a range of emotions for you. It may trigger past traumatic memories, current sources of stress and painful feelings, or both. If you have big emotions or if trauma reminders surface and you are overwhelmed in a way that is affecting you personally or professionally, we encourage you to seek professional help and support.

CHAPTER 1

The Neurobiology of Stress and Regulation of the Nervous System

When I was a few years into my role as principal, we had a student, LaTonya (Tonya), one of the oldest of seven siblings who attended our school. Tonya had the wisdom of a grandmother in a child's body. She was used to being a parent-type figure taking care of her siblings. I was amazed by her in many ways. I have known her since kindergarten, and now she is in the fifth grade. We had a good connection and often joked back and forth throughout the years. But one day, as I was greeting students and families as they arrived, I heard Tonya raising her voice while interacting with another student. In that moment, I was somewhat dysregulated because of the hustle and the bustle of a typical elementary school morning. In my heightened state of stress, I wanted to extinguish the altercation as quickly as possible because the office was filled with parents, kids, and many others. I raised my voice in a disappointed tone, "TONYA!" She stopped, didn't say anything, and simply froze.

I quickly realized that because of my own dysregulation, I reacted harsher than usual. And my escalated tone left this young child feeling alarmed and unsafe. After taking a deep breath, I knelt down, so I was at her eye level, and said, "Tonya, I am so sorry. I should not have raised my voice. I want you to feel safe at school, not scared. I sincerely apologize." Then I added, "Will you accept my apology?" (which I should not have done at that moment). But in her wise spirit, Tonya responded, "I'll think about it." A few hours went by before I made my way to her classroom to check in with her. As I walked up to her, she said, "Mr. P, I left you a note in your mailbox" (see figure 1.1). I thanked her and made my way back to my office. Her note said, "To: Mr. Portell; From: Tonya. I accept your apology Mr. Portell. Thank

FIGURE 1.1 Tonya's note

> To: mr porta
> From: Tonya
> ♡

> I accept rour apology
> mr. portell
> thak rou

you." I dated the note 8/15/2018, and I've kept it in my notebook ever since. It is a reminder to myself that I'm going to make mistakes with my own family, students, staff members, and the community. But mistakes must be followed by repair. Tonya ended her note with two words that struck me, "Thank you." She was thanking me for taking responsibility for restoring trust and repairing our relationship.

—M. P.

In this opening story, we see how an adult's stress-related behavior can activate and/or escalate a student's nervous system. And yet, when adults build self-awareness of their stress-related behaviors and learn specific strategies that they can use to de-escalate and calm their nervous systems, they can disrupt their reactive stress-related behaviors and instead model regulated and regulating behaviors that are essential for reducing students' stress and supporting them to feel safe at school. Prioritizing relational connection, trust, and repair of relational breakdowns before addressing behavioral consequences is essential for fostering supportive and healing environments within schools. Understanding the interplay between adults' stress-related behaviors and student responses sets the stage for the topic that we delve into in this chapter.

In this chapter, we discuss:

- Key regions of the brain.
- Healthy and unhealthy levels of stress.

- State-dependent functioning and the impact of stress on behavior.
- Mirror neurons and the contagious nature of stress.
- The four pathways to calm and regulate the nervous system.

BRAIN BASICS: THE IMPORTANCE OF UNDERSTANDING NEUROBIOLOGY IN EDUCATION

An understanding of the brain's structures is essential for educators and students, as it offers insights into how the brain and stress can shape behavior and learning. This is particularly important in the context of stress and trauma, where recent neuroscience reveals a complex interplay between different parts of the brain.[1] Next, we outline several critical regions of the brain involved when an internal or external threat is perceived, with a focus on aspects pertinent to educators (see figure 1.2). While our explanations align with contemporary neuroscientific insights, they are intentionally streamlined to emphasize the elements that are most relevant in an educational context. We recognize that, in simplifying as we do, we lose some of the complexity and nuance of a more technical discussion of neuroscience.

Hindbrain

The hindbrain, or brain stem, ensures our survival by managing basic life functions like breathing and heart rate. It's our automatic reflexive response in emergencies, swiftly reacting to threats and mobilizing our physiological resources

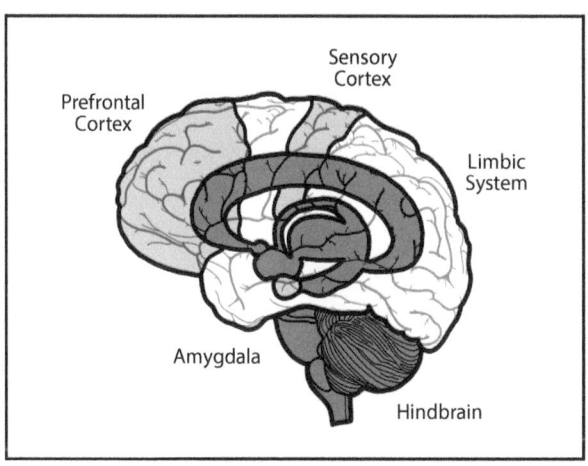

FIGURE 1.2   Brain regions and their primary functions in a threat response

to aid us for survival. In real or perceived emergencies, it dilates our pupils, increases blood pressure and body temperature, and shuts down nonessential functions such as higher-order thinking and reasoning. This primitive part of the brain operates automatically without moral judgment or logical reasoning, and it does not differentiate between real or imagined threats.

Sensory Cortex

The sensory cortex, a vital but less well known region, processes the wealth of information that we gather through our senses. It's like a sophisticated control panel that interprets sights, sounds, and textures, shaping our understanding of the world and our perception of the dangers within it.

Amygdala

The amygdala, often described as the brain's alarm, scans for danger and is quick to flag threats, triggering the hindbrain to react protectively (fight, flight, freeze, or fawn responses).

Limbic System

The limbic system, the emotional heart of the brain, nurtures our need to connect with others and to feel emotions. It plays a role in how secure we feel in our relationships, which can influence our stress levels. This system also plays a critical role in the development of relational health, the "positive, stimulating, and nurturing early relationships that ensure the emotional security and connections that advance physical health and development, social well-being, and resilience."[2] We feel connected and have a sense of belonging in our families and communities, and for students and teachers in their classrooms and schools, this sense of connection provides an important buffer that reduces stress. Conversely, when we perceive that we don't fit in or belong, the lack of connection can increase our perception of threat, which can then activate a survival response in the hindbrain. Individuals need many repeated positive emotional, social, and cognitive interactions to support the development of a healthy limbic system.[3]

Prefrontal Cortex

The prefrontal cortex, the brain's strategist, allows us to engage in more advanced processing capabilities. These include such functions as developing self and body awareness of perceived stress and emotions, using logic and reasoning, employing self-regulation strategies to calm significant emotions and disrupt reactivity, considering different perspectives, engaging in problem-solving, generating creative and innovative ideas, focusing with sustained attention, reflecting on past experiences and actions, and expressing empathy. The frontal lobe, within the prefrontal cortex, governs both self-regulation and executive functioning skills, which are essential for students' ability to learn and focus in school:

- *Self-regulation skills* involve the complex ability to develop self-awareness (e.g., indications of stress in the body), to disrupt unhealthy reactivity (e.g., fight, flight, freeze, or fawn stress-related behaviors), and to use strategies to calm the nervous system to prevent harm to self, others, or the environment.[4]
- *Executive function skills* include *working memory* (holding information), *behavior inhibition* (the ability to pause and consider the best option before acting), and *cognitive and behavioral flexibility* (the ability to change one's thinking and behavior in response to environmental stimuli).[5] Students use their executive functions to support their self-regulation, such as managing their emotions, focusing their attention on classroom activities, and engaging in social interactions in school.

Students Need Access to Their Cortex to Learn

Students need to be regulated to listen and learn in school. Yet the capacity to listen and learn is reduced significantly under stress. When students and educators experience high levels of stress, the more their cortex and limbic systems shut down and the reactive survival mechanisms of the hindbrain begin to dominate. Schools that intentionally work to reduce stress help students to be more regulated so they can access their cortex, increasing their capacity to learn academics and social and emotional skills.

Brain Integration

A well-functioning brain is characterized by the seamless integration of neural pathways that interlink its various regions.[6] Fostering such brain integration in students is our goal. This requires that we create safe and low-stress environments at school, enabling students to fully utilize all their brain functions, particularly those of the prefrontal cortex, which are essential for learning and cognitive processing. When stress levels are high for students and educators, their cortex and limbic systems become less active, allowing the reactive survival mechanisms of the hindbrain to take over. Educators can support their own and their students' healthy brain integration by:

- Learning about the brain and how different brain functions affect behavior.
- Developing self-awareness and emotional literacy.
- Learning a range of self-regulation strategies.
- Developing social emotional capacities, including problem-solving skills, to help them navigate daily stressors productively.

For educators, understanding how the brain responds to stress and perceptions of threat is crucial. This includes the ability to recognize signs of stress both in themselves and in students and to understand the difference between healthy and unhealthy levels of stress. This information can guide how classroom environments are arranged to minimize sources of threat and danger and to reinforce safety and belonging. Recognizing signs of stress and understanding their origin in the brain can also lead to more supportive interventions that help students feel safe, calm, and ready to learn.

HEALTHY AND UNHEALTHY LEVELS OF STRESS

Stress is defined as "any challenge or condition that forces our regulating physiological and neurophysiological systems to move outside their normal dynamic activity. . . . Stress occurs when homeostasis is disrupted."[7] The description by the Center on the Developing Child at Harvard University of three types of stress—positive, tolerable, and toxic—is a useful framework for considering thresholds of healthy versus unhealthy stress and their impact on our stress response systems.[8] The three levels of stress are defined in the following sections.

Positive Stress

Positive stress is a normal and healthy part of development. It results from stressors that children and youth are able to manage when they are in healthy environments with supportive adults. Examples may include starting a new school, studying for an exam, mastering a new skill, and taking on a class project with a deadline, where children may experience a brief increase in their heart rate and/or a mild elevation in the release of stress hormones, but they return to calm/stasis shortly after the stress activation. When children and youth face developmentally appropriate levels of stress in environments with adults who are available to provide support, they can develop coping skills that become an important foundation for them to develop resiliency and the ability to manage life's ongoing challenges as they mature.

Students learn how to manage their stress most effectively when they are in school environments with supportive adults who can buffer or decrease the impact of stressful experiences for them. This does not mean attempting to reduce all forms of stress for our students. Instead, it means that the adult provides just enough support that students can tolerate daily stressors at school without becoming overwhelmed.

Tolerable Stress

Tolerable stress occurs when students are faced with more severe, persistent, or longer-term threats. Examples include the loss of a loved one, experiencing a natural disaster (an earthquake, flood, hurricane, or tornado) or a similarly frightening experience (a car accident, medical procedure, or fall that leads to injury). The brain activates a survival "fight, flight, freeze" stress response, and the body releases stress hormones. The impact of this activation might adversely affect the brain and body if the student does not have a strong support system and at least one consistent, caring relationship with an adult who can buffer stress. If the activation of the stress response system is limited in time (versus ongoing) and a caring adult helps children cope with their stress, it is more likely to fall into the category of tolerable stress, as students can learn to manage this without long-term adverse outcomes.

Toxic Stress

Toxic (also called *traumatic*) stress occurs when students endure frequent, severe, and/or prolonged exposure to adversity without having consistent, caring adults to provide regulatory support. Physical or sexual abuse, physical or emotional neglect, caregiver mental illness, and exposure to persistent, cumulative risk factors (e.g., extreme poverty, racism, and war) are examples of the types of stress that, without the support of consistent, caring adults, can lead to toxic stress.

Toxic stress can lead to prolonged activation of an individual's stress response system and a significant release of stress chemicals throughout the developing brain and body. The fear associated with toxic stress overwhelms children's nervous systems and reduces their capacity to remain alert and attentive in school. Toxic stress harms and delays the development of neural circuits in a child's brain and impairs its functioning across all domains of development (physical, social, emotional, and cognitive).

> ### Educators Can Support Students to Develop Healthy Stress Response Systems
>
> Perry et al. explains that children who experience stressors characterized as predictable, moderate, and controlled are more likely to develop healthy stress response systems.[9] This turns out to be very important for students' success in school. Perry explains why this is so essential: "All learning—social, emotional, behavioral, or cognitive—requires exposure to novelty [and] novelty will activate the stress response system."[10] When students have healthy stress response systems, they are more resilient and capable of managing the daily stressors they face.
>
> In contrast, Perry warns that when children experience stressors that are unpredictable, severe, and prolonged, they are at risk of developing sensitized stress response systems that remain on high alert, telling them that they are unsafe and in danger throughout the day. This compromises their ability to manage daily stress and to concentrate and learn in school.[11] Students with sensitized stress response systems often find the daily challenges associated with being in school—for example, transitions between classes, introduction of new academic content, due dates, exams, presentations, and the demands of everyday social interactions—overwhelming and threatening. As a result, these students frequently display stress-related behaviors. This is especially true in schools located in underserved, unsafe, and over-policed communities where even the walk to school can be dangerous and dysregulating.
>
> *Students can develop healthy stress response systems by spending time in healthy school environments.* Students learn how to manage their stress most effectively when they are in school environments with supportive adults

> who can buffer or decrease their stress. Schools that intentionally cultivate environments where adults offer safety and nurturing relationships improve students' ability to navigate and cope with stressful experiences. However, this does not mean that they attempt to eliminate or reduce *all* forms of stress for students. Instead, they provide enough support that students learn to tolerate daily stressors at school without becoming overwhelmed.

NEUROCHEMICALS THAT ACTIVATE AND REGULATE THE STRESS RESPONSE SYSTEM

When faced with a stressful situation, our bodies release several chemicals to prepare us to effectively handle real and perceived threats:

- **Adrenaline.** Often referred to as the "fight-or-flight" hormone, adrenaline is produced by the adrenal glands after the brain's amygdala signals the presence of a potential threat. This hormone significantly increases our heart rate and energy level, helping us respond swiftly to immediate dangers. For educators, understanding this can explain why a student might react suddenly and intensely under stress.
- **Norepinephrine (noradrenaline).** Similar to adrenaline, norepinephrine heightens arousal and alertness, enhancing one's ability to be aware and responsive. It also adjusts blood flow, which can enhance performance during stressful situations but also might lead to someone feeling "on edge" during normal classroom activities.
- **Cortisol.** This stress hormone, also released from the adrenal glands, helps mobilize energy by increasing blood sugar. While cortisol is crucial for survival, prolonged exposure—as in chronic stress situations—can lead to negative health outcomes, such as weakened immune function and increased blood pressure.

However, our bodies also produce chemicals that help balance and regulate these stress responses:

- **Oxytocin.** This hormone helps promote relaxation and reduces the effects of stress. Oxytocin enhances feelings of trust and empathy, which can improve interpersonal interactions and create a supportive social environment.

- **Endorphins.** These are our body's natural pain relievers and mood elevators. Endorphins are released when the body feels pain or stress and during pleasurable activities (e.g., physical activity, eating, or playing). Endorphins are referred to as "'feel-good' chemicals," as they reduce stress, help us feel better, put us in a positive state of mind, and improve our overall sense of well-being.
- **Serotonin.** This neurotransmitter contributes to feelings of well-being and happiness. Balanced levels of serotonin can help stabilize mood and enhance overall mental health.

Understanding these neurochemicals can help educators recognize the signs of stress in students and themselves, enabling more supportive responses and strategies. Creating a classroom environment that encourages positive social interactions, movements, and moments of restoration can promote the release of positive chemicals like oxytocin, endorphins, and serotonin. This mitigates the stress response and fosters a more conducive learning atmosphere.

BRAIN FUNCTIONING AND BEHAVIOR ARE STATE DEPENDENT

Dr. Bruce Perry explains that all brain functioning is state dependent, which means that our brain is constantly processing sensory information to assess the state of safety or threat that we are in at any given moment.[12] This ongoing assessment influences our cognitive functioning and behavior.[13] For example, when the brain detects danger, people's stress increases, and they start to display stress-related survival behavior. Conversely, when the brain perceives minimal or no threat and people feel safe, their behavior is typically calm and regulated. Perry suggests that people cycle through five internal states along a continuum—calm, alert, alarm, fear, and terror—from a perceived sense of safety and calm to an acute level of threat and danger (see figure 1.3).[14]

When students and educators perceive threats, whether internal, external, or both, their stress response systems activate and their internal state changes. *The more distress and fear they experience, the further they shift from calm to states of alertness, alarm, fear, and even terror—the latter being the most extreme stress state.* In states of increased threat like alarm, fear, and terror, the amygdala signals danger and the hindbrain initiates a fight, flight, freeze, or fawn response (as discussed in chapter 2).

As our stress and threat perception increases, our brain functioning decreases, leading us to display more primitive (or regressed) behaviors.[15] This

THE NEUROBIOLOGY OF STRESS 35

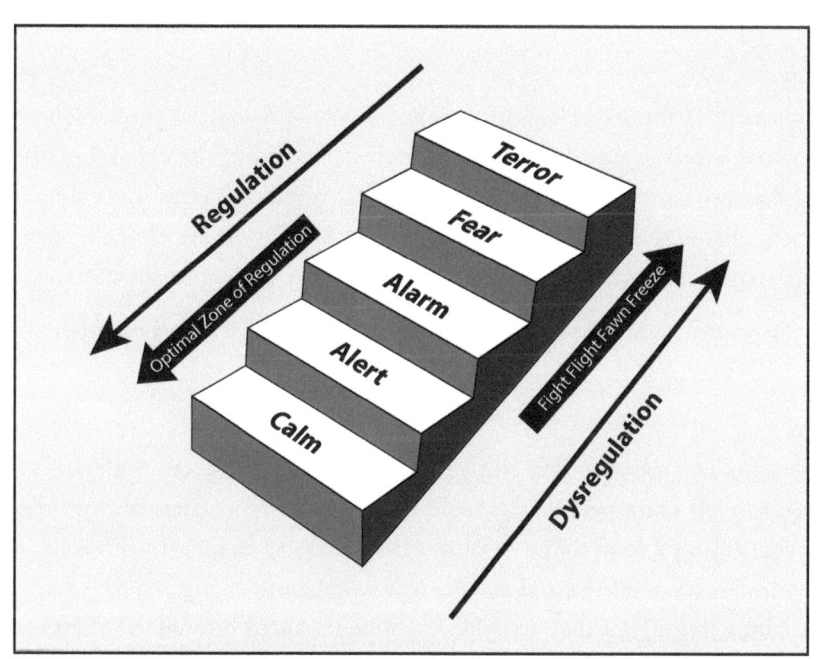

FIGURE 1.3 Dynamic states of the nervous system: From calm regulation to stress-induced dysregulation (Perry et al., 2018)[16]

[Figure showing a staircase diagram with steps labeled from bottom to top: Calm, Alert, Alarm, Fear, Terror. An arrow labeled "Regulation / Optimal Zone of Regulation" points down-left, and an arrow labeled "Dysregulation / Fight Flight Fawn Freeze" points up-right.]

is because fear will prioritize the use of certain neural networks for our survival, while limiting or shutting down access to others, especially to higher brain functions.[17] This is why students and educators in states of alarm, fear, and terror struggle with attention, concentration, and learning because their brains prioritize survival and monitoring for threats. As their internal states shift toward calm, they can think more clearly and engage their cognitive capacities more fully. It is important to note that individual responses to and perceptions of stress vary significantly. This is due to a range of factors, including but not limited to age, the nature and intensity of the threat, an individual's personal history of previous exposure to toxic stress and trauma, the person's temperament, gender, race and ethnicity, and the availability of support and protective factors.[18]

Teachers Observe Students in Each of These States

When teachers become careful observers of students, they can respond when they notice early warning signs of rising stress levels. Early intervention and supports can provide the buffers needed to reduce stress and prevent challenging behaviors before they escalate to stress-related behaviors that can be harmful to oneself, to others, or to the environment.

Calm

Students in a calm state feel safe; their nervous system does not perceive threats; they have access to their higher brain functions, including the use of the cortex; and they are better able to regulate their feelings and behavior. The calm state corresponds to the student's Optimal Zone of Regulation, which is the state in which a person is best able to learn in school. This state might look like this:

> *Clara arrives at school, smiling. Dhaisha is able to focus during a math exam during first period.*

Alert

When students' internal state shifts to alert, their nervous system is slightly activated as their brain perceives something that could be a potential threat (e.g., a student hears a loud sound or misreads a facial expression). In this state, the students are less reflective and more concrete in their thinking and they begin to feel a bit nervous, but they are still able to be reassured through relational support and a safe environment. This state might look like this:

> *Tanya bites their nails and twists their hair repeatedly. Ben texts a friend "that teacher is stupid and their class sucks."*

Alarm

In a state of alarm, students' stress response system has been activated and they begin to show physical signs of stress—their heart rate has increased, their pupils may be dilated, and their ability to process information is significantly decreased. This state might look like this:

> *Frankie does not turn in their assignment, which was due by the end of class. Alex rubs his face, looks confused, and shakes his leg under the desk for prolonged periods of time, and his eyes dart back and forth.*

Fear

When students' internal state is fear, they are fully displaying survival-based fight, flight, freeze, and/or fawning behaviors. This state might look like this:

> *Josefina's hoodie and sunglasses cover her face, and she displays freeze-related behaviors like looking out of the window and not hearing or noticing any of the sounds*

within her classroom. Mitchell displays flight-related behavior by asking to go to the bathroom. He can't sit still and is unable to focus in class.

Terror

In the state of terror, the students' lower brain stem/hindbrain has taken over completely. Their stress levels rise to a state of perceived terror, shutting down reasoning or problem-solving capabilities and resulting in behavior dysregulation. They no longer have access to their higher brain functions, as primitive survival instincts are prioritized, and learning becomes impossible. Importantly, this internal state of terror may not always manifest visibly; students might appear composed externally despite feeling significant distress internally. This state might look like this:

Ty becomes hostile during lunch with friends and gets into a physical fight with another student. Joey attempts to hide in a bathroom stall of the school campus, unable to interact or go to class.

Reflection/Discussion Questions

- What are some ways that students in your schools have displayed stress-related behaviors?
- What are the various ways that your teachers and school have responded to students' stress-related, dysregulated behaviors?

Understanding the continuum of internal states and how our internal states are affected by stress is an essential step for reducing stress in school. When educators and students develop self-awareness and learn to detect their own and others' stress-related behaviors, they can intentionally use strategies that calm the nervous system, increase regulation, and support access to the brain's full functioning.

Educators can learn to observe challenging behavior as a form of communication. Historically, teachers looked at challenging behavior as needing to be punished by using harsh disciplinary practices. Instead, in this new paradigm, a teacher looks past the dysregulation (stress-related behaviors) to the story that the challenging behavior is communicating about what the student feels or needs. The teacher can imagine that the student is trying to say, "I need support in finding ways to communicate the inner world of stress and big feelings that I am having." In that way, they can move from punishing to supporting the student to feel safer and more regulated.

ALL BEHAVIOR IS COMMUNICATION

The first reaction that educators often have when faced with a student's challenging behaviors is, "What's wrong with you!?" This perspective is based on the adult's stress response and often leads to more reactive and less thoughtful responses, including threats, blaming, shaming, exclusionary discipline, and bribing or ignoring students. These reactions are stress inducing for all students and increase their brain's unconscious perceptions of threat, which leads to their further dysregulation (expressed as an inability to manage and process emotions effectively). In addition, reactive and punitive disciplinary practices do not *teach* students what to do instead to manage their feelings—for example, identifying their emotions, recognizing when their emotions are too big to handle, and utilizing strategies to calm and regulate themselves.

When educators learn to recognize that all behavior is communication—and specifically, communication about how safe or threatened an individual's brain perceives the person to be—they have a new way to interpret students' challenging behaviors at school. By understanding that stress-related behaviors indicate that a student's brain has perceived danger or threat, adults can pause (e.g., take a deep breath) and prevent any harsh reactions, and instead respond with compassion and a belief that there is meaning behind the student's dysregulated behavior. They can ask themselves about what the behavior is communicating, specifically:

- What story is your nervous system telling me about how safe or threatened you feel right now?
- How can I relate to you in a manner that increases your feelings of safety and reduces your perceptions of threat?
- In essence, how can I be an effective navigator of your nervous system to guide you back to calm so you can think and reason once again?

In the following story, coauthor Dr. Tyisha Noise recalls an experience that she had as a high school principal with a student in distress who displayed fight-related behaviors. Her story highlights the importance of understanding that all behavior is communicating a story and what happens when adults first focus on the emotional well-being and safety of students:

> Feet stomping, kicking walls, tearing down bulletin boards. We assume it must be an intentional decision but we need to start to ask the question, what is this student's behavior communicating to me about how they feel? One time as a

high school assistant principal, I walked out into a hallway and a student was screaming and kicking her classroom door. I walked toward her slowly. I didn't want to escalate her. As she walked toward me, I could see the tears rolling down her face. By the time she got to me, she literally fell into my arms. She told me that it was the one-year anniversary of her brother being shot on their front doorstep. As she was running down the hallway trying to get to class on time, the bell rang, and her teacher closed the classroom door. When she got to the door, she broke. As she wept in my arms, I walked her into my office. I'm a human and I want to be a human with my students. I have learned that kids' behavior is telling us a story.

Dr. Noise did not initially know everything that this student brought inside her "invisible backpack" to school. The anniversary and loss of the student's loved one triggered her stress response system, resulting in dysregulated, stress-induced behaviors. Understanding that "all behavior is communication" allows educators to use an empathetic relational strategy to effectively de-escalate students. And once the students are calm, the educators can learn more about what activated their stress behaviors and teach them regulation strategies so they can learn to manage their overwhelming emotions in the future. As a school, everyone in the building needs to commit to seeing each other as human and showing up for each other with care and concern first and teaching second. Teaching and learning can happen only in an environment where individuals feel regulated, safe, and supported. Many times, we will never know the history or story of why the student is dysregulated. We don't need to know the story behind the behavior to help a student in distress. Just understanding that behavior is communicating a need will support adults in developing the empathy to mobilize their resources to prioritize regulation first and problem-solving second.

Stress Is Contagious: Mirror Neurons and Relational Contagion

The brain is neurobiologically wired to be socially connected, to be included, and to belong.[19] The mirror neuron system in the brain supports the ability to empathize, socialize, and communicate emotions to others, both verbally and nonverbally. Our mirror neurons lead us to absorb the emotional state of those around us, which is why *stress, calmness, joy, fear, anger, and other emotional states are contagious*. For example, if we are in the presence of someone who is highly stressed and displaying dysregulated behavior, we can begin to absorb that emotional state and find ourselves experiencing our own sense of personal distress. This process of taking in another's emotional state happens at a subconscious level, which means that individuals are neither aware of this process nor in control of it.

Because of our mirror neurons, when we are emotionally charged, we have the power to adversely affect everyone around us. When students do not have teachers who mirror safety, predictability, and caring for them, they have a higher likelihood of escalating their stress and dysregulation even further. In contrast, for students who are highly stressed or with histories of trauma, educators can play a really important role by mirroring messages of calm—sometimes for the first time in their lives—to develop a felt sense of safety and support.

Educators have the power to lead others to regulation through their tone of voice, facial expressions, and body language. Yet it is not easy to stay calm and mirror calm. Our brains have evolved to react fast for survival. By cultivating self-awareness, educators can learn to recognize when their stress response system is activated and learn strategies for regulating their nervous system. Only when educators develop self-awareness and use strategies to manage their own stress responses can they mirror emotional states associated with predictability, care, empathy, understanding, support, and safety.

If educators and other adults in schools want to mirror calm and regulation to students, it is essential that we create environments that minimize stressors and increase joy, connection, and belonging for them. Teachers with up to forty students in their classrooms, administrators and classified staff who supervise playgrounds and mealtimes with hundreds of students, and counselors who are inundated with one crisis after another cannot project a regulated emotional state unless we are taking care of them too. To model calm and regulation for students, it's imperative that we cultivate environments for adults within schools that minimize stressors, foster supportive environments, and create a sense of community connection. Achieving this requires prioritizing the adult's individual and collective well-being in schools.

Stress Is Contagious in the Classroom

Prior research demonstrates that higher levels of stress in school and classroom environments are associated with increased mental health problems, lower student achievement, and challenges adjusting to school.[20] Drs. Eva

Oberle and Kimberly Schonert-Reichl conducted the first study to examine explicitly if teachers' work stress is related to students' physiological stress regulation.[21] Specifically, the goal of their study was to investigate whether associations exist between classroom teachers' self-reports on their level of burnout and elementary school students' salivary cortisol levels. Neuroendocrine cortisol levels were used as biological indicators of children's stress-related experiences in the classroom.

This study was described as the "burnout cascade" that connects teachers' and students' stressful experiences.[22] This cycle begins when teachers work in environments where they are overworked, lack support and resources, and experience high levels of stress. These conditions increased their reactive, punitive behavior toward students and led to negative classroom spaces. In response, students did not perceive their school environments as safe, and they displayed more stress-related behavior, which increases teacher exhaustion and burnout and negative classroom environments—a vicious circle.[23]

What Were the Results of the Study?[24]

- This study provides evidence that teachers' stress is directly linked to students' stress levels.
- Specifically, students in classrooms with teachers who reported higher levels of burnout had higher levels of cortisol (stress chemicals) production.

Implications

- The findings of this study reinforce the importance of positive and caring student-teacher relationships for students' health and well-being.
- As a result, there is *a critical need to actively prevent teacher burnout and promote educators' well-being* through positive work environments that provide support and resources.

EDUCATORS AS NAVIGATORS OF STUDENTS' NERVOUS SYSTEMS: FOUR PATHWAYS TO REGULATION

Schools play an important role in supporting nervous system regulation for students. It is impossible for students to come to school each day and leave at the door their current life stressors and the impact of past traumatic events they have experienced. Students cannot turn off their stresses and turn on their cortexes like a light switch so they can engage and learn. Teachers and administrators are working with students who arrive at school with nervous systems that reflect their exposure to different levels of healthy and unhealthy stress. Some are calm and regulated, others are activated and showing signs of stress, and still others are sensitized and remain on high alert throughout the day. Educators can learn to become *navigators of students' nervous systems*—supporting students and buffering their stress throughout the day while also actively teaching them the skills they need to learn to cope with stressors in healthy ways, reducing their feelings of overwhelm, helplessness, and fear.

Perry outlines four main pathways to transition from a highly stressed state—such as alarm, fear, and terror—to a more regulated state of alert and calm.[25] These pathways can be used for prevention, to support adults and children to prevent the activation of their stress-response systems, and for intervention, to reduce stress and calm the nervous system once activated.

1. **Relational pathway to regulation: "Using relationships, co-regulation, and social supports to regulate and calm."** Our brains are wired for social connection.[26] As a result, relational pathways to regulation are the most powerful and effective ways to reduce stress and shift people from a state of alarm, fear, and terror toward a state of calm. In fact, continual micro-doses of relational connection with caring people who are trusted is one of the most effective ways to reduce stress.[27] Positive relationships and connections are so powerful that they act to reduce or even prevent the harm of stressors and adversity—an outcome evidenced in the growing literature on positive childhood experiences (PCEs).[28] Using relational pathways to regulate students and the adults in schools might look like the following:

For Students
- The crossing guard smiling, waving, and greeting families and students as they drive by or cross the street.
- A teacher recognizing that a student's emotional state is different one day and asking how she is doing.
- A teacher greeting students at the door as they arrive in class with a smile and/or a preferred greeting, such as a nod, handshake, high-five, or hug, as chosen by each student.

- A teacher asking a "question of the day" in the beginning of class for students to turn to a classmate and support them, in order to connect and strengthen their relationship.
- A teacher collecting informal student data via name cards at the beginning of the semester, where students can privately indicate the correct pronunciation of their names, preferred names or nicknames, favorite recreational activities, favorite snacks, learning goals, and other information that the teacher can later use to personalize learning and interactions with each student.

For Adults
- Taking time for connections and personal check-ins during staff meetings instead of rushing right into "business," allowing staff to name their current state of being using a mood meter or a check-in question like, "If you were a weather system, what would it be?"
- A principal remembering information about a teacher and checking in with that person, whether in the context of a formal meeting or during a trip down the hallway (e.g., "Your grandson came to visit this past week. How is he doing?" "I saw that the Little League team you coach won their game on Saturday. Congratulations!"); or by expressing impromptu compliments (e.g., "I saw the note the Robinson family wrote about how much their daughter is enjoying being in your class." "Thank you for teaching some of our newer teachers how you organize parent meetings.").

2. **Bottom-up pathway to regulation: "Using repetitive, sensory-based activity and movement to regulate and calm."**[29] This pathway is the most effective and fastest way of regulating an activated stress response system. These bottom-up activities stimulate the lower brain stem's regulatory network, effectively soothing the nervous system. To have this calming effect, bottom-up activities share several characteristics: (1) They are repetitive, (2) they are physical and involve moving the body, and (3) they engage our senses (sight, taste, sound, touch, and smell). Engaging in bottom-up activities can calm and regulate a stressed nervous system in a short amount of time. Investing in having one or more of these options available within classrooms and schools—to provide students and staff a chance to regulate without having to leave the classroom or assigned area—is an important

method of reducing stress in schools. Examples of bottom-up strategies to regulate students and adults in school might look like the following:
- Taking deep breaths or engaging in other calming activities
- Engaging in art-, sand-, or water-based activities
- Using fidget toys, sitting balls, and swivel chairs
- Embracing a therapeutic weighted stuffed animal
- Taking a coloring or drawing break
- Taking mini-breaks in class that involve movement or fun play (e.g., stretching, body movement)
- Listening to music, dancing, singing, chanting, or humming
- Building a regulation corner that contains a combination of activities that students can choose from independently
- Walking, jumping, or running (e.g., recess time, physical education class)
- Climbing, riding a bike or tricycle, or rocking back and forth (while standing or sitting in place)
- Jumping (e.g., on a mini-trampoline or in place)
- Playing with/petting animals
- Drumming and/or playing other musical instruments

3. **Top-down pathway to regulation: "Using the cortex (thoughts) to regulate and calm."**[30] This pathway is described as a "top-down" approach because it involves using the cortex (thinking and reasoning strategies) to reduce perceptions of threat and calm the nervous system. Using a top-down pathway to regulation requires access to higher brain functions, which may not be accessible in a highly stressed state. For this reason, it can be more difficult to use this pathway to regulate a highly activated stress response system. Using top-down strategies to regulate students and adults in school might look like the following:

For Students
- A teacher talking through a problem that a student has with the student after class. Talking helps regulate strong emotions.
- Having a parent/caregiver–teacher meeting to discuss strengths and concerns about a student, allowing the use of the cortex to strategize together on a plan of action to support the person.
- A meeting involving the student, their parent or caregiver, and a teacher or administrator, where the student has the opportunity to share their

classroom experiences, express their feelings, and discuss what they need to stay calm and focused.
- Students learn about bullying at a school assembly, allowing proactive teaching and discussion about different ways to reduce bullying in their school. Content from the assembly allows the school to create an environment where they have a common language, shared expectations, and a process for talking through bullying issues when they arise. Learning and problem-solving are top-down regulation strategies. At the secondary level, this presentation can be very impactful if it is given by students or co-presented by students and a respected adult.
- A student starts to become restless (i.e., talking to others and fidgeting) during an individual and quiet work assignment in class. The teacher, smiling, comes over and, in a nonthreatening way, stoops down and asks gently, "How is your assignment going? Do you have any questions?"

For Adults
- Tell yourself a mantra, quote, or reassuring thought—"Breathe and stay calm," "Don't do something you will regret," "This too shall pass," "Give myself grace," and "Will I remember this in five years?"
- In a staff meeting, a group of teachers voice a concern about a safety issue on the school campus. When teachers have an opportunity to voice concerns, it allows a space for thinking and talking through logical solutions to keep everyone safe.
- After a major campus occurrence that may have caused dysregulation, use restorative circles with teachers or students to share and process their feelings and create a safe space.
- Two teachers talk to one another in the lunchroom about a problem that one of them is having with a lesson plan. When one teacher is having difficulty with the lesson and feeling frustrated, and another teacher helps by offering ideas, it can be regulating to think and talk through those solutions with one another.
- Teachers remind themselves: "QTIP: Quit Taking It Personally"—for instance, when a student struggling in her math class storms out of the classroom calling the class "stupid." Teachers may also address the class and say something like, "We all have bad days and/or big feelings now and then."

4. **Intentional disengagement pathway to regulation: "Taking mini brain breaks to regulate and calm."**[31] This pathway involves a temporary shift of focus from the external world to essentially take a momentary "break from thinking." Taking "mini brain breaks" from all the stimulation and external sensory input has the effect of reducing stress and calming the nervous system. Using intentional disengagement strategies to regulate students and adults in school might look like the following:
   - Taking short brain breaks for students or adults (e.g., wandering through a school garden for five minutes while engaging all their senses or a fun icebreaker activity).
   - Playing soothing music allowing a "brain break" for a few minutes. Administrators can make a playlist of the staff's favorite songs and play different selections when needed. Alternatively, offering students during a transition from one lesson to another a song that is two minutes long, and when it ends, the transition is complete.
   - Reducing the amount of time devoted to lecturing or "talking at" adults in meetings or in class with students and increasing time for people's engagement and relational interaction.
   - Build in a short quiet break during class to let students take a momentary break from thinking and focusing (e.g., two minutes of silence or two minutes listening to music). During that two-minute break for the students, the teacher can build in a small, restorative mental break.

Relational Regulation + _____

Perry explains that the most powerful and effective approaches to regulating emotions and behavior happen when relational regulation is paired with one or more of the other pathways to regulation.[32] In schools, this might look like the following:

Relational Regulation + Top-Down

A high school student is tuning out in class more frequently (e.g., looking out the window) and not paying attention. This is new behavior during the past month. The teacher recognizes that there may be something happening for this student. After class, the teacher asks the student privately, "I noticed you have been less attentive during class, and I wonder how you are doing and is everything OK for you?"

Relational Regulation + Bottom-Up

A preK teacher leads the class in a "freeze dance" movement activity. He plays music, and the children dance. When the music stops and they hear the word "freeze," they have to pause in the dance position they land on, without moving. The teacher uses this fun, upbeat activity, while also participating and laughing and dancing/freezing together with his students.

Relational Regulation + Intentional Disengagement

Once a week, the teacher in middle school facilitates a "team-building game" in her class. This fun game creates connections and lets everyone intentionally disconnect from the academic rigor of class to take a mind break for a few minutes. This process can be scheduled into classes like an advisory or seminar so there is a regular opportunity for this connection and coregulation to occur.

Relational Regulation + Top-Down + Bottom-Up

An elementary teacher uses a beach ball in this five-minute activity. All the students stand in a circle, and one student tosses the ball to another, calling out that student's name (which reinforces belonging). The person who catches it answers the question of the day (e.g., "What are you thankful for?" or "Give yourself a compliment").

Relational Regulation + Top-Down + Bottom-Up for Staff

During a staff meeting, an administrator plans and facilitates an activity called "Touch Somebody Who . . ." The participants set up a small circle of chairs for half the staff in the open space in the room. The number of chairs should seat exactly half the staff. The administrator asks any group of staff to fill the seats and close their eyes. They then read a list of statements beginning with, "Touch somebody who . . ." (inspires you, makes you laugh, has a smile you like, etc.). Each time a statement is read, the standing staff

> circulate the room and literally touch someone on the shoulder. After about eight statements, the seated staff and standing staff switch places and complete a second round. This is a very powerful stress-reducing and -regulating activity that helps staff to connect while calming their nervous systems.

Intentionally integrating these four regulation pathways into schools and classrooms can significantly help students and educators to reduce their stress throughout the day. Regularly practicing these strategies will help those affected by toxic stress and trauma to rewire their overreactive nervous systems and will increase their ability to have access to activities that require the cortex, including listening, learning, and engaging in healthy ways.

CONCLUSION

Understanding the relationship between the brain, stress, and learning is essential for those working in educational systems. With this knowledge, we can design school systems and learning environments that proactively aim to minimize stress for both students and staff. Learning thrives in a context where children and adults perceive that they are safe. Educators need to manage not just academic content, but also the emotional climates of their schools and classrooms by becoming skilled at navigating the nervous systems of both themselves and their students.

CHAPTER 2

The Impact of Stress on Behavior

As a principal, I often would connect with students during recess or lunchtime. A student at my school was experiencing a lot of toxic stress at home. With Sean, given how much stress he was experiencing, we would go shoot a basketball, throw a football, or play a game. We would do things like that during the breaks in the day, and I noticed it would help him regulate through big body movement and connection with a trusting adult.

One day, I happened to see Sean in the hallway walking from his class to the bathroom and I asked, "How's your momma? How about your brother?" As we were talking, the school counselor, Jordan, came down the stairs and in a stern tone said, "Sean, what are you doing in the hallway? You don't need to be out here. I told you I would pick you up for our appointment." It jolted me, and I quickly replied, "Whoa! Slow down! We were checking in together and he was just going to use the restroom." As Jordan and I were exchanging words, Sean fell to the floor and began screaming and crying. Soon he was so dysregulated that he was struggling to breathe. I called 911. The paramedics arrived, put oxygen on him, and could not calm him sufficiently, so they transported him to the hospital. After the ambulance pulled away, Jordan said, "What was that all about? That was awfully dramatic, don't you think?" I quickly replied, "The way you addressed Sean was very triggering. Your tone of voice and body language was aggressive." Jordan's reply: "You coddle students too much." I could feel my own stress response system activating. My heart was racing, my hands were shaking, I was angry. I took a deep breath and said, "It is not a good idea for me to have this conversation now. Can we please follow up in the near future?" We were both so escalated that we could not even hear one another, nor look at ourselves and how we contributed to Sean's stress.

It took a few days before we could talk about it. Jordan and I finally had a follow-up conversation when we were both calmer and more regulated. I truly believe neither of us wanted to hurt Sean, but unfortunately, a student was left feeling profoundly unsafe, which triggered a cycle of dysregulation. Caught up in our own escalated feelings, neither of us at the time had any self-awareness about how our tone of voice, facial expressions, words, and nonverbal behavior were activating a student's stress response. I think this happens every day in schools. Much harm can be done when the adults in schools do not understand how our emotional states directly impact students' feelings of safety and/or threat. After Jordan and I both calmed, we had a very productive, reflective conversation, recognizing our own mistakes and learning together about what we could have done differently. It strengthened our relationship and helped us think of new ways we could handle an incident like that in the future.

To become trauma-informed requires unlearning the belief that expressing empathy for students is coddling them. It also involves giving ourselves and others grace as we learn new ways of understanding and practicing our work with students. We're all on a journey. It's not about perfection, but rather knowing that with ongoing practice and reflection, we can often take one step back and then leap two steps forward. Our willingness to reflect and repair is what matters most.

—M. P.

The story of Sean, who was experiencing a lot of stress at home, illustrates how stress affects behavior in educational settings. Sean's reaction in the hallway, Jordan's punitive stance, and the principal's initial response to Jordan all reflect the concept of state-dependent functioning described in chapter 1. Sean's distress and the subsequent reactions by the principal and the staff member, Jordan, highlight the significance of communication in shaping students' stress responses. The scenario underscores the importance of adults in educational settings using a calm and supportive demeanor, which can help shift students toward a state conducive to learning and social interaction. Conversely, students like Sean, whose nervous systems are wired on high alert from cumulative stress, may misperceive people and situations as unsafe or threatening.[1]

Understanding and addressing the effects of stress on behavior are essential for creating supportive educational environments. Creating supportive educational environments hinges on understanding and addressing the effects of stress on behavior. Educators can learn how stress affects the nervous system, potentially leading to dysregulated behaviors that challenge adults and hinder students' capacity to learn. With knowledge of the impact of stress, educators are better equipped to recognize that unmet needs—whether of students or of themselves—can trigger the body's stress response system.

In this chapter, we describe:

- How stress affects the body.
- Factors that activate the body's stress response system.
- Fight, flight, freeze, and fawn stress-related behaviors.
- Meeting students' and educators' needs as being central to stress reduction.

HOW BODIES "KEEP THE SCORE" OF STRESS AND TRAUMA

Dr. Bessel van der Kolk, author of the seminal book *The Body Keeps the Score: Brain, Mind, and Body in the Healing of Trauma*, draws upon his decades of experience as a noted psychiatrist, researcher, and clinician to outline the impact of stress and trauma on our bodies, leaving both immediate and enduring physical signs of distress.[2] He sheds light on how the autonomic nervous system—comprising the sympathetic and parasympathetic branches—reacts to perceived threats through immediate and prolonged physical responses. The sympathetic nervous system (SNS) is responsible for the body's response to stress or danger and is often associated with the fight or flight response, which prepares the body to face and survive a threat. When the SNS is activated, the heart beats faster, breathing accelerates, blood pressure and blood glucose levels increase, and the immune response intensifies. As discussed in chapter 1, these changes are driven by neurochemicals such as adrenaline, which boosts heart rate and energy; norepinephrine, which heightens arousal and readies the body for action; and cortisol, a hormone that modulates the body's stress response. In contrast, the parasympathetic nervous system (PNS), when activated, initiates a freeze response, slowing the nervous system and reducing the heart rate until the perception of danger has passed (the fight, flight, freeze, and fawn responses are discussed later in this chapter).

For preK–12 educators, understanding these physiological reactions in students is crucial. In educational settings, the release of stress chemicals will be observed as physical symptoms in students during stressful situations: a racing heart during a test, a headache during moments of high stress, or the stomachache that accompanies a challenging social interaction. As the threat subsides, these physiological responses should normalize. However, sustained toxic stress and trauma can contribute to long-term and chronic conditions including anxiety, depression, substance abuse, chronic pain, sleep disturbances, and various other mental and physical health conditions.[3]

When students' stress response systems are activated, especially when this happens repeatedly and for long periods of time without people and activities to buffer stress and reduce its impact, students will be both physically and emotionally affected. Their bodies "keep the score" of the accumulated stress in many ways (see figure 2.1).

FIGURE 2.1 How does a child's body "keep the score"? Recognizing signs of stress and/or trauma in students

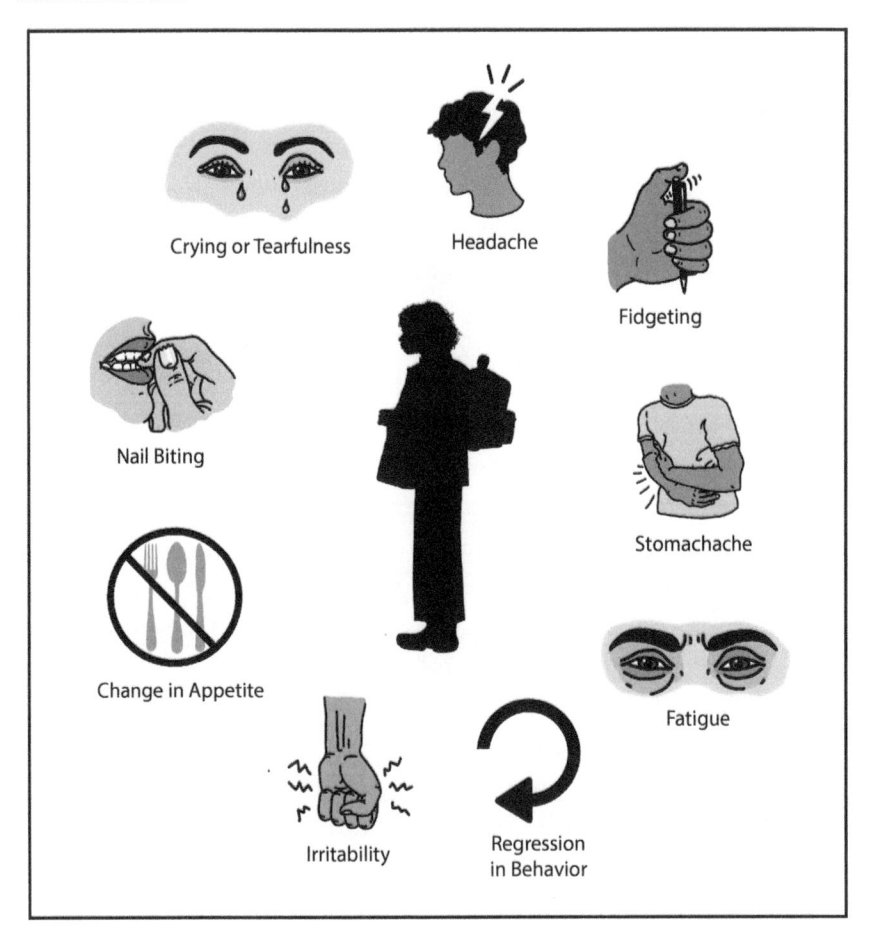

- Crying or Tearfulness
- Headache
- Fidgeting
- Nail Biting
- Stomachache
- Change in Appetite
- Fatigue
- Irritability
- Regression in Behavior

The body's response to chronic stress is further compounded in students from marginalized communities, a phenomenon that Dr. Arline Geronimus, a professor and researcher examining population-level health equity, termed "weathering." She described two distinct effects of stress on the body. First, our lived experiences affect our health at different levels of intensity. For marginalized communities, stress is continually wearing down their bodies. Second, people are not just passive victims; they "weather storms."[4] Relentless stress can recalibrate people's nervous systems to be in a continuous state of alert, increasing their vulnerability to a variety of health risks. Dr. Geronimus's work highlights why it is important to understand that ongoing stress factors without the buffers that can be provided in schools can result in long-term, adverse effects on the brain and body physically (physical symptoms), mentally (learning delays), emotionally (reactive behaviors and difficulty regulating), and socially (poor social skills).

FOUR FACTORS THAT SIGNIFICANTLY AFFECT INTERNAL STATES

Certain factors, including unfamiliarity, unpredictability/uncertainty, lack of personal control, and isolation, are particularly stress inducing for people. Understanding the following factors that increase stress is an important step for educators planning to reduce stress in schools:

1. **Unfamiliarity.** Events or experiences that are new and unfamiliar can increase the brain's perception of danger and activate a stress response. In schools, unfamiliarity might look like this:
   - A student, Rashmi, just moved from Nebraska to New York and is starting a new school for the first time.
   - Two parents communicate with the school that their child, Melissa, identifies as male and now will be called Michael.
   - The district is rolling out a new policy that teachers must follow.

   Schools that commit to reducing stress are intentional about increasing support for students and educators with events or experiences that are new and unfamiliar. Such situations might look like this:

   - Before new students start school, they meet their teachers, take a tour of the school, and attend a new student orientation meeting.

- When concerns are communicated, a meeting is convened to listen to the issues and collaboratively explore solutions that will be helpful for everyone involved.
- The principal loves a new curriculum that she learned about at a recent conference. Before bringing it back to her school to implement, she sends a few key teachers and administrators to learn about the new curriculum and provide input and feedback about it.

2. **Uncertainty/unpredictability.** Events and experiences that are unpredictable and/or involve continual disruption and change elevate the stress response. In schools, uncertainty/unpredictability might look like this:
   - A teacher gives verbal instructions about an assignment, and many of the students are unclear about exactly what the teacher wants when they leave the classroom. The instructions are not provided in writing.
   - The principal calls an English teacher and asks him to sub for a math teacher who is absent and to use his "free period" to cover the class.
   - A teacher receives an email Friday at 1:30 p.m. that the principal would like to meet with her Monday morning, but no additional details are provided.

Schools that commit to reducing stress are intentional about reducing uncertainty for students and educators. These situations might look like this:

- Teachers provide instructions both verbally and in writing. Ms. Kanza verbally assigns students to write two paragraphs defining the word "democracy." She writes the assignment on the board while providing verbal instructions. In addition, she posts the assignment on the school's communication app that the students use to review their current homework and future assignments.
- A principal requests a meeting with a teacher but provides some context of what the meeting will be about. Principal Bruno emails the teacher the following: "Thank you for providing your self-evaluation. I would love to meet with you next week sometime to complete your annual performance review."
- A parent asks the teacher in an email if she notices any changes in his child's behavior over the past month. The teacher responds, "I have noticed Jeremy continues to excel academically and maintains

participation and strong social connections with peers. There are no observed behavioral changes during our class time together that cause concern. If you would like to talk further about these observations, please let me know and I am happy to schedule some time to connect."

3. **Lack of personal control (real or perceived).** When students and adults believe that they do not have any control or ability to influence a situation, experience, or environment, feelings of fear can increase, activating the stress response system. In schools, lacking agency and control might look like this:
   - A school and the teachers are notified that one of their students just lost a parent. No further communication or resources are provided.
   - A student has a fear of speaking and was recently assigned a project requiring talking in front of the class.
   - A teacher has a habit of randomly calling on students, even when they don't raise their hands.
   - Administrators attended a conference and now want to implement a new program, even though the teachers believe that what they are doing right now is working.

   Schools that commit to reducing stress are intentional about increasing perceptions of agency and control for students and educators. These situations might look like this:
   - Students have the opportunity to share their cultural traditions and habits, preferred names, personal pronouns, gender identities, hobbies, and interests with teachers in a confidential way at the beginning of the year, and teachers incorporate that information into the way that they address and connect with students, as well as plan lessons.
   - Schools not only create steps and systems to handle emergency disasters, but a crisis response team to mobilize community strategies for things like death or loss of a student or the parent of a student.

4. **Isolation.** Isolation, loneliness, and a lack of belonging can significantly heighten stress. When individuals perceive themselves as outsiders, grappling with issues that no one seems to understand or acknowledge, it can intensify their feelings of isolation. This sense of disconnection, especially if people feel deliberately ignored or marginalized, can trigger survival

mechanisms in their stress response system. In schools, isolation might look like this:
- A student feels bullied and does not know whom to talk to about it.
- A student observes others doing drugs in the bathroom every day and does not feel safe going to the restroom or speaking up to anyone about it.
- Teachers feel disconnected from administrators, their decisions, and why they make them.
- A teacher is having a problem with a parent but does not have the time to talk to anyone about it.

Schools that commit to reducing stress are intentional about increasing feelings of connection, support, and belonging for students and educators. These situations might look like this:

- **Providing students safe and confidential ways to communicate stressful situations that happen to them or others on campus.** For example, (1) anonymous reporting systems can include online forms, suggestion boxes, or dedicated email addresses where students can submit their concerns confidentially; (2) a student helpline staffed by trained counselors provides students with a confidential pathway to discuss stressful situations or seek help; (3) peer support programs train students to provide confidential support to their peers facing stress or difficulties; (4) counseling services at school are offered for students to seek support for managing stress, anxiety, or other mental health concerns; and (5) an online platform or app is available, allowing students to anonymously or confidentially report a situation or access mental health resources.
- **Including teachers' voices, ideas, and feedback.** For example, (1) advisory committees with teacher representatives from all grade levels provide input on important decisions and regularly meet to discuss and brainstorm emerging issues; (2) open forums/town hall meetings are structured meetings available to all staff to voice opinions and communicate concerns and solutions; (3) feedback surveys are sent out to elicit anonymous feedback on identified areas of concern, positive success stories, and general input about ways to improve school systems; and (4) professional learning communities create opportunities for teachers to meet regularly with colleagues to discuss and share ideas and best teaching practices.

In addition to understanding the factors that significantly increase stress, it is very important that educators learn the signs of students' stress-related behaviors—fight, flight, freeze, and fawn.

LEARNING TO RECOGNIZE STUDENTS' FIGHT, FLIGHT, FREEZE, AND FAWN BEHAVIORS

Stress is expressed by students in a variety of ways. Understanding the spectrum of stress-related behaviors in students—fight, flight, freeze, and fawn—is crucial for educators, as they are signals that students are experiencing a level of stress that is intolerable for their nervous systems to endure, they are overwhelmed, and they do not have sufficient coping skills to manage their stress. When students get to this point, their bodies release stress chemicals (bringing about energy charges) that result in the following stress-related behaviors:

- Fight (directing aggression outward)
- Flight (directing attention away from perceived stresses by escaping)
- Freeze (turning inward and shutting down), or
- Fawn (pleasing at all costs to diminish perceived threats)

Each of these behaviors represents an automatic protective response to perceived threats arising from stressful situations or intense emotions. The hindbrain swiftly takes charge, prompting fight, flight, freeze, or fawn responses aimed at safeguarding the individual from real or perceived harm. This innate reaction applies universally to both students and adults, regardless of their trauma history. Educators can enhance their ability to identify early signs of stress-related behavior, remembering that all dysregulated behavior is a form of communication.

Stress-related survival behaviors from preschool to high school can look like . . .

Fight	**Acting out perceived danger**
	Fight behaviors arise from overwhelming stress that triggers perceptions of stress and/or threat. These behaviors serve as a protective mechanism for students in response to the perceived threat detected by their nervous systems. When students exhibit fight behaviors, it can seem as though they are intentionally causing harm to others or their surroundings. However, it's crucial to understand that this response is beyond their conscious control. Just as when an adult faces a sudden natural disaster like an earthquake, fire, or tornado, the ability to think

logically becomes nearly impossible. The body instinctively shifts into rapid mobilization geared toward life-saving strategies, as follows:
- Displaying emotional outbursts and reactions
- Destroying property
- Hitting or otherwise hurting others
- Having difficulty staying calm/reacting with angry, aggressive, and emotional outbursts/behavior

Example: "I don't know how many times in my career I would see kids balling their fists tightly. I learned that this is a stress response that signals, 'I'm feeling unsafe, I don't know what to do, it's too much and I can't take it anymore.' I stopped interpreting this behavior as a personal threat and instead, started to recognize it as an indicator that a student was extremely overwhelmed."

—Rachel H., seventh-grade teacher

Flight	**Moving away from the perceived danger** Flight behaviors are another coping mechanism that evolved as a survival response to the perception of danger. The function (i.e., the meaning behind the behavior) is to help students with intolerable stress levels to protect themselves by escaping the threat in question. Students displaying flight behaviors might look like they are: • Running away (out of the room or building) • Hiding from others • Covering their faces, eyes, or ears by wearing glasses, hoodies, or hats • Avoiding an activity, especially one that requires contact with others • Redirecting their attention elsewhere • Refusing to listen to adult directions or participate in class • Arriving late to school or class Example: "Wade was a tenth-grader with an IEP [individualized education plan]. Reading was a challenge for him, so at the beginning of English Language Arts class every day, he asked for a pass and disappeared for 20–40 minutes." —LaTonya W., tenth-grade teacher
Freeze	**Withdrawing to avoid the perceived danger** Freeze-related behaviors are coping mechanisms that support an individual to disconnect from an intolerable stressor. Students withdraw their attention to avoid the threat and instead focus internally, often disconnecting their attention from the immediate surroundings to reduce emotional and physical discomfort. These behaviors function to protect students from a threat that their nervous systems perceive: • Withdrawing or isolating themselves • Daydreaming or being "in another world" • Appearing apathetic or unengaged • Engaging in repetitive movements, fixating on something like picking at their skin over and over, head banging, rocking, or engaging in other self-injurious behaviors • Having difficulty focusing or remembering information Example: "Edward's parents were going through a contentious divorce. Since this happened and the parents were arguing with one another over custody, Eddie started to stare out the window and to daydream more frequently and it was so hard to bring them back." —Yoshira L., eleventh-grade teacher

Fawn	**Attempting to reduce the perceived danger**
	Fawning is a response to intolerable perceived stress characterized by individuals seeking to avoid conflict by pleasing others or putting others' needs before their own. They are continually checking for cues on how they should act or respond to a situation in ways that will be approved, avoiding conflict and negative attention and therefore improving their chances of safety. These students might not show outward signs of distress. Instead, they are internalizing stress in an attempt to avoid confrontation or criticism and to increase approval from the adult. Students displaying fawning behaviors might look like they are:
	• Constantly scanning the environment and changing their behavior to align with others around them as a form of self-protection
	• Excessively cooperative or overly compliant at the expense of their own needs and boundaries
	• Struggling to speak up about their opinions
	Example: "I know Cord's father is strict. I have seen him at our students' baseball games yelling at his son and correcting and directing him constantly. Cord always appears scared of his dad at the games. In my class, he seems to be so fearful of making a mistake. He won't speak up and avoids contributing anything verbally in class. If I ask him what he things about a particular topic in class, he responds 'I am not sure' as if he is scared to be reprimanded for the wrong response."
	—Joya K., fourth-grade teacher

Understanding the effects of stress and its influence on behavior, such as eliciting fight, flight, freeze, or fawn responses, enables educators to better identify how unmet needs—either their own or those of their students—can activate the body's stress response systems.

REDUCING STRESS IN SCHOOL BY ADDRESSING THE RANGE OF STUDENTS' NEEDS

In many schools, almost half of our students are missing from our classrooms on a regular basis, with disproportionate rates of chronic absence among historically underserved students of color. Equity issues are present in patterns of chronic absenteeism. Students of color, students from low-income families, and students with disabilities or involvement in the juvenile justice system are more likely to be chronically absent. The COVID-19 pandemic has further exacerbated these patterns. To address learning loss, we must first acknowledge a simple truth: *we can't help students learn if they're not present.*[5]

Chronic absenteeism, defined as missing at least 10 percent of school days or eighteen in a year—is one of the most important issues facing schools nationwide. Discussing chronic-absenteeism rates for the 2018–2019 and 2021–2022 school years for states across the United States, Dee (2024) explains, "Notably, every state experienced increased chronic absenteeism with magnitudes varying from 4 to 23 percentage points. During the 2018 to 2019 school year, the enrollment-weighted chronic-absenteeism rate averaged 14.8 percent. In the 2021 to 2022 school year, as students returned to in-person instruction, this average grew to 28.3 percent. This increase of 13.5 percentage points represents 91-percent growth relative to the pre-pandemic value." Dee explains that the increase in chronic absenteeism means an additional 6.5 million students have become chronically absent since schools returned to in-person instruction, reflecting a significant lack of student engagement in their education.[6] Research to date shows that the reasons accounting for millions of students' absences are complex and not yet entirely understood. Myung and Hough analyzed the many reasons to account for student absenteeism and the key factors necessary to encourage students to return to schools and to support their full engagement.[7] Although their analysis was focused on data in California, their results have important implications for understanding and effectively addressing these trends nationwide. They explain:

> Not all students find school to be a place where they experience health, safety, love and belonging, or esteem. It should then come as no surprise that these students do not feel compelled to attend school. . . . Even if students' basic needs are met, they may feel unsafe, may not feel a sense of belonging or care at school, or may not see how their time at school is aligned with their personal goals or values. Some attendance policies focus on reminding families and students of the importance of daily attendance, and of the compulsory nature of schooling; however, conversations about how schools can address rising rates of chronic absenteeism will be incomplete without attention to each category of needs.[8]

By applying Abraham Maslow's hierarchy of needs as a conceptual framework, they bring visibility to the "wide spectrum of needs that schools can address to increase motivation for engagement in learning" (see figure 2.2). We utilize this framework to shed light on how stress-related behaviors can stem from students' unmet needs within the school setting. A deeper understanding of the full range of students' needs equips educators to create and maintain learning environments that foster positive conditions and reduce the incidence of stress-related behaviors.

Reducing Stress in Schools by Addressing Students' Physiological Needs

The base of the pyramid represents the need for students to have their basic needs met before they can engage and learn in school. Students' motivation to attend

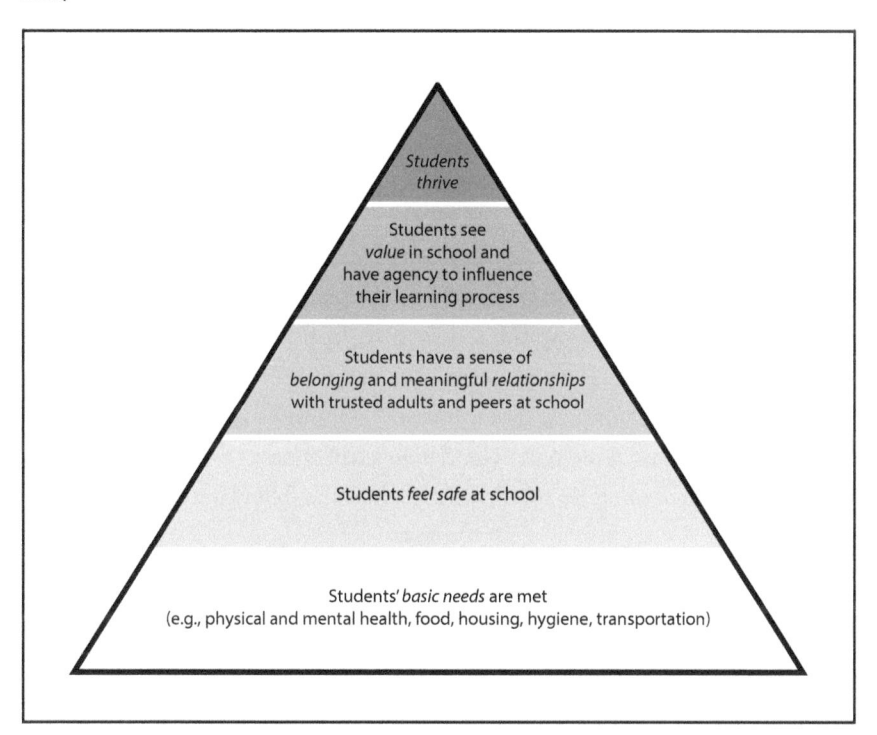

FIGURE 2.2   Meeting students' needs for safety and belonging in schools (Myung and Hough, 2023)[9]

Students thrive

Students see *value* in school and have agency to influence their learning process

Students have a sense of *belonging* and meaningful *relationships* with trusted adults and peers at school

Students *feel safe* at school

Students' *basic needs* are met
(e.g., physical and mental health, food, housing, hygiene, transportation)

school depends upon *whether they have their daily basic needs met* (health, nutrition, housing, mental health, transportation, and others). Absenteeism increases when students have health challenges and/or physical pain, anxiety, depression, and other mental health conditions. The Centers for Disease Control and Prevention's Youth Risk Behavior Survey found that more than 40 percent of youth reported feeling overwhelmed by sadness or hopelessness, to such a degree that it prevented them from engaging in daily activities.[10] Despite these feelings, many do not have access to mental health support.[11] There are many ways that schools are striving to meet students' basic needs. Some examples include:

- Offering free and reduced-price meals for students and a safe place to pick up snacks if meals are missed.
- Increasing access to local or nearby mental health resources.
- Providing laundry facilities for students and families or loaner clothing (including uniforms for schools that require them) and jackets.

- Sharing community resources and referrals (e.g., food banks, clothing donations, religious institution supports) with families.
- Collaborating with other public service offices to hold office hours at the schools so parents and families can come and find out what services are available and receive assistance in obtaining them.

Reducing Stress in Schools by Increasing Students' Perceptions of Safety

The second tier of the pyramid reinforces the idea that students' motivation to attend school is based on *how safe they feel in the school environment*. Absenteeism increases when safety is compromised by such factors as bullying and harassment on campus; policies or language that perpetuates racism, homophobia/transphobia, body shaming, or other forms of oppression and dehumanization; and exclusionary discipline practices. Schools can support students to increase their perceptions of safety in many ways, such as the following:

- Creating antibullying and harassment policies and procedures and teaching students how to be upstanders (students who actively stand up, speak out, or take action in support of their peers, especially in situations where someone is being mistreated, bullied, or excluded).
- Making explicit the multiple pathways (at least one of which should be anonymous) to report incidents and steps for investigating reports.
- Proactively promoting antiharassment and bullying campaigns and acknowledging student upstanders.
- Promoting inclusive environments for LGBTQIA+ students.
- Installing cameras in multiple campus locations.

Reducing Stress in Schools by Improving Students' Authentic Sense of Belonging

The third tier of the pyramid expands beyond basic survival and safety to emphasize students' intrinsic needs for love and belonging, as well as feeling safe. Students' motivation to attend school is based on whether they feel seen and heard and *experience an authentic sense of belonging in school*. Absenteeism increases when students do not have positive relationships with their teachers or other adults at school and do not perceive that they have support (for academics, mental health, and other needs that they have) from teachers and other school staff. Schools can support students to improve their sense of belonging in many ways, such as the following:

- Training teachers on trauma-responsive practices that promote relational and environmental safety and supports.
- Creating inclusive policies, procedures, training, and support, especially for more marginalized students who don't feel seen, supported, or included (those with disabilities, LGBTQIA+ students, and others).
- Creating opportunities for the school's most marginalized student populations to have a voice with administrators.

Reducing Stress in Schools by Improving Students' Feelings of Competence and Mastery

The fourth tier of the pyramid highlights that students need to experience esteem, or a feeling of competence and mastery, respect, and the freedom and agency to drive their learning process at school. Students' motivation to attend school is based on whether they find value and meaning in what they are learning and see themselves (their interests, strengths, cultures, languages, and histories) represented in the curricula and throughout the school. Schools can support students to increase their feelings of competence and mastery in many ways, such as the following:

- Proactively teaching social-emotional skills such as emotional literacy and emotion-regulating practices.
- Encouraging teachers to adopt student-centered teaching approaches that prioritize active learning, collaboration, and inquiry-based methods. This could involve incorporating engaging activities such as small-group discussions, project-based learning, hands-on experiments, and real-world problem-solving tasks.
- Providing opportunities for students to have a voice in their learning process by allowing them to express their interests, preferences, and opinions.
- Encouraging students to view mistakes as opportunities for learning and growth rather than as failures and emphasizing the importance of trying new approaches and being creative and innovative in problem-solving and learning activities.

- Ensuring that learning materials, resources, and curriculum content reflect the diversity of students' backgrounds, experiences, and identities.

Creating the Conditions for Students to Fully Engage and Learn in School

At this level of the pyramid, students can fully engage and learn in school. Attendance increases as students' have their basic needs met and they feel a sense of safety, belonging, and affirmation as well as competence as learners in school. Students who feel safe and have sufficient resilience/coping skills to buffer their stress in school may exhibit behaviors such as actively participating in class discussions, asking questions when confused, seeking help from teachers or peers without hesitation, and demonstrating a willingness to take risks in their learning. They may also display a sense of confidence, comfort, and openness within the school environment, engaging positively with both their peers and teachers. In addition, schools that proactively teach resilience and coping skills, which emphasize psychological, physical and emotional safety, will have an increase in the number of students and adults who are regulated and ready to access their cortexes to learn academics and resolve daily problems that they face in healthy ways.

Myung and Hough's research underscores the idea that when schools focus on reducing stress for students, one of the benefits/outcomes will be a reduction in chronic absenteeism.[12] For students, when school resonates with them on a personal level and they are supported in feeling seen, heard, and valued, they will have a greater sense of safety and belonging and feeling engaged in the educational process.

LEARNING TO RECOGNIZE EDUCATORS' FIGHT, FLIGHT, FREEZE, AND FAWN BEHAVIORS

Educators, like students, can exhibit a range of stress responses in the daily context of their work that reflect the spectrum of stress-related behaviors: fight, flight, freeze, and fawn. These behaviors in educators may manifest differently from those in students, influenced by their different roles, responsibilities, and adult coping strategies. An educator's *fight* response might emerge as a defensive or overly assertive stance in their interactions or pressures that they face from educational policies and constraints; *flight* can present as disengagement from stressful situations, avoidance of challenging discussions, or shutting down in the face of inequitable conditions in schools; *freeze* can show up as a total sense of overwhelm and feelings of powerlessness, to the point of inaction or difficulty making decisions; and *fawn* may appear as overcommitment or excessive accommodation to the demands of others or the district or educational system, at the cost of personal health and professional boundaries.

It is crucial for educators to recognize their fight, flight, freeze, and fawn behaviors because awareness allows them to better manage stress and provide stress-reducing supports to students. Understanding these responses in themselves and others can lead to healthier coping mechanisms, improved communication, and this self-awareness allows teachers to intentionally disrupt reactivity and instead implement stress-reducing teaching practices.

Stress-related survival behaviors for educators working in schools can look like . . .	
Fight	**Confronting the danger** Fight behaviors indicate that adults perceive a significant threat in their working environment. Teachers and administrators displaying fight behaviors in schools might look like this: • Overcontrolling the behavior of others (including students) • Correcting and directing students and others persistently • Arguing, yelling, or fighting with colleagues, supervisors, or students • Having an increasingly negative attitude toward everything • Experiencing a racing heart • Being critical of students, others, and self • Feeling agitation and irritability Example: "Ms. Lawson is constantly correcting and directing other teachers and telling them what to do and what they are doing wrong." —Wayne S., assistant principal
Flight	**Moving away from the danger** Flight behaviors are stress activated, based on educators' perceptions of danger. Protection and safety are increased by running away from/escaping the threat. Educators displaying flight behaviors in schools might look like this: • Calling in sick to work frequently • Avoiding others in the halls or the teachers' lounge • Leaving right after school and not talking to anyone • Avoiding school events and social functions such as pep rallies or making an excuse not to attend certain teacher training or meetings • Experiencing physical symptoms (headaches, stomachaches, back pain) • Loss of inspiration, joy, and desire to remain in teaching Example: "I have worked as a teacher for twenty years. I got into the profession to help kids and for the love of teaching. Now, I call in sick to work at least twice a month but think about doing so every single day." —Maddie F., third-grade teacher

Freeze	**Withdrawing to avoid the danger** Freeze-related behaviors represent a coping mechanism where adults withdraw their attention from something perceived as threatening. This is often a response when a "fight or flight" reaction is not accessible to the individual. Educators displaying freeze behaviors in schools might look like this: • Appearing withdrawn • Isolating themselves • Shutting down emotionally • Dissociating • Exhibiting physical symptoms that arise from increasing levels of stress • Appearing apathetic and uninterested in school activities or events • Lacking empathy for students, families, or others • Feeling alienated • Feeling constant fatigue/exhaustion • Engaging in repetitive movements, such as picking at their skin over and over, biting their nails, or twirling their hair • Failing to respond to emails, work requests, or other tasks • Falling behind in work • Having difficulty focusing or remembering information • Experiencing compassion fatigue Example: "Every day, I wake up and dread going to work. I can barely drag myself out of bed in the morning. I have a headache throughout the day and a stomachache. I have gone to the doctor a few times, and they can't find anything. I used to have empathy for the individual students' stories and a passion to help them. Now I come to school every day like a robot and don't really feel anything when I learn about my students and what they are going through. I am kind of numb to it." —Barbara H., preschool early childhood educator
Fawn	**Attempting to reduce the danger** Fawning is a stress-related survival response to danger that allows educators to reduce a threat through avoidance of conflict, appeasing others, and prioritizing others' needs before their own. Educators displaying fawning behaviors in schools might look like this: • Constantly scanning the environment and changing their behavior to align with others around them as a form of self-protection • Getting caught in self-doubt and self-critical mind loops • Being excessively cooperative or overly compliant, at the expense of their own needs and boundaries • Struggling to say "no" even when uncomfortable • Working to exhaustion to meet others' expectations • Getting involved in others' conflicts (that are not their own), just to make peace and to de-escalate the situation • Taking on too many tasks to please others or make others happy • Taking responsibility for others' mistakes and/or profusely apologizing when it is not their issue • Experiencing physical symptoms that arise from increasing levels of stress

> Example: "My supervisor gave me feedback about my performance. 90 percent of it was positive, but I perseverated on the few things they said I could do to improve. Now, I am bending over backwards to please them. Going out of my way to take on double the work. I have such a fear of failing that I am starting to have panic attacks every other day and I can barely breathe."
> —Terry A., fifth-grade teacher

When we detect these behaviors early on, it prevents stress from escalating and behaviors from deteriorating into unhealthy or toxic environments.

When Stress Escalates and Behavior Deteriorates: State-Dependent Regression

Dr. Perry explains that as people's stress levels escalate and their internal states shift from calm and alert toward alarm, fear, and then danger, the more their behavior begins to dysregulate in a cycle that he describes as state-dependent regression:

> You act less and less and less like an adult and more and more and more like a child and at some point, you regress and get to the point where you're completely self-referential. . . . You want your needs met, and you want them met now. . . . You are hard to reason with, you're emotional and reactive in the way you do things. . . . The more you get threatened, the less access you have to your cortex, and the more you basically functionally regress.[13]

Grasping Dr. Perry's concept of state-dependent regression is crucial for educational systems.[14] When administrators, teachers, and staff operate within schools that expose them to constant stress or do not act to intentionally buffer stress, it's inevitable that even the most productive, caring, and dedicated employees will exhibit signs of emotional, physical, and psychological wear, along with diminished cortical/executive brain access. Such regression affects not only educators' well-being but also the classroom and school environments. Stress has a contagious effect, leading to a cascade that can adversely affect employees, students, and families. The following are indicators that Perry describes as being related to state-dependent regression—signals that adults feel unsafe and are experiencing heightened states of alarm, fear, or terror—and how these might manifest in educational settings:[15]

- **Heightened reactivity.** This is a heightened state of emotion and worry, combined with an increased sensitivity to sound, light, and touch, others' behavior, and even the smallest stressors. Examples:

"Many times, in the morning when kids arrive, they come in escalated. We give them warnings with a consequence which is actually further stressing them and subsequently, the situation. Our harsher reaction can perpetuate students' stress which ultimately results in poor outcomes for everyone."

—Rina E., first-grade teacher

"Continue with this and you will have detention."

—Mark E., ninth-grade teacher

"When I am stressed, everything is overwhelming and overstimulating to me. Lights seem brighter, sounds echo even louder, and my entire body feels ready to break if one more thing happens."

—Laura V., elementary school principal

- **Vigilance and misinterpretation.** Stress can lead to hypervigilance, where educators become more sensitive and interpret even the simplest interaction as a stressful event. This state of alertness can result in misinterpretations and misunderstandings in communication and interactions. Examples:

    "I don't like the look you just gave me. Are you asking for trouble?"

    —Cynthia K., elementary school yard duty staff member

    "I swear our principal just walked by me and did not even say hi. They must be upset with me about something."

    —Louise S., school nurse

- **Exhaustion.** Chronic stress can lead to emotional and physical exhaustion. It is draining for the brain and body to be in a continual state of activation. The longer this stressed state lasts, the more adults will see themselves and others through a negative lens. Examples:

    "I feel like I walk through school days like a zombie, just doing what I need to do to get by, get the paycheck. But I feel checked out, shut down. I don't have any restored energy to deal with things other than teaching my lesson plans that day."

    —Johnny C., eighth-grade teacher

    "I don't feel very successful as a teacher. I can't seem to do anything right."

    —Corrine L., preschool teacher

- **Decreased creativity and reflection.** Stress impairs the ability to absorb new information and engage in creative and reflective thinking, as we need access to the cortex for such functions. As stress persists, the ability to take risks, problem-solve, engage in thoughtful analysis (including considering different perspectives beyond one's own), and generate new plans and effective solutions becomes increasingly challenging. Examples:

> "Administration just went to a conference and came back with an exciting new training for us. I keep thinking of how annoying yet *another* new thing sounds."
> —Connor W., fourth-grade teacher

> "I kept daydreaming during this staff meeting where everyone was asked to help explore creative solutions from some of the results of a recent school climate survey."
> —Edward N., school administrator

> "I sat through professional development that I was asked to go to, but I can't remember anything I learned."
> —Jillian R., sixth-grade teacher

- **Present focus.** High stress impedes educators' focus on what is happening in the "here and now." This affects the ability to plan for the future or reflect on the past, making forward-looking activities more difficult. It also causes the mind to worry constantly about the future or fret about the past, making it difficult to be present with others. Examples:

  > "My brain seems to always be in worry mode, scanning for all the things on my task list and trying to prevent what could go wrong next."
  > —Ethel B., school head cook

  > "I keep thinking about how I handled that interaction with the family. I can't stop thinking about it and replaying everything I said."
  > —Sylvia Q., elementary school family engagement coordinator

- **Impulsive and lower-quality decisions.** Under stress, educators might rush into decisions that are overly focused on meeting immediate needs instead of fully considering the long-term impacts or broader consequences of their decisions. In a state of high stress, it is very difficult to be thoughtful or to look at the big picture. Decisions are more simplistic and vulnerable to implicit bias/prejudices, and less likely to consider nuance, context, or specific circumstances, especially when many decisions need to be made within a short period of time. Examples:

"Your child is having many behavioral issues in class, and we need to resolve this right away, as he is at risk of being held back."

—Teresa C., school counselor

"I ran into my administrator in the hall and in passing, they said they needed me to drop everything and help them with an important issue that must be resolved by the end of the day."

—Karen L., school psychologist

- **Resistance to change.** Heightened stress levels can cause a resistance to new ideas, feedback, or changes. Educators may cling to familiar routines, even if they are less effective, because they provide a semblance of control and predictability. Examples:

  "I stopped listening and tuned out of the meeting when I heard the words, 'new district initiative.'"

  —Jamie D., eleventh-grade government teacher

  "This is the way we have always done things. Why does there need to be a change?"

  —Malika B., school crossing guard

Increased stress reduces access to higher-level cortical functioning, such as the ability to sustain focal attention, to engage in learning, to access healthy problem-solving strategies, to regulate impulses, and to maintain healthy relational interactions with others. Understanding our stress response system can help educators and school systems implement stress-reducing practices that will increase students' academic learning as well as reduce dysregulated behavior.

When stress increases and behavior deteriorates, we see state-dependent regression that results in students who are unable to focus and have difficulty problem-solving, and then their nervous system communicates distress in unhealthy and dysregulated ways, such as in the next vignette.

Vignette: "He Was Throwing Chairs and Flipping Desks": The Cascade of State-Dependent Regression

When a teacher and student have increased levels of stress, they both have the potential to react from the lower level (hind/survival: fight, flight, freeze, and fawn) of the brain versus the higher level (cortex: thinking, reasoning, and healthy problem-solving strategies). As seen in this vignette, without self-awareness and regulatory strategies in that moment, they may both exhibit behaviors that escalate one another. Principal Juan Ortega, of Ridge Blue High School, Amherst County, Virginia, shows that without self-awareness and regulatory strategies in that moment, teachers and students may both exhibit behaviors that escalate one another. When state-dependent regression happens with a student, Pedro, and Principal Ortega, they both have difficulty accessing higher-level thinking, listening, and problem-solving and resort to fight, flight, and freeze reactive and stress-related behaviors. Ortega explains:

> Pedro, a student at my school, was escalated in our library, throwing chairs, flipping tables, and being verbally aggressive. I tried to rationalize with him, which obviously was probably not the best move. Pedro was not in his prefrontal cortex. He was definitely reflecting signs that he was in a fight cycle. He began to verbally say things to me, which normally, I would understand were not personal insults. But because I was extremely stressed at the time, it began to activate me. Pedro grabbed a small globe and drew back as if he were going to throw it at me. In that moment, I went straight into my own fight response and my own stress was way out of control. I began to yell, raising my voice to try to get him to comply. I, too, was being controlled by my amygdala, and I dove into the ocean of dysregulation with him. I had allowed my overall stress levels to get to the point where I was adversely impacting my ability to support dysregulated students, and it also was impacting my interactions with the adults at school. It's really important to be willing to acknowledge to ourselves when this is happening, as our stress levels as leaders have a rippling effect on our students, staff, and our entire school community. We can harm others by not addressing our own stress, but we can also create healing through self-awareness, knowledge of stress, and the power of calmness being contagious. I've never met an educator that said, "I'm going to get into education to mess some kids up." But, due to the overwhelming stress factors that are currently happening in our education system, everyone needs training on stress and its impact on how our brains and bodies work, as well as strategies for de-escalating all the stress we are managing on a daily basis in schools.

Juan Ortega is a principal experiencing stress personally and professionally. He lives and works in a rural community, where many families have been hit hard by the national opioid epidemic. Ortega has personally had a close relative die of an overdose. There are multiple students who have developed drug addictions, and for that reason, or due to their parents' use of opioids and neglect of their children, students are developing adverse mental health issues. Pedro is one of those students; he lost a close uncle three months ago from an opioid overdose.

At Principal Ortega's school, a surge in stress-related behaviors poses a challenge for educators feeling unprepared to manage the dysregulation in their classrooms. Despite his efforts to secure district support for teacher training in social-emotional and trauma-informed practices, a vocal group of parents has successfully lobbied against such initiatives. In a reactionary move, the district has not only banned this essential professional development, but also instituted punitive measures (citations, expulsions, arrests, and other severe disciplinary actions) as the primary strategy for behavior management. In addition, district leaders created a reporting line for any school that chose to defy these policy changes. Principal Ortega feels stuck, and he knows that this approach is counterproductive and will only escalate stress and exacerbate the range of existing issues that he is always addressing, including the challenge to find and retain good teachers. Compounding this, Principal Ortega is working fifteen-hour days, which is adversely affecting his family relationships. Lately, he is beginning to have unexplained heart flutters, accompanied by migraines that force him to go home and be in a dark room until they subside. Key indicators of state-dependent regression in this scenario include the following:

- **Heightened reactivity.** Principal Ortega and Pedro are reactive with one another due to high levels of stress, limited self-awareness, and unintentional fight responses with one another.
- **Vigilance and misinterpretation.** Principal Ortega takes Pedro's anger personally instead of recognizing his cumulative stress personally and professionally, without the balance of restorative buffers.
- **Physical symptoms.** Principal Ortega's ongoing high stress begins to affect him physically and professionally (heart flutter, migraine, sick days, reactivity).
- **Decreased creativity and reflection.** Stress-induced fears prompt district leaders to make impulsive decisions, limiting their responsiveness, creative problem-solving, and effective long-term planning.
- **Present focus.** Under pressure, the district administrators prioritize reactive directives and control over thinking through strategic steps to reach the best outcomes.

- **Impulsive decisions.** The leaders make more impulsive, fear-based decisions, considering the loudest and most demanding voices while overlooking the needs of the entire school.

The effect of spiraling stress that ricochets from district administrators to Principal Ortega to his students and families, and even to his own personal life, reflects how stress is contagious and that state-dependent regression happens at a systems level. The cumulative impact of these stressors can be seen across the school system. Educators' calls for support are met with punitive responses, undermining their professional esteem and effectiveness. In this school and district, the following effects can be seen:

- **Compromised safety.** Policies are being enacted districtwide that significantly reduce resources and professional development that could support students and teachers and reduce stress in schools. Exclusionary discipline practices are being promoted, such as arrests, incarceration, and expulsion, which exacerbate stress and can create trauma.
- **Loss of care and belonging.** As stress levels increase at all levels of the community, districts, teachers, and administrators become more reactive, impulsive, and default to poor decision-making (e.g., yelling at students, banning Social-Emotional Learning/Trauma-Informed Practice training), resulting in a relational contagion that fuels collective feelings of a lack of safety and support, as well as isolation.
- **Reduced professional esteem and effectiveness.** Educators are asking for help, including professional development, so they will have strategies and resources to support students who are dysregulated. Instead, the district is making top-down decisions and threats (e.g., the reporting hotline), with punitive outcomes if compliance is compromised. The result is a workforce that feels increasingly frustrated and ineffective and the staff are left with feelings that they have no agency or control in their jobs.

Starting with the opioid epidemic in this rural region of Virginia, coupled with multiple community stress factors and parents using fear tactics to threaten the educational system, the district leaders react by micromanaging and implementing policies that are barriers for principals and teachers to reduce stress in their schools. These behaviors leave educators feeling unsafe, and therefore unable to support their high-need students—who are experiencing toxic levels of stress—to feel safe so they can engage and learn. Teachers and students can be taught to individually increase their self-awareness and learn ways to buffer their stress to take action to disrupt state-dependent regression. In addition, schools can prevent state-dependent regression by taking steps to intentionally reduce stress in schools. One way to reduce stress in schools and to prevent state-dependent regression is to reduce the stress of educators by intentionally striving to meet their human needs.

REDUCING STRESS IN SCHOOLS BY ADDRESSING EDUCATORS' NEEDS

Rather than placing the burden solely on educators to foster a positive climate for students, system-, district-, and school-level changes are also needed to support educators. As illustrated in figure 2.3, educational environments that foster educator well-being, prioritize the psychological and physical safety of educators, facilitate a collective sense of belonging, and embed strategies that allow

FIGURE 2.3 Meeting educators' needs for safety and belonging in schools (Myung and Hough, 2023)[16]

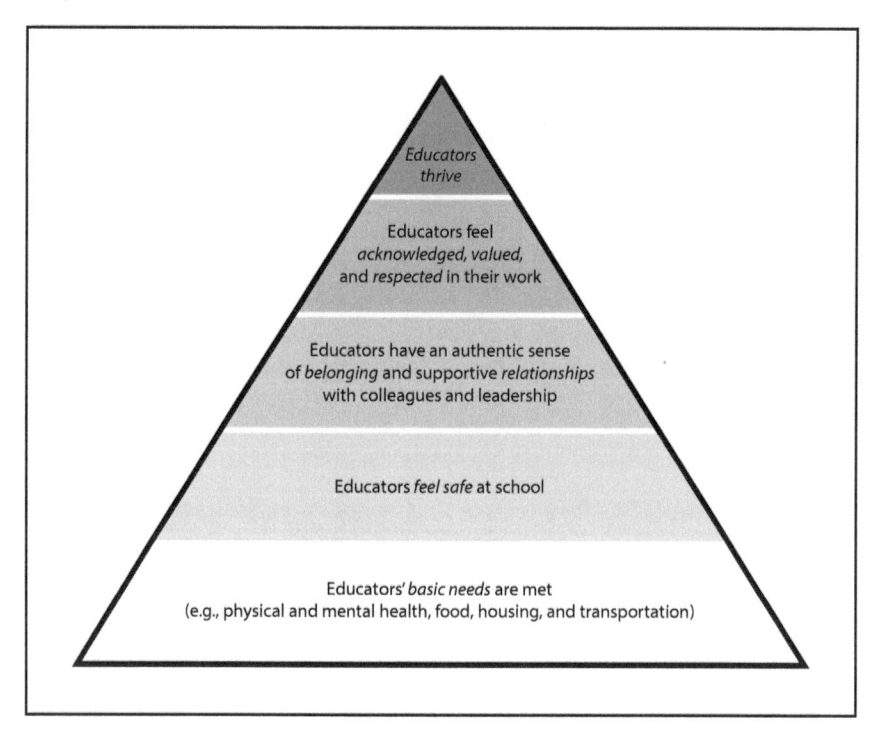

Educators thrive

Educators feel *acknowledged, valued,* and *respected* in their work

Educators have an authentic sense of *belonging* and supportive *relationships* with colleagues and leadership

Educators *feel safe* at school

Educators' *basic needs* are met
(e.g., physical and mental health, food, housing, and transportation)

educators to grow in the capacity and purpose of their profession to reduce stress and improve outcomes for everyone.

Reducing Stress in Schools by Addressing Educators' Basic Physiological Needs

The base of the pyramid represents the need for educators to *have their basic needs met* before they can teach in ways that align with their values. Teachers' and school leaders' motivation to remain in their jobs in schools depends upon whether they have met their daily needs for health, nutrition, housing, transportation, and other resources. Job dissatisfaction, burnout, and stress levels increase when educators experience health challenges and/or physical pain; anxiety, depression and other mental health conditions; financial insecurity; transportation barriers; housing insecurity; and/or community violence/danger and other threats to their survival. Schools can support teachers to address their basic needs in many ways, such as the following:

- Creating a safe and supportive school environment that prioritizes the physical and emotional safety of educators, including addressing issues of unsafe behavior, violence, and danger.
- Cultivate a culture of care and mutual support among staff, including peer-mentoring programs, support groups, and professional development opportunities focused on self-care and resilience-building.
- Providing healthy snacks and/or beverages in the break room, or a "happy hour" where teachers can gather and have healthy refreshments provided by the school.
- Advocating that teachers are paid as much as the district can afford and ensuring that when changes to benefits packages need to be made, teachers and front-line educational staff are the least affected.
- Listening to, surveying, and pulse checking with teachers often to address issues on campus as soon as possible.
- Using professional learning time to engage in stress reduction and reflection or wellness activities such as a walk to the park with a grounding exercise.
- Acknowledging teacher strengths and expressing appreciation on a regular basis.
- Establishing resources and support systems for educators facing personal or family emergencies, such as access to emergency funds or leave policies that accommodate unforeseen circumstances.

- Reallocating funds to create teacher leadership positions so that teachers in need of additional income can earn it on their school site or within the district, strengthening their connection to their work and their community.

Reducing Stress in Schools by Increasing Educators' Perceptions of Safety

This tier reinforces educators' need to feel safe in their school classrooms, schools, and working environments. Adults' capacity to work, engage, and be creative is rooted in *how safe they feel in the context of their daily work*. Job dissatisfaction, burnout, and stress increase when educators experience policies or language that perpetuate racism, homophobia/transphobia, or other forms of oppression and dehumanization; harassment, when school campus is not safe physically (poor lighting, ineffective policies, and threats to students and staff safety); and other experiences that compromise their feelings of safety. Schools can support teachers to increase their perceptions of safety in many ways, such as the following:

- Investing in physical safety measures, such as improving campus infrastructure and establishing security protocols.
- Addressing major campus safety issues or events before they escalate.
- Equipping school staff in de-escalation techniques.
- Providing training and professional development on cultural competency, implicit bias, and inclusive teaching practices.
- Establishing procedures for addressing harassment, discrimination, or bullying.
- Addressing campus safety issues or events early and often. Because of emotional contagion, a leader can short-circuit this phenomenon after safety events with a ten-minute emergency meeting (at break, at lunch, or immediately after school) at which they share the basics of the incident, where they are in the process, and what educators can expect to see next. They can reiterate their commitment to staff safety. These work better in person than in writing. Using a short video, so that the messaging is clear, concise, and consistent, is also effective.
- Equipping school leaders, mental health staff, and security to be the best de-escalators on the school campus. This minimizes the need for law enforcement presence and increases feelings of safety in educators.
- Facilitating staff surveys and conversations multiple times per year and asking staff for their safety concerns and suggestions. Once leadership has

reviewed the data and selected a course of action, reporting out to the staff on the data and next steps is also important.
- Bringing active shooter training to the school so educators feel equipped in case of incidents of that magnitude.

Reducing Stress in Schools by Improving Educators' Authentic Sense of Belonging

Beyond basic survival and safety concerns, educators need to feel *an authentic sense of belonging* at work. Job stress, dissatisfaction, and burnout increase when educators experience isolation, harassment, bullying, or lack of inclusion in decision-making. Schools can support teachers to increase their sense of belonging in many ways, such as the following:

- Asking for input from teachers before rolling out a new training program, project, or policy.
- Offering opportunities for teachers to communicate concerns or to provide suggestions for improving a system or process at school.
- Building positive relationships intentionally and connecting with teachers often (e.g., get to know your teachers' goals, interests, and favorite activities and hobbies).
- Showing appreciation often (teacher of the month type of awards and/or an award where teachers acknowledge one another, and provide breakfast or lunch during professional development sessions).

Reducing Stress in Schools by Supporting Educators to Feel Acknowledged and Respected

Educators should feel acknowledged and respected in the workplace. Adults' motivation at work is influenced by whether they find value and meaning in their jobs and see themselves (their interests, strengths, cultures, languages, and histories) represented in their workplace. Job dissatisfaction and burnout increase when educators feel continually overwhelmed and ineffective (e.g., with addressing students' learning gaps and challenging behaviors), which can lead to feelings of helplessness and anger; or when they don't know how to manage students' challenging behaviors effectively or don't receive guidance and ongoing support as new initiatives, curricula, and instructional frameworks are constantly rolled out that must be implemented to high standards by specific deadlines. Schools can support teachers to feel acknowledged, recognized, and supported in many ways, such as the following:

- Offering ongoing professional development opportunities tailored to teachers' needs and interests. By providing training sessions, workshops, and resources that enhance educators' skills and knowledge, schools can boost their confidence and sense of competence in their roles.
- Implementing regular supervision support and/or mentoring/coaching programs to help reduce teacher stress by providing educators with consistent support. Through regular meetings and feedback sessions, mentors and supervisors can help teachers navigate challenges, refine their teaching practices, and develop a greater sense of mastery in their profession.
- Advocating for manageable workloads and realistic expectations for educators, recognizing the importance of balancing professional responsibilities with personal well-being. Schools can implement policies and practices that promote work-life balance, reduce administrative burdens, and allocate sufficient time and resources for lesson planning, grading, and professional development.

Creating the Conditions for Educators to Thrive in Their Jobs

This level represents educators who not only have their basic needs met, but also feel a sense of safety and belonging, affirmation of their identities, and competence as professionals in their work. They can fully engage in their jobs, manage daily adversity, and plan and solve problems both effectively and creatively and ask for help and support when they need it.

Educators with reduced stress will have the internal energy and resources to respond to students' dysregulated behavior in a way that will guide them to a calm frame of mind rather than reacting with harsh and punitive disciplinary practices. In other words, the adults' calm demeanor will be contagious and create a collective environment that reduces stress overall in their classrooms, schools, and communities.

CONCLUSION

For educators working in preK–12 schools, comprehending the tangible effects of stress and trauma is crucial, as that directly influences the behaviors and responses of students, teachers, administrators, and staff. Reducing stress in educational settings means acknowledging that a student's emotional outburst, an adolescent's withdrawal, or a teacher's overcommitment might be an indicator of underlying stress. Manifestations such as fight, flight, freeze, and fawn behavior—whether defiant confrontations, quiet resistance, or a silent struggle behind a veneer of compliance—are calls for help that signal a need for safety and support. Effectively mitigating the impact of stress in our schools starts with recognizing the widespread presence of stress-related behaviors and the significant consequences of state-dependent regression when students' and adults' range of human needs are not met within schools. Building from this foundational knowledge, educators can create educational environments intentionally designed to alleviate stress, a theme that we explore in the subsequent chapters of this book.

CASE STUDY 1

The System Is Ill Prepared for the Real Lives of Young People Who Walk Through the Door[1] (see trigger warning)

One of our coauthors, Dr. Tyisha Noise, shares a story from her experience working as a high-school assistant principal to highlight the impact of stress and its toll on educators. This story illustrates the importance of reducing stress in schools by providing relational buffers and support systems that can help educators navigate triggering events. Dr. Noise explains:

> When I was an assistant principal in Watts, a community in South Los Angeles, there was a young Latina student, Teresa, at the school. Some kids, they're just like sunshine, and she was absolutely one of these kids. One day I got a call to come to the counseling office, and Teresa was in there with her mom. Mom begins to explain that Teresa had been inappropriately touched by another student on campus. My heart was in my throat because I'm just trying to take in what this means. As an administrator, I had to call the sheriff and the principal to share this information. When the sheriff arrived and Teresa saw that he was male, she asked me to sit with her while he interviewed her. So I had to listen to the details of her violation, including that it happened by a boy, Marcus, her same age. The entire process was uncomfortable and disconcerting.
>
> As school administrators, we went into the process of trying to determine exactly what happened, using multiple sources of information. As I sat down with the young boy's family to explain the discipline review board process, I asked mom, was this the first time she had seen this behavior? I told her, "I know this is really scary and uncomfortable. I have this unique job of needing to protect the child who was violated, but also still wanting the best for your son. Because whether or not Marcus

made this mistake and it was malicious or not, he is also ours." Mom hesitantly explained that when Marcus was younger and she was going through a hard time, she asked a family member to move in with them, and she believes he was violated by this family member very, very early in his life. Marcus then proceeded to violate his younger sister. She shared that nobody provided him with support, as nobody knew what to do. I learned that Marcus had multiple incidences in school before coming to us. Yet it went unaddressed in his individualized education plan (IEP) and at his previous schools. So now we were talking about expelling a fourteen-year-old African American boy from school when an entire system had failed to treat him for an issue that started when he was five. His family is terrified because systems tend to discipline us, but not to help or provide intervention or support.

I remember the deep, deep sorrow as the adult who had to walk both families through this process. There is no support for the person in my shoes, who sits and has to listen to every detail of these stories. The system is ill prepared for the real lives of young people who walk through the door from families steeped in trauma. Where do we bring healing, solace, resolution? Where do we do that for him? Because if we don't, we know he's going to jail. But we also know we can track this back to when he was four or five years old and all of these years that baby was in school.

This story reflects the reality that personal trauma never occurs in isolation, and the reality that healing interventions solely targeting individuals (e.g., therapeutic interventions to support Teresa and Marcus) are necessary, yet not sufficient. Limiting the focus solely to an individual level fails to address the root causes of the cycles of toxic stress and trauma at play. Instead, we need to consider both the interacting layers of trauma *and* healing to design and implement effective solutions for reducing stress in our schools.

By applying the RYSE framework, we analyze this story through three distinct dimensions—individual and interpersonal, school and community, and systemic—that affect students, families, and educators. The framework provides insight into creating intentional strategies for stress reduction, resilience, and healing across all levels. It underscores the school's role within an ecosystem that prioritizes the health and well-being of children, youth, and adults.

INDIVIDUAL AND INTERPERSONAL FACTORS THAT CONTRIBUTE TO STRESS IN SCHOOLS OR STRENGTHEN STUDENTS' AND EDUCATORS' WELL-BEING

Toxic Stress and Trauma

Both Teresa and Marcus were affected by sexual abuse, traumatic experiences that deeply affect an individual's beliefs, values, behaviors, and identity. The shame of child sexual abuse increases the likelihood of individuals and families suffering this type of abuse in silence, which leads to a high incidence of intergenerational transmission, creating a difficult psychological legacy for children and families to overcome. For example, Marcus is acting out his past traumatic experiences over and over as a protective and coping strategy to deal with the toxic stress resulting from his unresolved and untreated trauma. His trauma continues to be acted out behaviorally through a fight response that will cause ongoing harm until it is adequately addressed and resolved. Both students' individual and familial experiences were significantly affected by larger systemic impacts of stress and trauma.

Reducing Stress, Fostering Resilience, and Promoting Healing and Well-Being

To foster healing and resilience, it's crucial to provide customized support and opportunities that meet students at their current stage of development and align with their individualized needs. This approach is vital for all children, particularly those from underresourced and marginalized communities. School staff and administrators play a key role in weaving a network of supportive relationships that are fundamental to buffering stress, mitigating further damage and generational transmission, and supporting students to cope with adversities. Supporting the students and families in this story at a personal level might look like this:

- Acknowledge Teresa for bravely speaking up, telling her story, and emphasizing her many positive traits and strengths that have and will continue to help her buffer stress and build resilience. Also, recognize that Marcus's family was courageous in choosing to be vulnerable enough with a school administrator in a position of power to share his history and story. They had a sliver of trust that they used to give a cry for help for their child and family.
- Inform both Teresa's and Marcus's families about school and community resources and supports available (e.g., school counselors, referral for a school evaluation, access to therapeutic support based on their insurance, and/or free resources such as counseling if uninsured).
- Encourage and listen when Teresa talks about her feelings, inform Teresa's family how important it is that Teresa feels safe in her home moving forward, and facilitate peer support for Teresa and her family.

- Teresa might be at risk of saying, "Why did this happen to me?" or "I must be a bad person for this to happen, or there must be something wrong with me." With proper support from the adults around her, including counselors, she can process her experiences and feelings and begin to gain insight into them immediately after a traumatic event. The adults around her can help her to discover sources of strength, coping, and resilience with an alternative narrative: "I have discovered I am strong, brave, and a survivor."
- Administrators navigating intensive investigations like the one in this story experience enormous pressure. They can greatly benefit from having access to individual supervision and policy implementation support, like the following:
  - Having a safe and confidential place to process feelings, triggers, and other stimuli.
  - Having additional administrative support to help sort through the appropriate policies and determine the best course of action along the way.

  Having support like this can help with stress management, allowing administrators to remain regulated and better able to provide support to students and families, with outcomes that will be good for all levels of the system.

SCHOOL AND COMMUNITY FACTORS THAT CONTRIBUTE TO STRESS IN SCHOOLS OR STRENGTHEN STUDENTS' AND EDUCATORS' WELL-BEING

Toxic Stress and Trauma

Marcus's experience of sexual violence in his home as a young child at a critical time for his brain and body development, coupled with the total lack of support to help him organize this experience and work through it with the guidance of a caring adult, led to a traumatic reenactment of his original trauma as he continuously violated children in his presence. The trauma at the root of this story is the result of oppressive systemic forces that create unsafe conditions and deny resources and opportunities to families like Marcus's. Community distress disproportionately burdens communities of color and neighborhoods facing generational poverty. Marcus's mother lacked access to mental health resources (not attached to punishment) in her low-income community, and the severely underfunded schools that Marcus attended operate in survival mode, without the capacity to address students with significant mental health needs. Even the system put in place to help him via special education and an IEP failed to identify and address this issue throughout elementary and middle school. It is also likely that Marcus's mother had institutional distrust when it came to seeking assistance for Marcus due to the history of stigmatization and criminalization of the mental health needs of African Americans.

Reducing Stress, Fostering Resilience, and Promoting Healing and Well-Being

Resilience and healing stem from an awareness of the systems that shape opportunities and lived experiences. Recognizing that the prevalent distress in communities is often due to systemic problems, such as unfair policies leading to unequal resource distribution, can prevent children from internalizing oppression and self-doubt as they try to understand their communities. Supporting the children and families in this story at a community level might look like this:

- **Bringing in a bilingual advocate.** The school can connect Teresa's mom, for whom English is not her primary language, with a bilingual advocate who can explain treatment and support options to her and make her feel empowered to advocate for her child, given that most literature is printed in English.
- **Promoting the use of art as healing.** Art can reduce stress and heal trauma in children and adults across various settings, including schools. This is true for both creating art (e.g., dance, painting, writing, doodling, and other activities) and becoming exposed to literature, music, visual arts, and visual media. In light of research concerning the healing potential in the arts, schools can support children like Teresa by creating visually aesthetic places within the school or on campus where children feel safe and represented. Schools should also form meaningful partnerships with community-based mental health organizations that provide art therapy. Both Teresa's and Marcus's families could be referred to community-based mental health practitioners who intentionally incorporate art into their healing modalities. Schools and teachers should also develop relationships with diverse local artists and invite them into classrooms to share their art processes and encourage children to use art to handle their feelings and experiences. When it comes to children of color, the benefits of incorporating the arts as a way to heal can be magnified by prioritizing art, literature, and music that are culturally relevant and identity-affirming.

- **Incorporating a schoolwide or districtwide educational campaign about child abuse.** Programs such as Play it Safe!, Stop Child Abuse and Neglect, and other school-based childhood physical and sexual abuse prevention programs teach children to recognize abusive situations, respond to potentially abusive situations, and report abuse to someone who can help stop it.
- **Providing mental health support for educators.** For administrators receiving this type of report who are sexual assault survivors themselves, it is important that a counselor, social worker, or another administrator tasked with providing support is available for them, given that managing work like this can create secondary trauma for educators. Leaders cannot continue to serve other students when feeling triggered themselves, with no outlet or support system.
- **Providing mental health support for families.** It is important to connect to counseling and resources that help parents to support their children without feeling stigmatized or marginalized, and to advocate for equitable access to mental health services and culturally relevant healing methods for the family. For example, providing mental health support for Teresa's family could involve connecting her mother with a bilingual advocate who could explain treatment options and empower the family to advocate for Teresa effectively.

SYSTEMIC FACTORS THAT CONTRIBUTE TO STRESS IN SCHOOLS OR STRENGTHEN STUDENTS' AND EDUCATORS' WELL-BEING

Toxic Stress and Trauma

Throughout history, systems and policies have subjugated communities of color. The fact that Ed code (Education Code or the set of laws and regulations that govern public education within a specific state or country) required the administrator in this story to expel Marcus, even though she knew that his new school would only continue to fail him, is a tragic reflection of trauma at the systemic level. This story exemplifies how systemic racism operates. The educational policies that prioritized punishment of individual behavior—in this case leading Marcus to a future of acting out his unresolved trauma until he ends up in jail—exempt the society and educational system from any responsibility. Expelling

Marcus hides the lack of resources available to him and his family and the barriers that they faced when they were in great need of connection and support. Further, being removed from a supportive and familiar school environment in his community only adds to Marcus's trauma and exacerbates the feelings of loneliness, shame, and fear that may have led to this maladaptive behavior. Healing this level of trauma requires policy reform and confronting ongoing systemic inequities.

Reducing Stress, Fostering Resilience, and Promoting Healing and Well-Being

To enhance healing and resilience, it's essential to adopt restorative practices and policies focused on rehabilitation rather than punishment (see chapter 5). Such practices are especially pertinent in educational settings, where children and youth are particularly sensitive due to their young age, limited life experience, and ongoing brain development. These practices are key to establishing a secure educational environment where students can learn from their errors and engage actively, without fear of severe punishment or intimidation. Assuming a commitment to collective care shifts the responsibility for well-being to the school community rather than placing it solely on individual students and teachers. Supporting the children and families in this story at a systemic and institutional level might look like this:

- **Make child protection a priority across the state or as a condition of receiving state or federal funding.** There are many resources that schools can use to build awareness of how to prevent and effectively respond to child maltreatment and to improve child protection. For example, Second Step is a program that supports schools to make child protection a top priority through the development of policies and procedures, staff training, lesson plans for students, and family education.[2]
- **Provide training in trauma-informed practices for educators,** especially those in underserved communities in which students are more likely to encounter potentially traumatizing experiences.

Reflection/Discussion Questions
- As a school or district leader: What supports and/or resources are in place to support students who are traumatized at school, their families, and the educators involved in facilitating the processes and protocols for families?

- What lessons or campaigns are embedded in your school that teach students how to treat each other and how to report when they have been violated?
- What community-based resources are your counseling staff aware of and connected to so they can provide guidance and support to students and/or their families in an instance such as this?
- If the children in this story were your children, what would you want for them and your family after reporting an incident like this?

CHAPTER 3

Creating School Environments That Strengthen Adults' Nervous System Regulation

*C*reating regulated environments for adults in schools helps promote a positive, collective caring culture, ensures psychological safety, overall well-being, and a more regulated school environment. We incorporated intentional measures such as more soothing low LED lighting and designing inviting break rooms to play an important role in promoting wellness for our school educators. Our lounges and break rooms for teachers are designed to connect and recharge, including the creation of a "Be Well Room," emphasizing nature elements, uplifting quotes, and interactive elements like a compliment tree, calming diffusers, and napping pods, along with healthy snack options. Additionally, we've introduced support systems like "Tap in and Tap out" using a free phone app called GroupMe. If an adult was escalated and needed a break for any reason—if they were coping with something in their personal lives, if they needed additional help with a student who was dysregulated, or if they were having a stressful day . . . whatever the reason, it didn't matter, they didn't have to tell us—they would go to the app and say, "I need a Tap Out." Another staff member would step in temporarily to give the teacher a break (tap out) until they felt more regulated to enter back into the classroom (tap in).

This approach encourages a collective culture of care that supports the well-being of our teachers and staff. This tap in and tap out program reinforces that vulnerability and listening to your body are both essential aspects of working effectively with highly stressed students. As a principal, I emphasize to all our staff the importance of *prioritizing self-regulation over perfection, fostering a culture of collective care and mutual support within our school community. Ultimately, our goal is to create an environment where adults feel empowered to prioritize their well-being while knowing that they have the support of their colleagues and leadership. Systems like Tap-In and Tap-Out and staff wellness lounges are accessible interventions that we can build into our schools to support teacher and staff well-being. By intentionally building schoolwide collective supports, we reinforce the idea that the well-being of the entire community is a shared responsibility and benefits individual teachers but also contributes to a school environment that values teacher emotional well-being and resilience. Asking for help is not a sign of professional failure; instead, in our building, we have each other's backs.*

—M. P.

Foundational to building regulating environments in schools is the well-being of educators. They must feel secure and supported to maintain their own regulation. Ricky Robertson, a respected voice in education, encapsulates this succinctly, "We have to be focused on creating collective care in schools and *start by caring for the educators first*. This can only be achieved when educators feel safe, cared for, respected, and heard."[1] In line with this philosophy, the opening vignette reflects a school that has actively embedded structures and processes to convey care and safety for adults, thereby strengthening their capacity to handle their demanding roles with the necessary emotional reserves.

Prioritizing wellness and creating regulated environments in schools involve applying our understanding of state-dependent functioning to every facet of educators' work. Just as was conveyed in the opening story, schools can intentionally create environments that are designed to support individual and collective community sources of wellness that reduce stress. It is essential for adults because when regulated, they have the restored energy to cope with the day-to-day stressors. Reducing stress prevents long-term adverse outcomes (physically, emotionally, mentally, and socially) from the release of stress chemicals, and educators will have the energy to be more patient and less reactive in the face of dysregulated students.

In this chapter, we discuss:

- The significance of regulated environments for adult well-being in educational settings.

- Approaches to strengthening relationships and connection among school staff.
- Strategies to actively mitigate burnout.
- Techniques for responding to and de-escalating adults with activated stress-response systems.

STRENGTHENING RELATIONSHIPS AND CONNECTIONS

Positive relationships and supportive connections play a critical role in reducing stress for both adults and students in schools. Relationships play an important role in buffering the toxic impact of stress and improving emotional well-being. Perry reinforces how important it is that adults and children have sufficient doses of daily positive interactions.[2] Stress-reducing, regulating connections can take place in many contexts over the course of a day, and every individual has unique ways to define meaningful connections. Even brief, micro-level connections with others serve as significant buffers to stress and adversity in schools. These small doses of positive interactions for educators in schools might look like the following examples:

- **Structured connections.** Creating routines during formal scheduled meetings where employees have opportunities to share stories about what they are doing and/or working on—for example, by starting meetings with check-ins or using storytelling circles. This cultivates an environment where adults can feel seen, have a voice, and talk about what they are experiencing, and in doing so, reduce feelings of isolation in their work. Frequent doses of connection with colleagues help to build strong relationships and create a sense of community and belonging. Schools that support relationship building among teachers provide a crucial support system that buffers against the stressors inherent in the teaching profession. These relationships contribute to the well-being and resilience of educators.

Check-Ins

One way to build relational connections within staff is during faculty meetings. Begin each meeting by providing time for ten-minute "check-ins" based on the following three questions: Any announcements? Brags? Compliments?

- First, staff turn to an elbow partner and take turns responding to the prompt (five minutes).
- Second, everyone turns back to the whole group. Staff are asked if anyone wants to check in by responding to one of three prompts (announcements, brags, compliments).

Storytelling Circles

Storytelling circles are another effective method for fostering genuine human connections among the adults in schools. Creating opportunities for staff to share personal stories or professional experiences can create a positive school culture and foster connections. Staff are invited to sit in small-group circles, and then a volunteer facilitator poses a thought-provoking prompt, such as:

- What is one childhood memory that shaped who you are today?
- What kind of student were you in school (K–12 or postsecondary)? How does that shape your leadership now?
- Who was a teacher that affected you, and what qualities did they exhibit?
- Do you have an example of a student whom you affected positively this week?
- What is a professional experience that you are most proud of?
- Gratitude Tuesday: Name one or more things that you are grateful for.
- Who is your hero?
- "What's in a Name?" activity, with the following prompts facilitated in pairs: What is your name? What is the story of how you acquired your name? What does your name mean? How does your name reflect your culture? If you changed your name, what name would you choose?
- How do you identify racially or ethnically? How does this influence the work that you do here in the school?

The thought-provoking prompts initiate meaningful discussions in small-group settings, allowing genuine connection-building. After the smaller discussions, the entire group takes a few minutes to share and reflect on any insights or feelings associated with their experiences. The facilitator

> can encourage staff to identify connections based on their shared experiences. This activity can strengthen connections among team members and is a powerful way to create a positive school culture. By embracing this approach, everyone begins to view one another as humans with real-life experiences beyond what they know about each other as educators.
>
> It is important to note that participation and disclosure should never be mandatory, and this should be communicated to staff before implementing this practice.

- **Informal connections.** Involve micro-moments that organically present themselves throughout the day but can also be done with intentionality. A *spontaneous organic moment* would be when you walk past someone in the hall and say, "Good morning, Charlie, how was your weekend?" *Intentional organic connections* would look like a principal standing at the entrance each morning to welcome teachers and students for the day or walking down the hallway during passing periods to connect with and/or check in with staff.

  > "I often feel unseen and unwanted by certified staff. A simple 'hello' in the hallway can set the tone of a school culture."
  > —elementary school paraprofessional, comment shared in a staff meeting

- **Remembering.** When people hear that you remembered something they said, it can be a small but powerful dose of relational connection, sufficient to release the positive chemical called oxytocin, which buffers stress. For example, one teacher says to another, "So, how was your fiftieth birthday weekend? You mentioned you went up to the cabin." Or, "I know your knee surgery is next week. If I don't see you, I want you to know I am sending you all my best."

  > "As a superintendent, when I meet folks, I carry around a notepad and take notes about interesting things I learn about them. The other day, Teacher Benu shared with me that she was having a grandbaby in a few weeks. So next time I saw that teacher, I asked her how she was doing and was her new grandbaby born. I find that remembering the small things and connecting with each person meaningfully helps me build relationships and connection in a deeper way in our district."
  > —superintendent, preK–12 school district

Erin Groth, a veteran educator with twenty-five years of teaching experience and the current head of the science department at a large Chicago suburban high school, shares an example of informal connections and the concept of remembering at her high school and how important these forms of connection are for teachers and staff:

> What teachers really want is a genuine connection with their administrators—like "Julia, I walked past your classroom, and I saw you help that student in distress and I thought that was really powerful" or "I just heard that you are a grandparent, congratulations!" Consistent, supportive, and personalized communication between teachers and administrators means the world to us—and can solve a lot of the issues for staff who don't feel supported in their jobs. I don't expect my principal to know my résumé, but they should know something about me. Whether it's that a teacher comes in early and works out every morning or coaches football or is legendary for leading the school math team to always win. They could strive to learn something about every staff member so that when they see this person, they can make a genuine and personalized connection, "How are you today? I saw our math team did great. Congratulations! Keep it up!" These kinds of little connections make the staff feel visible and valued—"Hey, wow, my principal knows and appreciates something about me."

When individuals feel seen, heard, and valued within their school communities, it fosters a sense of belonging and contributes to their overall well-being. Creating environments where everyone feels important and appreciated is essential for nurturing communities of care and belonging. These acts of kindness not only promote supportive relationships, but also enhance collective community resilience and alleviate stress within schools.

In addition to being committed to building connection and relationships, schools that take educators' safety and self-regulation seriously will recognize how essential it is to know about the sources of workplace burnout and to actively work on preventing them.

INTENTIONALLY ADDRESSING THE ROOTS OF BURNOUT

Burnout is a response to chronic job stressors—high-frequency events embedded in workplace practices that have not been successfully managed. Over time, these stressors lead to an erosion of energy, involvement, and self-confidence in workers to the point where they feel exhausted, cynical, ineffective in their jobs, and burned out. There are many well-intentioned efforts to solve burnout in the world of work, but frequently, they address the effects of the problem, not its sources.[3]

Recent Gallup poll results report that K–12 educators have the highest burnout rate in the United States. In fact, almost 50 percent of K–12 employees in the United States (44 percent) say that they "always" or "very often" feel burned out at work. This percentage is greater than every other industry and professional group in the nation, leading to the conclusion that educators are among the most burned-out groups in the US workforce.[4] It's not surprising to hear the conclusion that school systems are having negative impacts on educators' health and engagement, which in turn adversely influences students' engagement.[5] Despite this crisis in our schools, few administrators are actively acknowledging and talking about burnout—or making plans to actively mitigate it. Instead, we have a quiet tragedy unfolding, as teachers and administrators are reporting their desire to leave the profession at unprecedented rates. Despite these conditions, many educators remain committed to their roles, supporting students and communities. However, their need for support and a strong commitment to alleviating burnout have never been more important.

Drs. Michael Leiter and Christina Maslach, two pioneering researchers on burnout, emphasize that *burnout is a management and organizational issue requiring a systemic solution, rather than an individual employee problem solvable through personal health and self-care activities.* To illustrate this point, they explain, "Think of burned-out employees as canaries in the coal mine. When the canary keels over, we acknowledge that the environment is hazardous—we don't tell the canary that it should take a long weekend."[6] Effective burnout management in the workplace begins with understanding its root causes. With this understanding, we can pivot from focusing solely on individual solutions to recognizing that meaningful solutions involve rethinking and redesigning our working environments. This shift aims to eliminate or significantly mitigate the factors that contribute to burnout. Leither and Maslach stress the importance of supporting employees in dealing with stress and burnout; however, they note that it is even more crucial to *proactively address the underlying causes* of burnout at the organizational and system levels.

FIGURE 3.1 Chronic job stressors that lead to burnout: Mismatches between a workplace and basic human needs

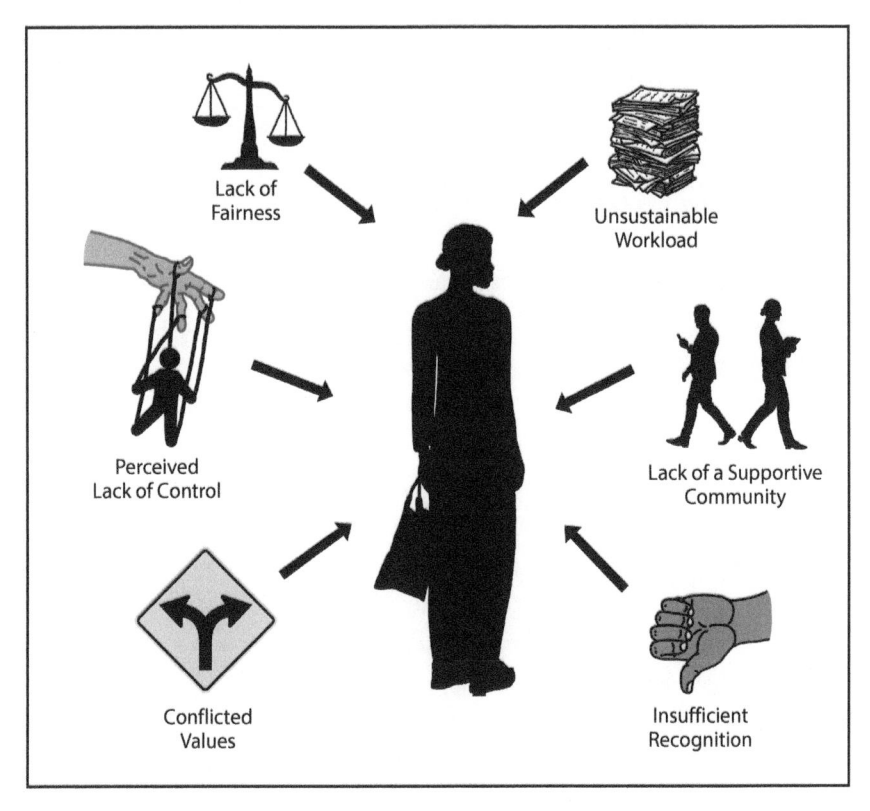

- Lack of Fairness
- Unsustainable Workload
- Perceived Lack of Control
- Lack of a Supportive Community
- Conflicted Values
- Insufficient Recognition

Mismatches Between a Workplace and Basic Human Needs

Leither and Maslach describe six main chronic job stressors that cause burnout and increase employee exhaustion, ineffectiveness, and cynicism and reduce feelings of competence, belongingness, and psychological safety at work (see figure 3.1).[7] They describe these factors as *mismatches between a job/workplace and basic human needs*. These mismatches occur across six core areas that are relevant for all roles and organizational contexts:

1. **Unsustainable workload.** A workload mismatch reflects conditions of high demand and insufficient resources (time, staff, information, etc.) to meet the demands successfully.

2. **Perceived lack of control.** A control mismatch involves inadequate autonomy to do a job well.
3. **Insufficient recognition for effort.** A recognition mismatch stipulates that effective and hard work is not receiving appropriate recognition and there is a lack of opportunity to continue to grow professionally.
4. **Lack of a supportive community.** A community mismatch displays that the workplace lacks mutual trust and support for employees and instead is characterized by incivility, bullying, harassment, or an inability to meet the needs for psychological safety at work.
5. **Lack of fairness.** A fairness mismatch is based on discrimination and inequitable policies, procedures, and/or practices in the workplace.
6. **Conflicted values.** A values mismatch happens when there are ethical, moral, and/or legal conflicts in the workplace.

These six chronic stressors contribute to burnout and can trigger state-dependent regression within the workplace. Supporting educators to reduce their stress and increase their regulation requires that we tackle these sources of burnout at their roots. Next, we outline several examples of strategies that educators, schools, and districts are using to reduce workplace stress and burnout proactively.

Mitigating Burnout by Redesigning Educators' Workloads

Working in demanding jobs that do not allow employees the resources that they need to be successful is a surefire way to increase staff burnout, ineffectiveness, and turnover. When people feel chronically overloaded and overwhelmed, they are likely to be less productive and successful in their jobs, even if they are highly skilled. If this happens over a sustained period of time, they will become emotionally and physically exhausted, and many will compromise their mental, physical, and social health and well-being.

Addressing the chronic stress caused by inequitable public investment in our schools—such as disparities in funding, resources, and support systems—presents a formidable challenge. However, it is critical to recognize that *unless we confront the root causes of excessive workloads, the cycle of burnout and high turnover will continue* in our nation's schools. The following are examples of the types of proactive measures being taken to mitigate educator stress through the creative redesign of workloads, making them more manageable, humanizing, and sustainable. Even small changes can reduce or prevent educators' feelings of overwhelm, self-doubt, guilt, and shame, while simultaneously increasing their sense of support in the workplace. Some ways in which schools can effectively redesign workloads for educators are to do the following:

- **Encourage partnering on tasks.** Because stress reduces people's capacity to perform in their jobs, the more stress that adults are experiencing, the greater the need to create opportunities for employees to work in partnership to maintain efficiency and effectiveness.[8] Working together, adults can provide one another with relational regulation—acting as buffers for stress—and share responsibilities so they are able to maintain the quality of their work. There are many examples of schools creating opportunities for partnering among staff:
  - A school counselor working in a middle school, who provides ongoing support and services to the students, classrooms, and teachers and feels stressed and isolated, began checking in with the vice principal. Having opportunities to partner with, get support from, and take time for reflection and dialogue with the vice principal acted as a buffer to reduce the counselor's stress and decrease her isolation, and it also allowed her to be more present, restored, and engaged in her interactions with the students and teachers.
  - A team of teachers collaborated to develop lesson plans and share resources. By working together, they reduced their individual workloads, supported one another, exchanged ideas, built relationships, and reduced the stress level of each team member.
- **Prioritize workload.** When employees are overwhelmed by too many tasks and limited time, stress can increase and become intolerable. Helping staff members prioritize their workloads and know when to complete each task and what can be reduced can make their stress levels feel more manageable.
  - Jane, a dedicated teacher, has been feeling overwhelmed and stressed due to an increasingly demanding workload. Recognizing the signs of burnout, the school administrator, Mr. Rodriguez, decides to address the situation proactively to ensure Jane's well-being by helping her to

prioritize, delegate tasks, and let go of some of the perfectionistic standards that she sets for herself. Mr. Rodriguez is also coaching Jane about the importance of setting boundaries and saying "no" when the task might adversely affect her health either mentally or physically.

- **Reduce meeting fatigue.** Another way to alleviate workload stress is by addressing meeting fatigue by evaluating the number and duration of meetings. The first step is to evaluate necessity. Can the information be communicated via email? If so, draft a clear, succinct, and thoughtful email with a link to a form for giving feedback and asking questions. For step two, if a meeting is essential, limit it to the minimum amount of time necessary to accomplish the task and identify the core essential attendees. For step three, always begin with a brief check-in to support building relationships and relational regulation, while maintaining a set time for efficiency.[9]
- **Build in short regulation breaks throughout the workday and during meetings.** In working with adults, the more stress that they are experiencing, the more frequently they will need short regulation breaks (just like students!). Short regulation breaks lasting from thirty seconds to five minutes, when used intentionally and proactively, can keep the cortex "open for business" so educators can maintain optimal regulation.[10] These mini-regulation breaks can be as simple as offering a body stretch, doing a deep breathing activity, or taking a short break during a staff meeting. For individuals, it may be going to make a cup of tea, listening to a minute of music, or saying a mantra, prayer, or quote to themselves. Many teachers incorporate these regulation breaks for themselves, but they also can do them with students. Sharing a regulation break with students can contribute significantly to the calming of the entire classroom *and* the teacher, allowing both to have increased access to executive cortex capabilities (e.g., thinking, reasoning, and problem-solving).
- **Provide opportunities to reflect.** Relationships and taking time for reflection regularly are important strategies to support adults' regulation. Talking to another person helps reduce and buffer stress. When schools create opportunities for teachers to reflect on their practices and to talk about difficult experiences, they are in essence creating organizational care routines. As Venet states, "Teachers need time and space to reflect on their relationships with students. Administrators can support this work by

devoting a portion of faculty meetings to gathering teachers in small groups or community circles to reflect on the social-emotional experience of their work."[11] They can also provide this by scheduling regular one-to-one supervision and/or coaching meetings or check-ins.

Creating Healthy Professional Boundaries

Creating healthy professional boundaries and redesigning workloads can be the antidote to burnout and stress. Prioritizing relationships requires that educators create healthy professional boundaries to prevent them from being perpetually on call for school, the principal, and students/families who are in communication all hours of the day and night. When we set boundaries, those around us will have an increased sense of safety, and we will protect ourselves from absorbing too much stress from our work demands each day. When educators create healthy boundaries with their colleagues, supervisors, and students, they are communicating when they are on and off work, protecting themselves personally and emotionally, and in doing so increasing their sense of safety, much as a fence around a home provides people with privacy and increases their sense of security.[12] By prioritizing relationships and implementing healthy professional boundaries, educators can redesign workloads to match their capacity, thus preventing a mismatch that leads to burnout and stress.

There are many ways that educators can and do create healthy boundaries in the context of their daily interactions in schools. This might look and sound like the following:

- A teacher who is asked to join a school committee at a time when she is taking care of her mother, preparing for the holidays, and generally feeling overwhelmed with life. She responded to the email request by saying, "Thanks so much, I would love to, but I am overcommitted right now, and if I participated, I could not give it my all and contribute in a meaningful way."
- A principal deciding that he will leave no later than 5:30 p.m. each day, and also learning to be honest and direct with staff when they request his time. He explains, "Sometimes when a staff member asks me, 'Do you

have a minute?' I now respond, 'My brain is fully occupied right now, and I want to give you the attention you deserve. Can I find you in a bit?'"
- A teacher who uses lunch to catch up on emails and work. Many times, students like to hang out after class and stay through lunch and request help on an assignment. Sometimes they are allowed to stay. Other days, the teacher tells them, "I appreciate that you want to be in here, but I need to prepare for class. Staying here is not an option today. I do have an office hour, as shown on your syllabus, every Friday, where you can sign up to talk or ask for help. If you sign up, I would love to see you then."

By setting clear boundaries, educators create a sense of safety for themselves and a balanced work-life dynamic, ensuring that they maintain their physical and emotional well-being while still fulfilling their job expectations successfully. A sustainable workload is crucial for establishing and maintaining healthy boundaries, but when demands are excessively high, even those who value boundaries find themselves taking work home or staying late.

Reflection/Discussion Questions
- Is setting a boundary in the professional workplace easy or difficult for you to do?
- Do you have an example in the past where you set a boundary to take care of yourself?
- What are the signs that you may need to set or reset a boundary in your current context?

Mitigating Burnout by Increasing Educators' Agency and Control

When educators work in conditions where they perceive that they have little agency and control, their stress will naturally increase, as will their risk of experiencing burnout on the job. Many education policies have reduced teacher autonomy and instead greatly increased the pressure on teachers to devote the majority of their time to adhering to standardized curricula, predetermined scripts, and high-stakes testing. We can reduce the risk of burnout in schools by increasing opportunities for educators to have input in and influence on school decisions and to have more time and autonomy for creative planning for their students (e.g., the "whole" child: social, emotional, and family engagement, lesson planning). Schools are increasing educators' shared power by giving voice, agency, and control in their daily work in many ways, such as the following:

- **Soliciting feedback in multiple ways.** Actively seeking feedback for improvement and following through by reporting out on how and if that feedback was implemented. This can be done through one-on-one discussions, regular staff meetings, monthly consultations with team leaders, and the administration of staff surveys quarterly.
- **Letting go of perfect.** Supporting teachers in having agency, voice, and control is facilitated when leaders emphasize and give permission to make mistakes as opportunities for growth, while also modeling vulnerability through sharing their own mistakes, learning edges, and areas for improvement.
- **Create a meeting agenda.** Asking for agenda items from teachers empowers them by giving them agency and control over the direction and focus of discussions, fostering a sense of ownership and investment in the decision-making process. This can be done by (1) sending the meeting notice in advance and asking if there are any agenda items they would like to add; and/or (2) incorporating previous meeting discussions with unresolved issues back into the next meeting so that teachers feel you have not disregarded unresolved issues that were important to them.

Mitigating Burnout by Increasing Recognition for Educators' Effort

If teachers consistently invest substantial time and effort into their jobs but feel as though their work is going unrecognized and unappreciated, even the most dedicated may become disheartened. Mitigating stress and burnout requires schools to be intentional about offering educators with recognition, appreciation, and benefits to acknowledge their efforts and accomplishments. There is no single best way to acknowledge and appreciate educators, as different things resonate with different people. There are many ways that schools are recognizing educators for their efforts, including the following:

- Providing a public acknowledgment of recognition (over the school morning announcements or at a district award ceremony).
- Taking the time to ask others how their day is going—and really listening.

- Emailing or sending a handwritten note or card to someone to let them know that you appreciated something (a thank-you to a teacher for covering Ms. Jana's class during his free period).
- Displaying student-created artwork to show appreciation for their teacher (the principal creates a tree with leaves and asks each student to list one thing that they appreciate about their teacher on a leaf).
- Creating space for teachers to acknowledge one another publicly and privately.
- A one-on-one affirmation/feedback conversation on specific strategies that an administrator has seen a staff member using that resulted in academic or social success.
- Offering to fund and find coverage for a teacher to attend a professional development (PD) session focused on an area or skill that they are interested in.
- Creating opportunities for high-performing teachers to facilitate PD (full or mini) for other teachers on or off your campus.
- Inviting a teacher with a specific strength in a particular area to join a paid committee at the site or district level.
- Creating opportunities during one-on-one meetings to discuss teachers' goals and connect them to opportunities that support it.

Mitigating Burnout Through Increased Support for Educators

Amplifying support for educators is paramount for cultivating healthy work environments. When educators feel supported, this not only enhances their well-being, it also positively affects their ability to be patient, creative, and responsive to the needs of their students. By investing in support systems to enhance the well-being of educators, schools are investing in the success and happiness of the entire school community. Schools are increasing support for educators in many ways, such as the following:

- **Increasing access to mental health support.** This is becoming a recognized priority in school districts, despite the financial investment required. Schools are now providing essential mental health resources for staff, such as on-call services available for educators whenever needed, as well as reflective sessions facilitated by therapists to help teachers discuss classroom challenges and stress management. By investing in adult mental health resources, schools convey to their staff that they acknowledge the daily stress and trauma in classrooms. They further support teachers by offering services like mental health professionals (e.g., social workers, school counselors, and others) who assist with managing students' stress-induced behaviors, as well as supporting staff mental health needs. Some schools that do not have formal mental health support create time during their social-emotional learning team meetings to speak about the types of support that the adults need.

- **Creating staff wellness lounges.** These spaces can provide opportunities for restoration, with comfortable seating options to encourage relaxation and relational connection. Create a calm and inviting atmosphere with warm and calming colors on the walls, soft and natural lighting, and a peaceful atmosphere that might include nature elements such as plants, flowers, or even a small indoor garden. Post inspirational quotes to uplift and inspire, and even add an interactive community element like a monthly theme board where staff can add personal mantras, express gratitude, or give kudos to colleagues. Some schools have added a suggestion box for staff to share ideas for improving the lounge or proposing wellness activities, and others include wellness resources such as books, magazines, calming music, stress balls, fidget toys, and/or adult coloring books. Another example is utilizing a wellness calendar in the lounge to highlight monthly activities, workshops, or wellness programs offered at the school for teachers.

Mitigating Burnout by Reducing Values Conflicts in the Workplace

Our nation's sociopolitical climate over the past decade has been mired with values conflicts. This has been exacerbated by the collective trauma of the COVID-19 pandemic, but polarizing issues like political partisanship, generational differences, school funding inequities, systemic racism, the plight of LGBTQIA+ children, and other value-based issues in our society have made our nation's schools a values battleground. This environment has led to an increase in burnout, moral injury, and ethical dilemmas among teachers, administrators, and other school personnel. School can alleviate stress and create regulated environments for school personnel by reducing value conflicts in these polarizing times in many ways, such as the following:

- Having clearly defined and culturally responsive shared set of values. These values should be part of a living document that is periodically reviewed and, if needed, updated to reflect the collective needs of both the student body and school personnel. School policies, procedures, and practices should also be periodically audited to ensure that they align with agreed-upon shared values.
- Fostering environments where teachers feel comfortable discussing differences and conflicts without fear of reprisal (e.g., using protocols and decision-making processes to ensure that all voices are heard and different values considered in school policies and practices). One of the ways that school leaders can do this is through modeling and facilitating conversations that allow adults to practice discussing differences in respectful ways.
- Offering continuous PD and/or structured opportunities for reflection and dialogue on ethical dilemmas so that educators have support in considering strategies to align their practice with personal and professional values. Schools can offer training on such topics as empathy-centered dialogue and communicating across difference, which helps educators discover their own stress activators, reflect on their personal values in comparison to school-wide values, and communicate their concerns in safe and healthy ways.
- Partnering with community organizations, such as local conflict resolution nonprofits, to navigate conflict and facilitate restorative practices among school staff.

Mitigating Burnout by Improving Fairness in the Workplace

Unfairness in the workplace stems from discrimination, harassment, and inequitable policies, practices, and procedures. Addressing unfairness in the workplace is critical to cultivating healthy work environments. When educators feel a sense of belonging and psychological safety, this not only enhances their work performance and enriches their interactions with students, but it also reduces the likelihood of staff burnout.

Creating a regulated work environment in schools is beneficial to all school personnel. It is especially beneficial to school personnel of color, as they too often experience high levels of harassment in work settings. All school personnel have a role to play in ensuring fairness and belonging in the workplace. However, school leaders must be proactive in creating a fair and just work environment, which includes intervening when they observe or learn about comments or behavior that reflects harm, prejudice, or discrimination in the workplace.

The following vignette reflects an example of a teacher who, during a staff meeting, directed a series of damaging comments toward a new colleague. These remarks represent *microassaults*, which are often subconscious behaviors or verbal statements that express disrespect, exhibit lack of sensitivity, and/or degrade a person's racial heritage or identity.[13 (see trigger warning)] In this story, the school leader failed to address the harmful comments, leaving the targeted teacher unsupported and unprotected. We outline how the situation could have been managed differently, detailing proactive steps that the principal should have taken to intervene and stop the hurtful comments, thus reinforcing and promoting a respectful and fair school environment.

Vignette: "Your Style May Be More Entertaining, But Toning Things Down Might Get Better Results"

Principal Williams is an elementary school principal in a small suburban community. He has recently hired a new teacher, Ms. Fetuga. Ms. Fetuga is African American and recently graduated college and moved to the area to take on the new position. Soon after joining the team, Principal Williams becomes impressed with Ms. Fetuga's ability to engage her students and decides to give her kudos during a staff meeting, where veteran teacher Mr. Clark is seated next to Ms. Fetuga.

Principal Williams: Good morning, everyone. This is a busy, short week due to the holiday, so let's jump right into our agenda. We may be able to get out of here early. Before we get started, I want to give kudos to our newest teacher, Ms. Fetuga, for her ability to really engage with her students. I was able to observe her class last week briefly, and her energetic teaching style really invigorated her students.

The other teachers and administrators clap and give votes of encouragement.

Ms. Fetuga: Thank you, Principal Williams. I appreciate it.

Mr. Clark: I think it's great that the students were engaged, but I wonder if that will lead to better performance.

Ms. Fetuga: Generally, engagement leads to attentiveness and better grades. I guess we will see how the students respond.

Mr. Clark: Yes, it's just that I know you are new here. Your teaching style is very different from the rest of us. Our students are not used to such an energetic teaching style. It may be overwhelming for them. Your style may be more entertaining, but toning things down might get better results.

Ms. Fetuga: My students seem to enjoy my lessons. What do you mean by "toning it down"? Do you have specific concerns or suggestions?

Mr. Clark: I'm just offering advice. I've been here for a long time and know the students well. No need to be defensive. I believe a more toned-down approach would be better suited for the children we serve.

Principal Williams: I appreciate your feedback, Mr. Clark. Let's table this discussion and get into today's agenda. We have a full week and have much to discuss today.

This interaction reflects a lack of fairness in this workplace—the type of toxic interactions that greatly increase stress and lead to burnout for valued staff. In this conversation, Ms. Fetuga's fellow teacher, Mr. Clark, is making publicly judgmental and hurtful comments that imply during a staff meeting that Ms. Fetuga is different from the other teachers in the school and not fully able to serve her students due to these unstated differences. His remarks are not constructive or specific, but more focused on "othering" Ms. Fetuga and insinuating that her style of teaching is not compatible with the current school culture.

In addition, Principal Williams is not responsive in this situation and is, instead, focused on moving quickly through the weekly staff meeting due to having a tight schedule. In this instance, Principal Williams has not properly supported Ms. Fetuga, who is a new teacher and is likely very motivated to fit into and acclimate to the new environment. It is obvious, based on Principal William's kudos, that he is making an effort to encourage the school's new staff; however, by not addressing Mr. Clark's comment, which qualifies as a microassault, Principal Williams is not creating an environment where all teachers feel safe and have a sense of belonging. Hurtful comments such as these could potentially negatively affect Ms. Fetuga's enthusiasm for teaching or even lead to her looking for another school where she will feel more supported and welcomed.

Improving Fairness in This School Setting

In this scenario, Principal Williams should have considered the psychological safety of all the staff present, especially Ms. Fetuga. He must also model the appropriate reaction to witnessing a microassualt for the other school personnel in the meeting. Since staff meetings are very important, Principal Williams should have taken advantage of the opportunity to immediately, directly, and publicly address the issue. Here are some steps that Principal Williams could have taken to address this situation:

- **Be direct.** Instead of rushing through the staff meeting, it is important that administrators do not shy away from discussing harmful statements and behavior in the moment. The principal should have modeled how a difficult conversation could occur. This would include being direct in stating to Mr. Clark that he has engaged in harmful behavior, regardless of his intentions. He could then remind Mr. Clark that Ms. Fetuga is a new teacher in a critical stage, and it is essential that she feels respected, welcomed, and supported at this time. He would need to take care not to shame Mr. Clark but still hold him accountable for the potential impact that his words and actions have on others.
- **Be clear.** Principal Williams should have made his stance on microaggressions and discrimination clear. He could state clearly that fairness and openness are central to healthy work environments and hurtful comments have no place in work environments that strive for fairness. Moving forward to minimize the likelihood that this would happen again, Principal Williams could have created a set of meeting norms that create a set of guidelines and standards for how we should address and behave toward one another.
- **Disrupt harmful behavior right away.** Principal Williams let the conversation go too far. Ms. Fetuga should never have had to defend herself. When Mr. Clark made his first comment, Principal Williams should have set the standard by interrupting earlier and affirming that different teaching approaches are essential to reaching the school's student population. He then could have followed up and had a private conversation with Mr. Clark.
- **Be responsive.** In lieu of this incident, Principal Williams should have followed through by creating opportunities for professional development and other structured interactions that were meant to build connectedness, deepen the listening and conversation skills of his staff, and reduce the likelihood of this type of incident happening again. He should have examined

policies, procedures, and formal and/or informal practices that may need to be fairer and more equitable at his school. For example, he could ensure that the policies associated with welcoming new school staff included verbiage about microaggressions and their potential impact on new staff. He could also schedule opportunities for his staff to engage in training on implicit bias and bias mitigation and encourage his staff to be upstanders (individuals who take action to support others and stand up against injustice, bullying, discrimination, or any form of harm or wrongdoing) for students and one another.

Here is an example of how the interaction could have gone had Principal Williams acted with fairness in mind:

Principal Williams: Good morning, everyone. This is a busy, short week due to the holiday, so let's jump right into our agenda. We may be able to get out of here early. Before we get started, I want to give kudos to our newest teacher, Ms. Fetuga, for her ability to really engage with her students. I was able to observe her class last week briefly, and her energetic teaching style really invigorated her students.
The other teachers and administrators clap and give votes of encouragement.
Ms. Fetuga: Thank you, Principal Williams. I appreciate it.
Mr. Clark: I think it's great that the students were engaged, but I wonder if that will lead to better performance.
Principal Williams: Yes, Ms. Fetuga's style is different, and we as educators should embrace diverse styles because schools have lots of kinds of learners, and there is much to be gained from finding new, different, and creative ways to engage them. Furthermore, we know that higher engagement generally leads to higher performance, and we will be glad to support Ms. Fetuga's efforts in her development as a new teacher. We have to move on, we have a full agenda, but Mr. Clark, I'd like to continue this conversation at a later time.

Be Proactive in Preventing Burnout

Educators today are managing unprecedented levels of stress. According to Leiter and Maslach's research, burnout stems from management and organizational challenges that require systemic solutions that prioritize collective care, not just individual efforts like personal health and self-care activities.[14] Effective strategies to alleviate stress in schools involve rethinking and reshaping our work environments. To proactively address the root causes of burnout and improve regulation, schools can take the following steps:

- Redesign educators' workloads for better balance.
- Increase educators' agency and control over their work.
- Enhance recognition and rewards for educators' efforts.
- Provide more direct support for educators.
- Promote fairness within the workplace.
- Foster alignment with the values that underpin the school's mission and vision.

Reflection/Discussion Questions
- Consider the six mismatches to human needs. How do any of these show up in your work? What is being done or could be done to address these sources of burnout in your school or district?

RESPONDING IN WAYS THAT DE-ESCALATE ADULTS' STRESS AND PROMOTE REGULATION AND CALM

Creating regulated environments also involves understanding appropriate responses to individuals whose stress response systems have been activated, aiming to calm and regulate them rather than exacerbate their distress. Table 3.1 compares behavior that escalates state-dependent regression with those that reduce threat, calm the nervous system, and allow individuals to return to a state of calm so they can access their cortex for more effective thinking, reasoning, and problem-solving.

Next, we introduce the concept of reflective questions as a tool to reduce stress and enable individuals to engage their cortex for problem-solving aimed at achieving beneficial outcomes.

USING REFLECTIVE QUESTIONS TO SUPPORT DE-ESCALATION

Another way to support regulation among adults in schools is to embrace the practice of asking reflective questions. Reflective questions support regulation because they encourage individuals to pause, reflect, and engage their prefrontal cortex, which is responsible for reasoning and problem-solving. By using the reflective prompts given here, individuals slow down enough to consider their

TABLE 3.1 Responses that increase educators' stress and dysregulation versus those that calm and regulate

INSTEAD OF...	TRY THE FOLLOWING...
These reactions are likely to: • Increase stress or perception of threat • Increase dysregulation and state-dependent regression	These reactions are likely to: • Reduce stress or perception of threat • Support de-escalation • Provide a healthy outlet to expel energy charge from activation of the stress response system
Prioritizing directing, correcting, or solutions while the individual is dysregulated. Seeking compliance *without* conveying care and concern about the individual. Words that correct, direct, or criticize ("Why did you do that?" "You will get written up if you don't accomplish this by the deadline.") or jumping to questions and solutions while they are escalated and unable to access the prefrontal cortex ("This is what I did—why don't you try this").	Prioritizing listening and supporting, first to calm the person and then focus on solutions once the adult is regulated. Being able to talk about big feelings first to calm them is important before moving to finding solutions. Listening to people's stories and how they feel allows a space for them to release the built-up tension from their perceived experience. Using words that de-escalate, such as "Something happened that caused you concern. Do you want to talk about it?" Communicating verbal messages of calm, safety, and connection through your words: "I am here to support you" or "You are not alone—we can work this out and find a way."
Moving too quickly toward the person, with escalated energy and emotion. Not reading the cues as to how much interaction, conversation, or physical proximity the person can handle while dysregulated.	Approaching individuals in a way that their nervous system can tolerate. Understanding that some people can tolerate close proximity, and it is regulating for them to connect, process, and talk about how they feel with a trusted person. Recognizing that for others, moving too quickly toward them and/or pushing them to talk, may dysregulate them even more. They might need to know that you are there (and have not ignored or abandoned them), but they require some personal space to feel safe.
Facial expressions and body language that convey a threatening stance (frowning face, turned-down brows, and clenched jawline). Using stern or harsh voice tones (escalated voice, rapid speech).	Facial expressions and body language that communicate empathy for what the adult is feeling and body language that reinforces messages of safety and can help guide the adult back to a regulated state. Holding the body with open or relaxed hands, speaking with gentle, soft tones, and slowing down speech prosody (i.e., speed of voice).

Continued

TABLE 3.1 *continued*

INSTEAD OF...	TRY THE FOLLOWING...
Sending a message of abandonment, like walking away and leaving a person and saying, "You need to calm down" or "You are out of control." When someone feels abandoned and ignored in distress, it increases perceived isolation and threat, which results in more dysregulated behaviors.	Reinforcing your presence by saying, "You are not alone. I'm here with you." Clearly sending a message that people are important and worthy of time and attention when they are ready to reengage: "I see you need some space right now. I am here for you when you are ready. I will check back in with you to see how you are doing."
Calling someone out in front of others. In a faculty meeting, the principal observes a teacher becoming visibly flustered during a discussion. In front of everyone, the principal says, "I notice you seem flustered. Do you care to share with us all more about that?"	Creating a sense of privacy and confidentiality so people feel comfortable sharing their stories. Asking people (offering a choice) if they would like to go somewhere more private to talk together or what would be helpful to them in the moment.
Minimizing, ignoring, or dismissing what the person is feeling. "This doesn't make any logical sense." "At least you don't have [this situation]." "You should be thankful that you at least have _____." "It is not that big of a deal. You are making a bigger deal of this than it really is." "You are so emotional and overreacting."	Helping people tell their stories without agreeing or disagreeing, and without correction or direction. Listening to people's stories and feelings before responding helps them regulate big feelings and return to calm. Helping people notice and name their feelings and sending messages that you care for them and what they have experienced. Using words that de-escalate or are neutral such as, "That happened to you," "How did that feel?," "You must have felt X," "I wonder if..."

thoughts and feelings, to gain insight into their emotional state, and to make more intentional choices. Reflective questions also help individuals come up with their own answers, which ultimately creates a sense of individual efficacy. When individuals have high levels of stress, they have limited access to their prefrontal cortex and executive functioning skills. Therefore, they become emotionally reactive, making it hard for them to think clearly or use their problem-solving skills effectively. We introduce here two types of reflective questions.

Reflective Questions That Regulate (use with someone outside the Optimal Zone of Regulation)

These questions support restoring the nervous system back to calm. When you observe an individual (student, teacher, staff member) who is escalated, these inquiry questions can help reduce stress and calm the person. The function of these questions includes the following:

- Information gathering
- Listening to and attuning with nonverbal body language and facial expressions
- Downloading the person's story to calm the significant emotions (research shows that telling a story and naming emotions in the presence of a trusted person is regulating)
- Co-regulating and letting the person borrow your calm
- Expressing empathy
- Tracking patterns in your own mental file cabinet

Examples of reflective and regulative questions and comments:

- What I heard you say was . . .
- I notice that . . .
- How do you feel right now?
- What was that like for you?
- I'm wondering . . .
- What did you think about that?
- I'm curious about . . .
- I'm interested to know more about . . .
- What did you notice happened when . . . ?
- Let me make sure I got this right . . .
- What did it feel like in your body? I notice that your fists are clenched. You are holding your stomach.
- This is what I hear you are feeling . . .
- I can see you have [*name something you notice that is a nonverbal/sensory cue, such as clenched fists*] when you talk about this.
- I heard you say . . .
- Can we pause for a moment . . . ?
- What I hear you saying is . . . you want to help the family, but they are not listening to your suggestions.
- I think I hear that [*you believe that children cry for attention and you feel that you should ignore them, or they will be spoiled*].

- It sounds like you all are on the same page about [*wanting to help this child, you just all have different beliefs and strategies about how to help him and this is causing conflict*].
- You have been crying a lot lately and you are worried that this is affecting your job performance.
- When that family said that to you, you felt hurt.
- What has been your experience with . . . ?

Reflective Questions That Reframe and Engage the Cortex (use when the individual is calm)

When individuals are more regulated and their stress has reduced, they are able to access their cortex to begin to think, reason, and map effective outcomes and solutions. The function of these questions includes the following:

- Considering potential or desired outcomes
- Exploring potential solutions and outcomes
- Exploring the intentions and feelings of everyone involved to find common ground
- Promoting growth versus fixed mindsets (Can we be open to compromise?)
- Connecting patterns and themes that you are hearing and observing
- Restating in words that involve a connection to a possible solution
- Expanding a perspective or mindset

    Examples of reflective questions that reframe and engage the cortex:

- Do you imagine _____ also has that experience?
- What are some of the things that _____ behavior might be communicating?
- What was the experience like before the event/feeling/thought . . . ?
- What was the experience like during . . . and after . . . ?
- Let's take a moment to sit and reflect and see what we come up with.
- If you were there now, what would you want to do differently? The same? How would it feel to do _____?
- What else could support you?
- What would you have done differently now that you look back?
- Let's think about what you can try . . . ?

- Can we pause for a moment so I can make sure I got it all . . . [*repeat back and connect it to a summary*]. "I heard you say that the family said they won't go to therapy, but you feel they need it. Is that right?"
- Let's play with how that strategy might work . . .
- What are some other ways?
- How would that affect others?
- How would that affect you?
- What are small steps to begin to resolve this conflict?
- If you had a magic wand, how would you solve this?

In the next vignette, we see the application of these reflective practice questions and the concept of relational regulation in the authentic story of a supervisor who used these strategies to support a staff member who entered her office dysregulated.

Vignette: "I Quit, I Am Done with All of This": A Supervisor's Toolbox of Strategies to Support a Dysregulated Staff Member

Dr. Anissa Cummings, a school psychologist in rural northern Texas, takes pride in her two decades of service. In recent years, she has been fortunate to work under an exceptional supervisor who has significantly alleviated her work-related stress. An example of this was when several students entered her office crying and reported incidents of bullying, including one female student who disclosed incidents of sexual harassment. These accounts resonated painfully with Dr. Cummings's own childhood experiences, leaving her feeling emotionally frozen and uncertain about how to proceed with handling these allegations. She remembers that day walking into the office of her supervisor, Kay Mantle, and unloading in a manner that she describes as "not a pretty picture."

Dr. Cummings's frustration poured out as she closed the supervisor's door with force. Her outburst was verbal, expressing a desire to quit, citing excessive stress and the school's lack of consistent procedures to addressing bullying. In this state of heightened distress, her capacity for logical reasoning was compromised. Initially, the words that spilled out to her supervisor started with the sentence, "I quit, I am done with all this."

Ms. Mantle remained calm as Dr. Cummings entered her office with escalated energy. She had a nonthreatening facial expression and ensured that she slowed the prosody of her voice, saying gently, "Would you like to sit down and talk about it?" When Dr. Cummings remained standing, Ms. Mantle asked her if she would like to talk while walking—"It looks like this has been a hard day, would you like to go for a walk and talk about it?"—allowing the two of them to discuss the situation confidentially while in motion. During this time, Ms. Mantle primarily listened to Dr. Cummings with compassion, giving her an opportunity to describe what happened and how she was feeling.

They walked around the perimeter of the school and talked, and while they did, Dr. Cummings began to show signs of a calming nervous system—her speech slowed in pace, her facial expressions looked less distressed, and she started walking slower. After about seven minutes, they arrived back to Ms. Mantle's office, where she sat down. Ms. Mantle then asked her, "What solutions can we think of together to address this problem?" Together, they started to strategize. First, they reviewed the school policy on bullying. Second, they agreed to consult with the principal to come up with a plan to address the bullying happening to these students at school. Third, Ms. Mantle said that she would engage the school safety committee to develop a comprehensive and coordinated plan to both investigate and respond to the reports of bullying and the various ways that, as a school, they could create more safety for students.

Without the grounding space provided by her supervisor, Dr. Cummings might have remained in an emotionally reactive state, unable to access her cortex. Reflecting on the experience, Dr. Cummings emphasized the value of working with a compassionate leader who could co-regulate her in times of extreme stress. Dr. Cummings knows that when adults in schools are absorbing the stress of work and the stress and trauma that students bring with them into school, they also need a person to go to who will help them to de-escalate and return to regulation. Ms. Mantle used several tools to support Dr. Cummings to calm her nervous system and regulate:

- A calm voice, friendly tone, and nonthreatening body language (e.g., slowing the prosody of her voice, having relaxed shoulders and facial expressions that convey a calm, safe person who is here to listen).
- Naming feelings to reduce their intensity (e.g., "Tell me more about it" and "How did it feel when that happened?").

- Inviting movement as a bottom-up activity to increase regulation and release excess stress (e.g., offering to walk and talk).
- Starting with support to regulate Dr. Cummings first and then, once her cortex was available, brainstorming and identifying solutions together.

Reflection/Discussion Question

- In reviewing the regulating strategies used here to support Dr. Cummings, can you identify any practices that you have used to support another person or colleague to return to regulation?

CONCLUSION

This chapter highlights the profound influence that regulated environments and strong relational connections have on educators' health, well-being, and capacity for effective leadership, teaching, and student support within our schools. To alleviate student stress, we must first focus on supporting adults, taking proactive steps to lessen their stress, and helping them to forge healthy relationships and connections at work. It's crucial to address burnout at its roots, equip educators with strategies for calming and de-escalating stressed individuals, and mitigate behaviors triggered by stress. By prioritizing educators' well-being and deliberately crafting school environments that minimize stress, educators can build stronger reserves, which enables them to better support and regulate students and maintain their dedication to teaching.

CASE STUDY 2

"Either You're Going to Let Me Take You Off Work, or Your Body's Going to Take You Off of Work"

In the landscape of today's schools, stress is a pervasive challenge, not just for teachers but for administrators as well. One of the coauthors, Dr. Tyisha Noise, shares a story from the front lines of being a middle school leader, which serves as a poignant reminder of the systemic pressures within the educational system and the urgent need for intentional stress reduction measures for all educators, including administrators. She offers a powerful bird's-eye view of the challenges faced by so many within the education system and highlights the need for improved support systems for everyone, including administrators. She invites us to consider the implications of more and more work being added to educators' plates without adequate support, and how too many educators end up sacrificing their health and well-being for their careers. Addressing burnout and turnover while prioritizing the health and well-being of staff is crucial for creating a sustainable and productive work environment. She explains:

> One of the things I've learned in the system of education is that the better you are at what you do, the more stuff they give you to do. So getting good at your work doesn't give you margin—it just gives you more stuff to do. Positionally, I am an African American woman. I grew up in poverty, so there's a general underlying anxiety about being good at work and keeping a job. I didn't learn how to step away. My health took me away. I had a big scare

around my blood pressure being sky high about my third year into administration. And I remember when my doctor gave me a screening called the Becks Depression Inventory and the Becks Anxiety Inventory, and the results of both were awful. And she said, I need to take you off work. And I remember crying in the corner of her office because I was telling her, "We're in a transition year. We've changed leadership. I can't be off now." And she said to me, *"Either you're going to let me take you off work, or your body's going to take you off of work."* So, I listened to her, and I took six weeks of medical leave. My supervisors weren't happy. Nobody asked if I was OK. Nobody asked what I needed. They just said, "Fine." Because by law, they didn't have a choice.

While I was off, I didn't hear from my supervisors, I heard from my peers and the teachers whom I closely supervised. It hurt a lot. I felt like a failure—like I was supposed to be able to manage the kind of pressure and trauma and the things that were constantly happening in our school. I was five years into my work in one of the most impacted communities in the nation. My body was breaking down, and I felt guilty about that. When I came back, nobody could figure out what to take off my plate. So when I went back to work six weeks later, I went back to the exact same job I left, in the exact same format, and nothing had changed—absolutely nothing. Even after coming back and performing and being lauded for being able to do the work and do it well, I was burned out and came to the conclusion that I was not supposed to be in school leadership. If I was burned out and other people were not, then I must be doing it wrong. *There was nobody from leadership to say, "Hey, let us help you figure this out."* It was like they didn't care. So I started to look for another job.

Dr. Noise's experience underscores that within the demanding context of education, proficiency often translates into a heavier workload rather than recognition or relief. Her story is a testament to the need for educational systems to not only recognize the signs of burnout, but to actively engage in creating solutions that will alleviate the burden on educators. By applying the RYSE framework, we analyze this story through three distinct dimensions—individual and interpersonal, school and community, and systemic—to identify how the lack of institutional support during Dr. Noise's medical leave—a time when she needed empathy and assistance—illustrates the shortcomings of the current system, which significantly contribute to cycles of stress and burnout for even our most passionate and committed educators. The framework also allows us to imagine this story from a very different perspective—a system designed to prioritize the health and well-being of educators.

INDIVIDUAL AND INTERPERSONAL FACTORS THAT CONTRIBUTE TO STRESS IN SCHOOLS OR STRENGTHEN STUDENTS' AND EDUCATORS' WELL-BEING

Toxic Stress and Trauma

Dr. Noise's status as a single, childless, African American, female, first-generation college graduate in her first school leadership position provides a unique set of stressors. First, diversity, equity, and inclusion (DEI) and unconscious bias research by Cornell University's Dr. Lisa Nishii demonstrates that women in leadership in general, and women of color more specifically, are judged more harshly when in leadership positions, even when they are highly qualified and perform well.[1] Dr. Noise not only served in a historically underserved community, but she served in a location that had long-term challenges addressing the behaviors and needs of African American girls. Furthermore, nearly all of her teammates had families with children, and as such, they were more likely to take off work, leave earlier, and request coverage for events occurring outside the school day. In an attempt to be a "team player," Dr. Noise often covered for her colleagues so leadership responsibilities were addressed. This habit was never acknowledged or addressed by district leadership, creating a cycle in which others were able to rearrange and adjust their responsibilities and Dr. Noise was often tasked to pick them up.

Despite her extensive support of others, her teammates would sometimes complain that she was not contributing enough to the team. In these cases, she was rarely offered the opportunity to engage in a restorative conversation and to clear the air. Concerns were often brought to her by her leaders as truths requiring her adjustment, but without opportunities to work on building a cohesive team where everyone contributed equally. The kind of toxic stress created by being one of the few African American leaders on her site, with additional scrutiny, more responsibilities, less time off, and little concern for her needs, while carrying vicarious trauma from addressing intense student situations, was a recipe for toxic stress, which affected Dr. Noise's health and required her to take off work. Continued exposure to toxic stress and overwhelming circumstances without an adjustment in responsibility or support ultimately caused burnout and forced her to leave a community that she loved serving.

Reducing Stress, Fostering Resilience, and Promoting Healing and Well-Being

Supporting the administrator in this story at a personal level might look like this:

- When Dr. Noise's boss noticed that she was uncharacteristically short and less patient, instead of just generically asking if she was happy, her boss could have asked, "What's wrong, and how can I help?"
- When Dr. Noise encountered microaggressions, those issues should have been addressed right away, and she should have been offered opportunities to converse with the teammates who were responsible and had a chance to have these relationships restored.
- When Dr. Noise and another colleague were asked to take on the work of two other administrators cut from the budget, she should have been fairly compensated for the additional work, provided with additional professional learning or coaching since she was going to be leading teams of her former peers, and offered protected time off since the new role required her to work over built-in breaks.

SCHOOL AND COMMUNITY FACTORS THAT CONTRIBUTE TO STRESS IN SCHOOLS OR STRENGTHEN STUDENTS' AND EDUCATORS' WELL-BEING

Toxic Stress and Trauma

Students living in poverty are more likely to be exposed to unsafe and unhealthy social and physical environments, higher crime, and contaminated air and water, as well as lower-quality municipal and social services. In impoverished communities, students' caregivers are less able to create ideal trusting environments to nurture healthy attachments, increasing their likelihood of exposure to adverse childhood or possibly traumatic experiences. For these reasons, students in these circumstances are more likely to develop mental health and nervous system regulation challenges than their more affluent counterparts. Schools located in impoverished and underserved communities often double as the central hub of care for the entire community including students and their families.

Reducing Stress, Fostering Resilience, and Promoting Healing and Well-Being

Supporting the administrator in this story at a personal level might look like this:

- Build more partnerships with community agencies to provide intervention and support services for students to relieve some of the weight on campus administrators and teachers.
- Reduce class sizes to give teachers a fair and manageable opportunity to meet students' diverse needs.
- Hire other equally qualified and effective team members so that work responsibilities were distributed in a more manageable way instead of hiring more new team members that needed training.
- Dr. Noise's work responsibilities should have been adjusted to maximize her strengths, not to compensate for others who lacked cultural proficiency or the ability to manage their relationships with difficult staff.
- Dr. Noise should have heard from her superiors when she was on leave to communicate that her contributions were missed and appreciated, as well as to wish her a speedy recovery.

SYSTEMIC FACTORS THAT CONTRIBUTE TO STRESS IN SCHOOLS OR STRENGTHEN STUDENTS' AND EDUCATORS' WELL-BEING

Toxic Stress and Trauma

In the year that Dr. Noise experienced her increased anxiety, major depressive episode, and extremely high blood pressure, her school was in a transition. It was being forced to downsize staffing in a very high-needs school located in a very underserved community where the staff and leadership were already overworked and overwhelmed. While Dr. Noise has spent her career in Title I schools located in underserved communities, no other transition affected her so intensely. While the district's justification for downsizing the school was a dwindling student population, it seems that what had not been considered was the level of need presented by students in this highly affected community or the mental and emotional capacity required of the adults to love, support, teach, and lead students in a context where high numbers of students arrive dysregulated and/or mentally and emotionally undernourished every single day.

Reducing Stress, Fostering Resilience, and Promoting Healing and Well-Being

Supporting the administrator in this story at a systemic level might look like this:

- District leadership should have looked more extensively at alternative paths to managing budget cuts that did not add pressure on an already overwhelmed team.
- During a transition, district leadership should have considered the weight of systemic change on every person in that entire system and scaled back certain expectations to give administrators and teachers the mental and emotional space to plan for the impending changes.

Reflection/Discussion Questions
- As an educator, do you know when you are feeling overwhelmed? How good are you at setting boundaries for yourself until you can regain equilibrium?
- How do you set boundaries when you are being encouraged to work beyond your limits by your boss? Can you do so without fear?
- How do you repair or restore your mind, will, and emotions when you are tired, drained, or overwhelmed?

CHAPTER 4

Creating School Environments That Reduce Stress and Strengthen Students' Nervous System Regulation

Regulated environments in schools are holistic, encompassing both the physical space and the emotional climate. Intentional planning is essential to create elements such as low lighting or covers for incandescent, bright lights, flexible seating arrangements that accommodate student movement during lessons to improve focus, and specifically designated areas that assist students in self-regulation. For example, the "Be Well Room" served as an individualized de-escalation space for adults and students that was furnished with calming amenities. Another key feature was the inclusion of "calm down" corners in classrooms, where students could self-refer when feeling emotionally overwhelmed. These corners, equipped with calming tools, had clear purposes and clear expectations set for their use, including protocols for sharing the space. Similar spaces were provided outside classrooms, including in the gym and music room, even extending to the principal's office, transforming it from a punitive space to one that promotes regulation. Granting students the autonomy to utilize these areas as needed was crucial, highlighting the value of teaching and practicing de-escalation strategies. The focus on emotional support fostered a culture where students were better regulated and more prepared to engage in learning.

—M. P.

For students to be calm, regulated, and able to learn—to have the full capacity of their cortex engaged—we must emphasize relational regulation throughout the entire school setting. This includes designing classroom environments to promote safety and nervous system regulation throughout the school day. Most critically, adults must explicitly teach resilience skills to students beginning in early childhood and continuing through elementary, middle, and high school. This instruction is essential so students can confront life's challenges with adaptability and strength and navigate inevitable stressors without becoming overwhelmed by their stress-response systems.

The innovative practices described in the opening vignette bring this philosophy to life. Through intentional planning and the creation of dedicated spaces like "Be Well Rooms" and "re-set/regulation corners," this elementary school has successfully embedded the practice of self-regulation into the entire school environment. Students have the autonomy to use these spaces, which are integral to teaching them to recognize and manage their emotions constructively. By doing so, the school is not only acknowledging the complex emotional needs of students, but also equipping them with the tools that they need to navigate challenges that they will face both inside and outside the classroom.

Students who feel safe and are regulated, as well as those who acquire the skills to manage the intensity of their emotions as outlined in this chapter, will be better equipped to engage their prefrontal cortex. This enhances their ability to:

- Listen and absorb academic content in school.
- Learn social, emotional, and resilience-building skills.
- Engage with social activities and peers at school.
- Discuss problems and solutions to stressful situations that they encounter.
- Be receptive to reminders about classroom or school expectations and rules.
- Maintain sustained focus and attention in class.
- Have logical discussions to reflect on their behavior and consider more appropriate actions.

In this chapter, we discuss:

- Strategies for facilitating relationships and connection for students.
- The use of co-regulation to calm and regulate students.
- Arranging the environment to support students' nervous system regulation.
- Addressing microaggressions in the classroom.
- Supporting students to build their own emotional emergency tool kit.

EDUCATORS AS FACILITATORS OF RELATIONSHIPS AND CONNECTION FOR STUDENTS

Relationships and connections play a crucial role in reducing stress for students. When students feel connected to peers, teachers, and supportive adults, they are less likely to experience the adverse effects of social isolation, mental health vulnerabilities, and toxic stress. Being part of a supportive network provides students with a sense of belonging and security, allowing them to share experiences, seek advice, and receive emotional support during challenging times. This relational support, where students feel that adults at school really care about them, is the most important and effective way to buffer students' stress.

Purposefully carving out time for relationship-building and fostering genuine connections throughout the school day are highly valued in schools committed to reducing stress. Daily classroom meetings and regular schoolwide gatherings are important opportunities for reinforcing a sense of connection and belonging among students and between students and educators. Students benefit from peer connections and community relationship building in schools because the limbic brain, responsible for emotions and social bonding, is wired for relational connection.[1] By fostering strong relationships, educators provide a foundation of safety and belonging that significantly reduces stress. In addition, peer connections serve as important resilience factors and stress buffers, especially during challenging times. When students feel connected and supported by their peers, the school becomes a place where they can explore, learn, and grow not only academically but also socially and emotionally. By emphasizing the value of making connections, building relationships, and offering students ample opportunities to engage in forging peer connections, schools can reduce students' stress and foster a regulated and positive learning environment.

The following are several examples of the ways that schools support students to build relationships and connection with peers and adults in ways that strengthen students' regulation:

- **Smart Start.** A child who arrives at school with a dysregulated nervous system is experiencing internal overwhelm. Because of mirror neurons, dysregulated students' stress can negatively affect others in the school environment from the moment they walk through the door. This is why the time of arrival at school is an important opportunity to make that transition a soft landing, where relational regulation can buffer students' stress at the start of the day. In one elementary school, Teresa Manning, a first-grade teacher, uses the power of relationship and co-regulation to support her students to begin their day regulated so they can learn. She dubs it "Smart Start." As the kids arrive, she makes it her mission to connect personally with each one, ensuring that they're settled before the day begins. Her classroom ritual involves quiet activities. She doesn't put out toys or have loud, engaging activities. Instead, when they arrive, students can choose playing with Play-Doh or kinetic sand or going to the calming space, the writing center, or the class library. She makes sure that she connects with all students at the beginning of the day to support their efforts to regulate. She offers extra support as needed, whether sending children to the cafeteria for breakfast, giving them an extra hug, keeping them close to her, or arranging for them to meet with the school counselor. When she first started this routine, it took close to forty minutes before everyone was regulated. Practicing on a daily basis, her students now regulate within fifteen minutes. She feels strongly that it is worth the time investment "because kids can't learn until they are calm and regulated. Now, that we have our morning routine, they are ready to roll and learn each morning!"

- **Community circles and classroom meetings.** These can play a vital role in reducing student stress in school. Weekly community circles are facilitated within advisory periods, homerooms, or seminar courses in grades 6–12 and are inspired by restorative practice models. Led by an adult, these community circles aim to build peer connections and foster relational regulation through engaging games and activities that promote fun and camaraderie. Beyond just fostering community, these gatherings are pivotal to addressing and processing stressful incidents within the school environment. For instance, at the high school level, community circles can be instrumental in helping staff and students work through the grief of losing a fellow student. In middle school, they provide a structured space for students to discuss their reactions to traumatic events, such as a police-involved incident on campus, thereby assisting them in navigating and understanding emotions linked to such stressful experiences and reinforcing that they have support to navigate through adversity.

- **Peer check-ins.** Peer check-ins provide brief but meaningful opportunities for students to engage with and learn about their classmates. Our human brain is always scanning to determine if we belong, fit in, or are seen; and when we perceive that we do not, the stress response system is activated. Teachers who include peer check-ins as part of their daily and/or weekly routine support students to forge connections with peers—a process that can reduce stress and increase their sense of belonging. Peer check-ins for different age groups might look like this:
  - **Early childhood/elementary.** Pairing students together and asking them to share one thing that they are excited about that day or week; or using a feeling poster and having students point to how they feel about their day or week to their peer.
  - **Middle school.** Having students discuss a recent book they've read or a movie they've watched, sharing their thoughts and opinions with each other; using icebreaker questions about hobbies or interests to encourage students to engage with one another; or asking students what they enjoyed doing last weekend or are looking forward to for the upcoming weekend.
  - **High school.** Encouraging students to discuss current events or topics in their classes with a peer partner; or providing such prompts for discussion as: What characteristics do you hope to have when you are thirty years old? Who is a hero (past, present, imaginary character) you admire? What is one profession that you have thought of doing when you get older?

  To address issues of exclusion of one or more students, peers can be assigned to a partner through random selection and then rotating partnerships regularly. For students who find talking with peers stress-activating, alternative peer check-in methods can include writing reflections in a shared journal, using digital apps for communicating input, and joining the teacher for small-group discussions.

- **Clubs, interest groups, and gathering places at school.** Student groups play a crucial role in providing students with a sense of connection and belonging, ultimately contributing to stress reduction. Joining a community gathering or special interest group allows students to connect with like-minded peers who share similar interests and passions, creating a supportive community within the larger school environment. This sense of belonging fosters a feeling of acceptance and reducing isolation. The camaraderie and shared experiences within these social groups help to build strong social bonds and give students ways to navigate the complexities of school life with a network of supportive friends.

> **Roses and Thorns**
>
> Venet describes using a "Rose/Thorn" five-minute check-in with her students at the beginning of the day, where they are invited to share one thing that's going well for them that week (a "rose") and one thing that's not going so well (a "thorn").[2] She uses this to establish a tone of mutual support and care in the classroom. Other names for this activity include "Highs and Lows" or "Thumbs Up and Thumbs Down."
>
> This activity can be done with students in pairs or small groups to encourage connection and reflection. Here is the way it can work in a classroom setting:
>
> - **Description.** Explain that the rose symbolizes something positive or enjoyable or that we are thankful for in our lives, and the thorn represents a challenge or difficulty.
> - **Individual reflection.** Encourage students to take a minute to gather their thoughts and ideas or to write them down as they prepare to go next in small groups/pairs.
> - **Pair and share.** First, provide the designated time to discuss roses, and then signal the next time frame for thorns. Remind them that they are not fixing or solving problems or advising anyone, only listening.
> - **Deepening reflection** (optional). Ask students to go deeper and discuss how they are dealing with the thorns or overcoming their challenge now or in the future.
> - **Closing.** End on a note that is uplifting by asking the entire group to list one coping strategy that they use to cope with stress and to overcome challenges in healthy ways.

There is a critical need for inclusive spaces within schools that are important and safe sanctuaries, providing an atmosphere where students can authentically express themselves. As the number of students reporting high levels of stress, anxiety, and other mental health challenges soars, creating supportive environments in schools has never been more urgent. Middle school student Ashley describes how a school club was a life-saving environment for her friend Byron:

> My BFF, Lola, decided she's gonna be Byron now and start using he/him pronouns. He's figuring out who he is. He opened up to his parents about being trans, but it didn't go down well. They were *not* accepting at all. His folks totally flipped and were not cool with it. It hit him hard, and he was dealing with some heavy emotions. I'm talking about the D-word, depression, and even some messed-up thoughts. It was a wild ride, and I felt super helpless seeing her go through that.
>
> Our school has this LGBTQ club. It's like this awesome place where we can be ourselves. Being in that club literally saved Lola's, I mean Byron's, life, no joke. Having a spot where he feels loved and accepted turned things around for him. It's like where we got each other's backs. We're all about that support. So, shout-out to the LGBTQ club for helping my friend Byron through some tough times. There's always a place to find acceptance no matter what.

This club was instrumental in alleviating the stressors that Byron encountered during a challenging period, underscoring the vital importance of inclusive school environments in helping students manage stress. In some instances, such communities can even mitigate the effects of trauma or create lifelines for students who are at risk for self-harm or suicide, reducing their feelings of isolation and helplessness and supporting students' coping capacities and overall emotional well-being.

When Students Resist Forming Relationships and Connection

Some students, particularly those who have experienced trauma in the context of relationships, will not find it comforting or even safe for them to form connection with others, and they will resist efforts to do so. For these students, educators will need to find alternative routes to build connections with them that prioritize what allows their nervous systems to feel safe. The following is a vignette describing Cora, a school psychologist, who is struggling to connect with a tenth-grade student, Lourdes, who exhibits stress-related behaviors and struggles to trust adults due to past experiences. Recognizing the need for a nonrelational pathway, Cora decides to share a video as a way to connect with Lourdes. The video, on a phone, was the first point of entry for the student to feel safe in building a connection and trust with the adult. Some students take time to build trust, and the starting point can be a neutral shared interest, like the video that Cora shared with Lourdes.

Vignette: "Do You Want to See a Funny Video on TikTok?"

Cora is a high school psychologist in Laramie, Wyoming. Lourdes, a tenth-grade student referred through the individualized education plan (IEP) process, is referred to her for counseling. Lourdes has poor grades—she is failing two classes—and her teachers report that she is "unmotivated and has a lack of engagement and initiative." Her parents share that they are concerned that Lourdes seems depressed. Cora explains how it took some time to discover what did and did not work with Lourdes, and eventually how she identified how to support Lourdes to feel safe and to trust her in counseling. Cora explains the arc of their time together:

> During our first few counseling sessions, Lourdes did not talk or engage in conversation with me. She sat in silence, scrolling on her phone. I understand that it takes some time to build a relationship with a student. I also know it is important in counseling to first build a trusting relationship where a student will feel safe and comfortable. Pressuring Lourdes to talk would only shut her down more.
>
> Each week, I put several things on the table: snacks, markers and paper, a few fidget toys, and a meditative sand tray with rocks and a mini-rake. During our third session, Lourdes asked if she could have a snack. This was the first time she said any words to me. In the fourth session, Lourdes picked up some of the blank paper and opened a bag of chips and started to eat them while doodling on the paper in between scrolling through TikTok on her phone.
>
> In her fifth session with me, Lourdes asked if I wanted to see a funny video on TikTok. We began watching some funny videos and laughing at them together. When Lourdes shared her video with me, I took this as her first invitation for connection. This was a sign that her nervous system was beginning to feel comfortable and safe with me.

At first, relational regulation was not an accessible strategy to use to reduce Lourdes's distress because there was not yet trust built. The regulating strategies that helped to calm Lourdes's nervous system included the following:

- **Agency, choice, and voice.** Students that are experiencing stress may feel a loss of control. By giving Lourdes options of how she wanted to engage and

interact and providing her with various choices of activities to do during the session, Cora reduced her stress and helped her begin to feel safer.
- **Relational regulation.** Even though Cora does not necessarily like or advocate the use of TikTok, she observed that allowing Lourdes to scroll through the app was the only activity that allowed her to tolerate staying in the first few sessions. Looking through her phone allowed Lourdes to manage and regulate her uncomfortable feelings of being with someone new in a counselor's office. Cora knew that this could be the entry to further discussions and possibly meaningful conversations that would reveal how Lourdes was feeling.
- **Bottom-of-the-brain regulation.** As discussed in chapter 1, bottom-up approaches to regulation—repetitive somato (movement) sensory activities—engage the core regulatory networks and are the fastest and most effective and direct way of regulating stress for adults and children.[3] Providing Lourdes with several options to support bottom-up regulation (e.g., the ability to draw, fidget, have a snack, or draw in the sand tray) helped her to calm her activated stress response system without having to talk and share her feelings or talk about what was bothering her.
- **Patience.** It takes time to build a relationship. Cora recognized that pressuring or asking a lot of questions would drive Lourdes further away and increase her stress level. Further, when students are in a state of high stress and dysregulation, they have less access to their cortex and conversation is often much more difficult. Cora focused on regulating activities that would bring Lourdes's cortex back "online" before she tried to identify what specifically was challenging her and come up with problem-solving strategies.

Relationships and connections are the most powerful factors in decreasing stress among students within school environments. When students experience a sense of belonging and connection with their peers, teachers, and in school, the adverse impacts of social isolation and heightened stress levels diminish significantly. Once teachers build a trusting relationship with a student, they are better equipped to support the child and reduce that child's stress through a concept that we introduce next, called "co-regulation." In other words, when students trust their teachers, when they are under distress, they will be more likely to seek out regulatory support from an adult they feel safe with.

Co-regulation

Co-regulation typically involves teachers communicating messages of calm, empathy, care, and safety through calming words and/or nonreactive body language. It is one of the most effective methods of relational regulation available to us, particularly within the school environment. Just as stress is contagious, so is calmness. When educators remain calm and regulated, the power of their mirror neurons goes into action, and students begin to absorb the educator's regulated state to calm their own nervous systems. In the following vignette, Timothy, a middle school science teacher, uses co-regulation to create safety and support for a student whose stress response system was activated after hearing about the requirement to do a presentation as a class assignment.

Vignette: "Let's Take a Deep Breath and Then Count to Ten Together"

Timothy is a middle school science teacher in Lansing, Michigan. One of his students, Ama, approaches him after class once all the other students have left for lunch. She appears to be in distress. She has shallow and rapid breathing, her hands are shaking, her eyes are darting back and forth, and she can barely get a whisper out, "I can't do this." He does not know what she means by "can't do this," but he knows that she is in distress. Timothy is worried as he hears these words. He thinks that she might be suicidal and that he may not know how to handle this situation adequately. His own heart starts racing rapidly. He pulls up a chair for Ama, and they both sit down. He calmly says, "It looks like something happened that upset you. Do you want to talk about it?" She isn't able to say anything right away, so he says, "Let's take a deep breath and then count to ten together." He starts with one, two . . . and continues all the way to ten.

    She does not join him in counting but shows signs of calming—her breathing becomes less rapid and shallow, her hands stop shaking, and her eyes become more focused. Timothy sees physical signs (breathing slowed, fists unclenched) and behavioral signs (able to talk and see potential solutions) that his student is more regulated. She starts to explain how hard it is to focus on all the lessons in school and to do homework, and how she feels out of control because she is falling behind. Timothy recognizes that Ama is in distress, so he creates a safe space, carves out time, and uses several strategies to co-regulate her activated nervous system and return it to a more optimal state of regulation.

During this short interaction with Ama, Timothy used several strategies to provide co-regulatory support to her. These strategies can help her to build new and healthier neural pathways over time so she is able to manage her stress without her nervous system activating a survival response. These regulating strategies include the following:

- **Self-awareness.** Timothy recognized the signs of his own internal stress response system feeling dysregulated. Worry (feelings) that he might not be able to deal with a situation that may potentially involve suicidal ideation (even though he did not know what the issue was) caused him to feel a sense of urgency and panic (feelings), and he felt his heart racing (sensations) and heard an internal voice telling him to run (thoughts and his flight response kicking in). Recognizing all these factors internally (thoughts, feelings, sensations) was a crucial first step to prevent a reactionary response that might lead this student to increase her dysregulation, and instead choose a response that will lead her to regulation.
- **Pausing.** What helped Timothy from having his own stress-related reaction was to use a mantra (top-of-brain strategy) to regulate. He said to himself, "This student doesn't feel safe, and she came to me for help." He recognized that when a student comes to an adult in distress, that is a sign of trust and a call for help.
- **Relational co-regulation.** To reduce the feeling of standing over a student, which can cause further dysregulation, he got down to Ama's same level, which subconsciously reinforced a message of safety for her brain. He also invited her to breathe and to count slowly from one to ten, both bottom-up strategies to achieve regulation. It is important to recognize that Timothy must have taken time to build a trusting relationship with Ama, or else she never would have approached him for help. Indeed, if Ama did not trust Timothy, she likely would have darted out of the room (flight response).
- **Wait for the cortex to open, and then move to problem-solving.** Recognizing that Ama likely had reduced access to her cortex while she was in her state of activated stress, Timothy used very few words and prioritized co-regulating her nervous system (breathing, counting) first. Once he observed signs that Ama was gaining access to her cortex (she started talking about her stress with words), he asked her, "What is worrying you the most that led you to feel so overwhelmed?"

To successfully co-regulate a distressed student, educators must actively work against the contagious nature of the dysregulated student's stress. This is because the educator's own internal state will be subconsciously influenced to "mirror" the student's stress and dysregulated emotional state. As Winfrey and Perry remind us, a dysregulated adult will *never* regulate a dysregulated child.[4] This is why it is very important for educators to build self-awareness of their own internal states. Whenever they are in the presence of a distressed and dysregulated student, they will either begin to mirror the student's distressed nervous system and follow the student into dysregulation or, ideally, do the opposite—remain calm and influence the student to mirror their own regulated state, as Timothy did with Ama. He could have reacted by ignoring or dismissing her (a freeze response), by using words that were directive, correcting, or shaming (a fight response), or even by saying he did not have time, as he was urgently trying to make it to another appointment (a flight response). Instead, he recognized his own worry (feeling), his own stress (heart racing), and his negative thoughts ("I have no idea how to help—I am not a counselor"). While recognizing his inner stress experience, he still took action to say to himself, "This student is dysregulated, and she came to me for help." In the middle of his own emotional storm, he found his calm and used it to co-regulate Ama.

Co-regulation is being intentional about bringing students into adults' calm instead of being drawn into students' storms, essentially modeling for students how self-regulation works. Delivering co-regulatory support with repetition over time helps students build their own self-regulation. When consistent and supportive adults use co-regulation to disrupt the activation of a child's neural pathways associated with fear and stress, they are supporting the child's brain to develop new and healthier neural pathways.[5] As this happens with consistency over time, students will not need as much co-regulatory support from teachers and other adults, as they will have developed their own capacity to cope with stress.

Co-regulating a Distressed Student

Co-regulating a distressed student can be very challenging and emotionally draining. Being a model of regulation for students requires adults to do the following:

- Have self/body awareness of their emotions within a specific moment.
- Prevent themselves from absorbing the students' stress and responding with their own dysregulated behaviors.
- Employing one or more strategies to regulate their own stress.

ARRANGING THE ENVIRONMENT TO SUPPORT STUDENTS' NERVOUS SYSTEM REGULATION

Educators can arrange learning environments in schools in ways that intentionally promote regulation of students' nervous systems. School environments designed to support nervous system regulation are arranged to increase familiarity and predictability, give students opportunities for agency and control and strengthen relationships and connections between and among children and adults. Next, we introduce several strategies for arranging classroom and school environments that reduce stress and provide regulatory support for students throughout the day.

Increasing Predictability Throughout the School Day

Change can be hard for some students and triggering for many who have trauma histories (uncertainty can trigger that sense of threat and danger). When there is not an understanding of what is coming next, this uncertainty will activate the stress-response system. This can happen at the beginning of the year, when students enter a new classroom, or when there is a change in their daily routine (e.g., a pop quiz, an assembly, an unexpected fire drill, or a guest speaker). Teachers who create a predictable, daily schedule with regular routines repeated each day with consistency support students to decrease their feelings of anxiety and stress, increase feelings of safety, and have a sense of control in the school environment (which increases access to their executive brain, allowing them to think, engage, and listen).

Establishing Predictable Schedules

Predictable daily schedules help students across all grades understand what to expect during their school day. For learners who may struggle with transitions or changes, a predictable schedule offers a sense of security and reduces anxiety. Utilizing visual schedules and incorporating images for each activity can significantly support students in understanding what is coming next. A visual schedule communicates the order of activities from the beginning to the end of the day using photographs, images, and/or words. A visual schedule tells a student where to be and when (time of day) that activity will take place. A single one can be posted on the wall for all students to see, or individual visual schedules can be created for each student. Educators use visual schedules to decrease uncertainty, increase predictability, and as a result improve students' perceptions of safety at school. A visual schedule can also be helpful to students who do not respond well to verbal prompts or instructions or to children who are new to a school or classroom. When the cortex is unavailable due to stress, it can be hard to listen, remember, or focus. Visuals help the cortex to track, even while a person is stressed, the tasks at hand that need to be accomplished. The following are examples of the different ways that teachers use visual schedules with students from early childhood through high school to increase predictability and reduce their stress:

- **Early childhood: PreK-kindergarten.** A child is crying for a parent. The teacher uses the visual schedule to show the student when the parent is coming and where the student is in the day.
- **Elementary school.** A teacher welcomes a new group of students at the start of the year. She reviews a visual schedule that shows the daily routine during the first week of class. The schedule is visually posted in the classroom at eye level for the students. She takes photos of the students doing each activity and adds them to the visual schedule. It might look like this:

MRS. DARNIE'S FIFTH-GRADE CLASS SCHEDULE	
8:00–8:30 a.m.	Arrival and morning activities
8:30–9:00 a.m.	Homeroom and attendance
9:00–10:00 a.m.	Math
10:00–10:15 a.m.	Morning recess
10:15–11:15 a.m.	Language arts (reading/writing)
11:15–12:00 p.m.	Lunch and lunch recess
12:00–1:00 p.m.	Science or social studies
1:00–1:45 p.m.	Specials (art, music, PE, library, etc.)
1:45–2:30 p.m.	Quiet reading or independent study

2:30–3:00 p.m.	Afternoon recess or brain break: Short break for students to stretch, move around, or engage in student choice and self-directed play activities
3:00–3:30 p.m.	Review, wrap-up, and pack up
3:30 p.m.	Dismissal: Students are dismissed to go home or to after-school programs, clubs, or activities

Note: The schedule may vary depending on the school's specific routines, grade levels, and curriculum requirements. It may also include periods for interventions, assemblies, guest speakers, or special events.

- **Middle and high school.** A teacher uses a white board to write the homework assignment for the week in one column and the due dates for future projects in another column, as follows:

HOMEWORK	DUE DATE
Math Assignment: Pages 27–28, problems 1–15 in textbook	October 12
Middle School Geography Assignment: Choose a country from any continent (except your own country). Research and create a detailed PowerPoint presentation (no more than 10 slides) on the following aspects: • **Geography:** Describe the physical features, climate, and natural resources of the country. • **Culture:** Explore the traditions, languages spoken, major religions, and cultural practices.	January 10

Adding Predictable Routines to Daily Schedules
Routines create a predictable transition that falls within the daily schedule (e.g., transition from outdoor play to indoor English class), and they are incorporated into predictable schedules (e.g., transition room outdoor play to indoor English class).

Transitions
Transitions are sensitive moments during the day for many students. Moving from the known to the unknown (changes in the schedule or experiencing a transition) can activate the nervous system. A simple transition or change for one child may only elevate stress levels momentarily, and then they quickly adjust back to their calmer baseline. However, for a student whose nervous system is wired to be on high alert due to toxic or traumatic stress, a transition can further activate the stress response system into fight, flight, freeze, or fawn survival behavior. It is helpful to pair a verbal prompt that a change is coming ("five more minutes") with visuals (a countdown timer) and auditory cues (chimes).

Students who have experienced toxic stress may have difficulty following verbal prompts. Their bodies may be wired to be on high alert, significantly limiting their access to the cortical regions of the brain and making it difficult for them to listen and follow instructions.

Tips for Increasing Predictability during Transitions

- Minimize the abruptness of transition by giving advance warnings.
- Provide a verbal cue ("five more minutes") paired with a nonverbal cue, such as a visual aid (a visual timer) and/or an audio signal (chimes).
- Individualize supports and cues for students who need extra support (e.g., a teacher getting down to students' level to support them; using an individualized timer for a particular student).
- Create rituals for each transition so it becomes a fun activity and a familiar and predictable routine.

Using Visual and Auditory Aids to Support Transitions

Visual and auditory cues again support the cortex under stress to open and focus on the task that is coming next. It helps all students (and particularly those with increased stress) stay in their Optimal Zone of Regulation while transitioning between activities throughout their school day. Such aids include the following:

- **Playing music or singing a clean-up song as a signal that a transition is coming.** It is especially helpful if the same song is used for the same transition each day. Repetition creates a sense of safety and predictability.
- **Playing a game to support younger children in transitioning from one activity to the next.** Slither like a snake; crawl like a spider; hop like a bunny; pretend to be a truck driver zooming to the next activity.
- **Using an auditory or visual cue.** For example, chimes, musical instrument, five-minute timer, visual countdown timer.
- **Turning lights on or off to provide a visual cue.**
- **Sharing a glimmer.** Give directions: Turn to a classmate next to you and share one good thing that happened this week (or any other question of the day).
- **Supporting a relaxing, mindful, calming activity** like a breathing, movement or stretching activity, playing a fun game.

Using Predictable Routines and Schedules to Reduce Stress in a Seventh-Grade Math Class

Teacher Tyson, who works in a metropolitan school district with students in the seventh grade, has learned to use predictable routines and schedules in his classroom as effective methods for reducing students' stress. He explains:

> I got into this work to teach academics and slowly learned that I am working with humans with different levels of tolerance and experiences with stress. I have learned many lessons, but one in particular is how to handle transitions to reduce challenging behavior. I used to say to the students, "Put your papers away and take out your math textbook." My transitions were abrupt and jarring, and there were always kids in my class who became dysregulated. Now, I give my students both a verbal ("five more minutes") and visual/auditory queue (visual countdown timer with music) that a transition is about to happen. I learned in one of our professional development trainings that this will prepare their cortex (thinking brain) to listen and their regulatory system to slowly move from one event to the next, while minimizing the number of students who might move outside of their window of tolerance. I now repeat the same predictable transition each day at the same time. For this daily transition, I use a visual countdown timer projected to the white board, with gentle music playing and a timer counting down from "5, 4, 3, 2, 1" to support our transition to a math lesson. Since implementing this simple, predictable routine and transition, I have noticed much more regulation with all my students in class.

How is Teacher Tyson supporting nervous system regulation for his seventh grade students?

- He shifted from abrupt transitions to providing verbal and visual cues beforehand, allowing his students to anticipate and mentally prepare for the upcoming change. This approach reduces the element of surprise and helps the students to transition smoothly, without feeling rushed or overwhelmed.
- By giving students verbal cues like "five more minutes" and using visual countdown timers with music, he engages the students' cortex (thinking brain), signaling them to prepare for an upcoming transition. This proactive approach helps them shift into a change gradually, reducing the stress that comes with sudden changes.

> - Implementing the same predictable transition routine daily establishes a sense of consistency and predictability for his students. They know what to expect, which promotes feelings of safety and security, both of which are essential for reducing stress levels and maintaining emotional regulation.

When Predictability Is Not Possible, or the Schedule Needs to Be Changed

When modifications are necessary, educators should aim to provide advance notice to students, along with additional support to help them navigate changes effectively. Many students, especially those affected by trauma or toxic stress, are living with a nervous system on high alert. A simple change in the otherwise predictable schedule can activate their stress response system. Advance notice can prepare them more readily for the change to come.

Calming Corners, Reset Zones, and Regulating Spaces

These are all terms describing the practice of designating a semiprivate area in the classroom where students can go to regulate themselves when they have big emotions and their stress-response systems have been activated. These spaces provide students an opportunity to navigate and manage their big emotions in productive ways. *They are never used as a time-out or punishment.* Instead, they are introduced with rules and expectations, but they always provide students with a safe place to go if they need to regulate their bodies.

Materials in a Reset Space

These spaces can be equipped with various tools and resources to help students calm, refocus, and regulate. Examples include:

- A beanbag, small soft chair, or cushion
- A small shelf or basket to place calming items (e.g., fidgets, stuffed animals, bubbles, pinwheels, coloring books, journals, and noise-canceling headphones)
- Books that teach about feelings and/or calming strategies: *Calm Down Time (Toddler) Listening to My Body,* by Gabi Garcia (4–10), *Understanding My Brain, Becoming Humane* (4–10)

- *My Moods. My Choices* flip book, which has feelings on one side and then on the back of each page a suggestion for regulating significant emotions
- Coloring books and crayons
- Worksheets in which to journal or draw to express feelings

> **But . . . I Am Worried That Kids Won't Learn If They Leave to Use a Reset Space**
>
> The biggest worry that teachers have about implementing this type of space in the classroom is that "students won't be learning and will be missing out on academic content." This is the paradigm shift. Districts, schools, and educators who understand the neurobiology of stress (as described in chapters 1 and 2) will understand that these reset spaces actually create pathways for students to calm their activated nervous systems so they can access their cortex and allow learning to happen.

Students who are dysregulated have a hard time accessing their prefrontal cortex to listen and learn. The following vignette describes how one elementary school in northern California uses a reset space to support students to calm themselves and bring their cortex back online.

Vignette: "I Need My Five Minutes"

Robin Pence, a restorative practice specialist, and Lauren Menchavez, principal at Lynwood Elementary in Novato, California, explain how they use calming spaces with all the students at their school:

> Robin: Every single classroom in our elementary school, from Transitional Kindergarten all the way to fifth grade, has a corner where a student can go to reset and calm when they feel overwhelmed. Some have a little carpet, a beanbag, or a soft chair, maybe some fidgets, sensory objects, or a stuffed animal like a sloth that helps them slow down and breathe. The corner may have social-emotional books or a journal to write about their feelings. Each teacher designs their own reset calming corner.
>
> Lauren: It is important teachers do not use these spaces as a punishment or time out. When a student perceives the space as a place they are sent when in trouble, it will activate their stress response system and no longer be a pathway to safety but instead will be one that represents a threat.

Robin: There's an equity element to these spaces. Before, in our school, children were being sent to the office or outside when they were dysregulated, and often, the students being asked to leave the classroom were our boys of color. We know that when we isolate students, we are causing more dysregulation and increased stress. In contrast, we now give all students this opportunity to regulate and be successful in the classroom. Students know that they can "take five" to reset their nervous systems and then integrate back into the classroom more engaged and focused. Children do really well using these spaces. We have normalized it so it feels like something we all can do to help our bodies feel safe and regulated again.

Reset and calming zones are a wonderful way to invite students who are dysregulated to find calm so they can reengage with the learning process. Setting expectations, rules, and instructions on how to use the space is important so that when an emotional emergency happens and students are dysregulated, they have the opportunity to default to the strategy (or new habit) that was practiced rather than to their reactive, primitive fight, flight, freeze, or fawn behavior.

Students need to be taught how to use reset spaces, and doing so will take time and practice. Teachers can set up rules for how to use the space or co-create them with students. The following are recommendations for introducing a calming space to students:

- Co-design the calming space with students so they feel a sense of belonging and connection to it. When students feel included and involved (e.g., being allowed to help create rules and expectations), they are likely to be more interested, invested in, and comfortable using the space.
- Create the space such that it includes items, objects, and activities that do not disrupt the class but will be regulating to the nervous system for students.
- Create posted rules that describe how to enter the space, how to use the space, and how to reengage with the class. For example: (1) Student picks up red/green cards from a teacher's desk, indicating that they want to enter the reset space. (2) They set the five-minute quiet timer and pick a regulation strategy that will help them in the reset space. (3) When the five minutes is up, the students decide if they are back in the green (calm zone) or still in the red (dysregulated zone). If in the red, they reset the timer for five more minutes. (4) At the end of five minutes, they return the cards to the teacher's desk.

- Emphasize that only one child at a time is allowed, but students can seek a teacher's help if they are available (e.g., to process how they felt after before returning or to think of better ways that they could have handled a situation).
- Practice with real-life scenarios or examples of things that students may experience when they move to the red zone (dysregulated), and have each of them practice how they would enter the space, regulate their bodies, and then leave the space.
- Establish a code word for the students to use. For example, if a student says, "I need my five minutes" or the teacher asks a student, "Do you need five minutes?" this is the code word signaling that the calming space may be needed.
- Practice with students how to use the reset space when they are calm. The more they practice, the more they are wiring their brain (neurosynaptic connectors) to build a new habit and remain calm and use coping strategies when their stress response system is activated. It helps the body prepare what to do when students have a real-life, in-the-moment emotional emergency.

Teaching Students to Use a Reset or Calm Space

The following is how Robin Pence recommends introducing the reset space to elementary-age students:

- "In our classroom, we have an area called a reset space." (*Indicate space.*)
- "Has anyone here ever had big feelings? Maybe of frustration (sadness, anger, missing family, etc.)?" (*A helpful gesture to teach and use is the sign language sign for "me too."*) "Yes, I sometimes get those feelings too."
- "Sometimes when we have those kinds of big feelings, it can be hard to focus on learning. We might need a few minutes to care for ourselves and calm our body. When I get big feelings, it often helps me to take a break to help my body calm down. Anyone else feel the same?"
- "In our reset space, we have a few things you can do that could help calm your body. These items stay in the reset space since they are there for everyone." (*Demonstrate the calming materials.*) (Tip: You may

> not want to put too many calming materials out at first. Two to three choices are good to start.)
> - "We use this five-minute sand timer to help you and me know when it's time to return to your seat." (*Demonstrate how to use the timer.*) (Tip: You might teach a sign that students can use when they need to use the reset space, and also a sign for if they need five more minutes.) "When you see the timer finish, it's time to clean up and return to your seat."
> - "It's important that we use this space only when we need it and that it's left ready for the next person. Who can give us an example of how to use the reset space?"

Reset spaces have many benefits for teachers, students, and schools. For example:

- **A dysregulated child cannot think, learn, engage, or focus.** Teachers who teach students to find a pathway to regulate their bodies will have fewer challenging behaviors in their classroom. These spaces provide a designated place where students can practice emotional regulation strategies. By utilizing calming activities, such as deep breathing exercises, mindfulness, or sensory tools, students can learn to manage and express their emotions in a healthy way so they can be ready to reengage with academic learning.
- **As school environments can be overwhelming for some students, these areas offer a retreat where students can take a break to help them reduce their stress levels.** By providing a calm and quiet space, students can regulate and then return to their classroom activities ready to learn.
- **They support students to develop self-awareness by recognizing their emotions.** When students understand and acknowledge their feelings, they are better able to implement healthier problem-solving strategies.
- **Engaging in calming activities can help students refocus their attention.** By taking a short break in the calming space, students can reset and return to the classroom with better access to their logical thinking and listening part of the brain (cortex).
- **These spaces provide opportunities for students to practice and develop coping skills for managing their stress.** This helps them build resilience in the face of future life challenges.

Not all classrooms have room for reset spaces. If so, they can be designed and placed outside the classroom to serve students across the school campus throughout the day. An example of reset spaces located in a central location is the Mariposa Restorative Room, described next.

> **Mariposa Restorative Room: A Schoolwide Reset Space**
>
> Across many cultures, butterflies are associated with transformation and metamorphosis. Robin Pence drew upon this metaphor when naming a restorative room at the elementary school. "Mariposa" is Spanish for "butterfly," and the Mariposa Restorative Room at Lynwood Elementary School serves as a proactive and intentional space. It is a central resource hub for promoting social-emotional skills, offering tools for managing dysregulated behaviors, referring to the school's family liaison to make community referrals, and facilitating professional development for teachers in implementing stress-reducing practices. Through its multitiered approach, it works to support students in developing self-awareness and effective self-regulation techniques while fostering a culture of emotional well-being within the school community. There are many uses for the Mariposa Restorative Room:
>
> - **A reset space where the school principal and teachers can request timely support for individual students who are dysregulated.** Students are invited to go to the Mariposa Restorative Room to not only find calm, but to also reset their brains and bodies so they can return to the classroom environment, ready to learn. Students also have adult guidance and support to build critical social and emotional skills to strengthen their emergency emotional tool kit (e.g., self-awareness, emotional literacy, and self-regulation skills).
> - **Referrals for students and families to the Mariposa Restorative Room are made by the principal, teachers, support staff, counselors, and/or the restorative practice specialist.** The school recognizes that when students come to class feeling dysregulated, they may struggle to choose kindness, lose focus, and display behaviors that could harm themselves or others. To address this, the Mariposa Restorative Room is used as a space to help reset students' nervous systems, allowing them to return to class and reengage in healthy ways.

- **The center is also a central location for teachers seeking resources to teach social-emotional and resilience skills and to manage students' dysregulated behaviors.** Teachers can find resource books, children's social emotional books to read to the class, one-page handouts with strategies to address various student behavioral challenges (e.g., bullying, attention issues, talking back in class, and community referrals), and displays and samples of classroom tools (e.g., feeling charts, laminated thermometers indicating the size of emotions, visual schedules, etc.).
- **Staff and families can be referred to the school's community/family liaison to receive resources and referrals such as counseling, food banks, free clothing drives, and financial counseling specialists for families.** Many families are experiencing ongoing stress related to basic survival needs, such as food and clothing. Connecting these families to resources that address cumulative risk factors can help reduce their overall stress levels. Alleviating family stress can directly benefit students who may absorb their family's anxiety and bring their overwhelmed nervous systems into the school environment.
- **Professional development for teachers to teach de-escalation strategies, how to introduce reset spaces in their class, and other tips on promoting social-emotional and trauma informed practices in their classroom.** This approach focuses on teaching social and emotional skills rather than relying on harsh and punitive disciplinary practices.

> We had a student and he had outbursts. It felt like he'd go from green to red so quickly and start hitting and throwing things. In the beginning, I was getting calls to come get this student to help him reset. In working with this student, he learned all these new skills, how to name his feelings, understand the size of his emotions, and some key regulatory practices to calm his body (e.g., box breathing—inhaling for a count of four, holding the breath for four counts, exhaling for four counts, and holding the breath again for four counts). After working with him for several weeks, we found this past week when he became dysregulated, he used the regulatory skills (breathing) to calm his dysregulated behavior on his own in class, without even needing to come to our Mariposa Center for support.
>
> —Robin Pence

ADDRESSING MICROAGGRESSIONS IN THE CLASSROOM[6 (see trigger warning)]

In schools, confronting and mitigating stress caused by racism are essential. Fu et al. emphasize the critical support needed for minoritized students during early adolescence—a pivotal period for racial-ethnic identify formation.[7] Unfortunately, it is also when many encounter increased prejudice and discrimination, including less overt (but equally damaging) *racial microaggressions (RMAs)*.

Defined as "brief and commonplace daily verbal, behavioral, and environmental indignities, whether intentional or unintentional, that communicate hostile, derogatory or negative racial slights and insults, directed toward racial and ethnic minorities," RMAs contribute to a toxic educational atmosphere.[8] These behaviors are notably harmful to minoritized youth, fostering environments rife with psychological distress manifested in the forms of social withdrawal, heightened anxiety, depression, aggression, defiance, elevated stress levels, and a spectrum of physical health problems.[9]

The obligation of schools to counter racism is unequivocal. Educators require comprehensive training to develop the skills and confidence to identify and intervene in instances of racism, including microaggression. Proactive strategies are not just necessary; they are imperative for the mental and emotional well-being of affected students and crucial for cultivating an inclusive, supportive school environment.

Three Subcategories of Microaggression

Microinsults

Microinsults are unconscious behaviors or verbal remarks that "convey rudeness, insensitivity and demean a person's racial heritage or identity."[10]

A high school teacher nonchalantly remarks to a student of color, "I'm impressed by how well you are doing in this advanced calculus class," which sounds good but may imply that she did not expect the student to perform well academically.

Microinvalidations

Microinvalidations are often unconscious, verbal comments or behaviors that exclude, negate, or nullify the psychological thoughts, feelings, or experiential reality of a person of color.[11]

> A Latina student tells a counselor that she feels like she is not being called on as much as other students during class discussions. The counselor responds, "I'm sure your teacher is just trying to give everyone a fair chance. Maybe you just need to raise your hand more often."
>
> **Microassaults**
>
> Microassaults are explicit racial derogations, characterized primarily by violent verbal or nonverbal attacks meant to hurt the intended victim through name-calling, avoidant behavior, or purposeful discriminatory actions.[12]
>
> During recess, a white student tells a Black student, "You don't belong in this school" and tells other children to exclude the student from play.

In the following story, witness how a teacher's timely intervention was able to disrupt microaggressions in an algebra classroom to support one of her students. As young Imani navigates the complexities of the group dynamics in her high school, she encounters dismissive and undermining behaviors that challenge her sense of belonging. Her teacher, Ms. Rasheedat, not only provides Imani with a voice but also fosters a classroom dialogue that cultivates awareness, empathy, and a commitment to an inclusive educational environment.

Vignette: "Can Anyone Tell Me What a Microaggression Is?": Disrupting Racial Discrimination in a High School Class

Soon after entering high school at age thirteen, Imani, a curious and eager student, finds herself facing a series of subtle and strange encounters. During algebra class, the first group project is assigned. Imani is the only student of color in her group, and she quickly finds that two of her fellow group members consistently interrupt her or undermine her contributions by ignoring her or making dismissive remarks. Whenever she attempts to contribute to the assignment, she feels as if she is invisible or her intelligence is being questioned. The interactions are subtle but still leave Imani feeling saddened and frustrated. Imani's third groupmate also seems to witness her experiences but doesn't say anything or intervene.

As the week goes on, Imani begins to have stomachaches and dreads going to algebra class. Her interactions with her groupmates also grow tense as Imani begins to take an argumentative or defensive tone as the group project progresses. By the end of the week, Imani begins to shut down and is no longer contributing to the project at all. Fearful of getting a poor grade, Imani decides to share her experiences with her mother. Imani's mother reaches out to her teacher immediately.

The following Monday, Imani's teacher, Ms. Rasheedat, asks Imani to share her concerns and feelings about the group project. Imani confides in Ms. Rasheedat, who is aware of the research on microaggressions in school settings.[13] Due to Imani's courage, Ms. Rasheedat is able to facilitate conversations with the class about the importance of fostering inclusion and respect in classroom settings. The conversation gives Imani the space to share her feelings with the class. In response, several other students share similar experiences that they have had with microaggressions centered on race, but also gender, accents, and disabilities. The following is how this conversation unfolds in class:

Ms. Rasheedat: Good afternoon, class. Let's have a class discussion today instead of jumping right into group work. It's an important discussion, so let's set some rules. First, we've already discussed the importance of respecting one another and allowing everyone to feel heard and seen. Second, this is not about punishment. If you have questions or concerns, we can discuss them without fear of punishment. Third, you don't have to engage in this conversation; it's not mandatory. A recent incident concerning microaggressions was brought to my attention. One of our classmates shared that she experienced microaggressions during group breakouts. I want to create a safe space to discuss microaggressions and understand their impact. *Can anyone tell me what a microaggression is?*

Angel (student): Isn't that when someone is being racist?

Ms. Rasheedat: Angel, many microaggressions are based on race, but they can also be based on gender, income, or appearance. Microaggressions are subtle ways that we make others feel as if they don't belong. Sometimes people aren't aware they are being harmful, but that doesn't excuse the behavior. We need to be aware of our behavior and words so that we don't harm others.

Imani: I'm the one who told Ms. Rasheedat about the microaggressions. I have been feeling very angry working on this project with my team. They are constantly ignoring me or acting like I'm not smart enough.

Ms. Rasheedat: Imani, do you feel comfortable telling the class why this experience made you angry?

Imani: I felt like they were treating me this way because I'm Black.

Luke (member of Imani's group): We're not racist. I was just trying to complete the assignment fast and get a good grade.

Ms. Rasheedat: Luke, that may be the case. It's important to recognize that microaggressions are often not intended to be hurtful. However, microaggressions cause harm. We need to be mindful of our impact on others. We can only do this with awareness and empathy.

Bea (student): What if we witness someone else experiencing a microaggression? I saw how Imani was being treated, but I didn't say anything. I wasn't sure about what to do. I'm sorry, Imani. I felt bad.

Ms. Rasheedat: Bea, as long as we follow our class rules and do so respectfully, it's OK to speak up for the person you see experiencing a microaggression. Let the person who is being harmful know that their words or actions are inappropriate. Explain how they could be affecting others. You can also offer support to the person who is experiencing the microaggression. Ask them to share how they feel.

Student: I'm glad we're having this conversation. I have definitely experienced microaggressions at school, not just from students but from teachers too. I don't know if they are trying to hurt me, but they do hurt my feelings.

As the conversation continued, several other students shared their experiences with microaggressions. Ms. Rasheedat acknowledged the harm that had been done and praised the students for their courage and transparency. The students agreed to co-create a safe and inclusive classroom environment. Ms. Rasheedat also brought up the class discussion with the principal and at the following staff meeting. As a result, the school implemented a values education campaign and restorative practices program focused on microaggressions.

The Essential Role of Teachers in Detecting RMAs and Disrupting Peer Bullying

Building on the story of Imani, where teacher intervention played a crucial role, Fu et al.'s research underscores the necessity for educators to be vigilant and proactive in their classrooms.[14] Drawing from their review of RMA research, the authors offer several recommendations for educators and schools:

- **Teachers, school psychologists, and parents are essential to positive racial–ethnic socialization for minoritized youth.** By actively engaging in open conversations, providing support, and challenging biases, they can help foster resilience and a positive sense of identity among these youth.
- **School staff should increase awareness of RMAs' impact on student well-being and behavior.** Support and care from teachers can have a significant and positive effect on students who are struggling and can make the difference in creating a racially inclusive and responsive classroom climate.
- **Implementing microintervention strategies can validate students' racial experiences, affirm their identities, and provide support against and buffer the negative impact of RMAs.** Students need to experience microinterventions frequently in the context of daily interactions with staff at school. Educators need to learn, practice, and rehearse their skills in learning how to implement microinterventions.

What are Micro-Interventions

Micro-interventions are "the everyday words or deeds that communicate to targets of microaggressions (a) validation of their experiential realty, (b) value as a person, (c) affirmation of their racial or group identity, (d) support and encouragement, and (e) reassurance that they are not alone."[15]

- **Collaborative efforts between parents and teachers are important to address the racial challenges that minoritized students face.**
- **Development of school-based antiracism programs targeting microaggressions is necessary to benefit both minoritized and white youth.**[16]

Reflection/Discussion Questions

- How have you observed microaggressions in your school, and how does this phenomenon alter a student or teacher physically, emotionally, mentally, and/or behaviorally?
- Imani's teacher facilitated a class discussion. What are some other ways that teachers and administrators can address microaggressions among students? What can be done when microaggressions occur among school personnel?

- Often, in the case of microaggression, students like Imani actually endure consequences for their reactions to these types of identity assaults, while microaggressors often receive no consequences. How can you help educators be attentive to microaggressions and the resulting physiological signs of stress in their students? How can educators address microaggressors in a trauma-informed manner?

TEACHING STUDENTS TO BE THEIR OWN EMERGENCY FIRST RESPONDERS IN TIMES OF STRESS

Schools routinely conduct drills for earthquakes, fires, tornados, and active shooters. These proactive drills help build a solid habit, forming memories of what to do to be safe in life-threatening situations. This preparation ensures that in a real emergency, the brain will mobilize these learned behaviors rather than defaulting to fight, flight, freeze, and fawn responses. Similarly, we can provide students with tools designed for emotional emergencies, which enable them to manage their emotions and react constructively in stressful situations (see figure 4.1). As students master these skills, they can also apply them proactively to stay regulated in school. Developing these abilities helps students to strengthen their resilience, equipping them to handle both significant and minor stressors effectively.

Introducing the Tool Kit to Students

Begin by setting the stage for students by having them imagine for a moment that each of them is a superhero. But instead of being able to fly or have superhuman strength, their superpower is being able to understand and regulate their feelings and reactions to stress so they can help themselves and others around them to feel safe and calm. Teachers might explain:

> Our aim is to help you become detectives of your own feelings and reactions to stress so you can better manage stressful situations. Imagine your nervous system like a superhero's control center that needs to know when and how to remain calm and when to spring into action. You can learn how to tell when you are calm and when your stress-detecting alarm starts to ring louder. If your alarm gets too loud—like when you're scared, worried, or have high stress—your emergency tool kit will help you turn the volume down. Think of the skills you learn with this tool kit like your emotional superpowers. The more you

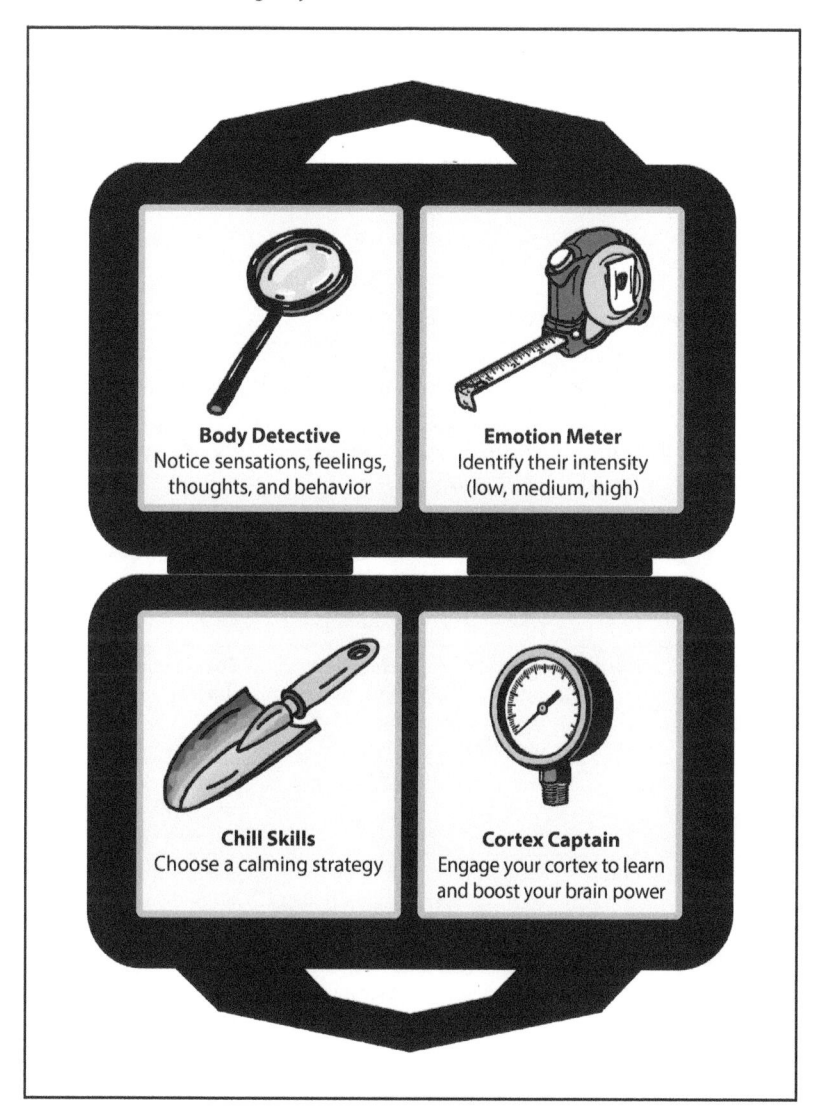

FIGURE 4.1   Emotional emergency tool kit

Body Detective
Notice sensations, feelings, thoughts, and behavior

Emotion Meter
Identify their intensity (low, medium, high)

Chill Skills
Choose a calming strategy

Cortex Captain
Engage your cortex to learn and boost your brain power

practice and use these skills, the better you will become at handling big feelings and difficult situations. You will have responses to help you tackle problems effectively instead of feeling overwhelmed by strong emotions or directing them inappropriately toward yourself, others, or the environment around you. In doing so, you will harness your strengths—your unique superpowers—ensuring you and those around you can have the best day possible.

Body Detective

This tool is represented by a *magnifying glass* because it symbolizes the importance of being a careful investigator, paying close attention with curiosity to the inner world of their sensations, feelings, thoughts, and behaviors that they have in the moment. Building self-awareness is an important skill that includes being a detective, carefully observing and noticing the cues that the body provides to detect stress levels. Learning to notice calm or stress in the body happens by learning to identify and recognize the sensations, emotions, thoughts, and behaviors in the moment (see table 4.1).

TABLE 4.1 Becoming a body detective to learn about the body's reaction to stress

STRESS-ACTIVATING EVENT	FEELING (LIMBIC BRAIN)	SENSATION (HIND/SURVIVAL BRAIN)	THOUGHTS (CORTEX)	BEHAVIOR (CALM, FIGHT, FLIGHT, FREEZE, OR FAWN)
The teacher pulled a pop quiz on us.	Nervous	Racing heart	I might fail because I did not have time to study.	Ditching class (flight)
My best friend's mom has cancer and is in hospice.	Helpless	Difficulty catching my breath; broke out in hives	Why would this happen to somebody so nice?	Daydreaming in class (freeze)
At lunch, no one wanted to sit with me.	Sad	Trembling	No one likes me.	Shutting down, isolating myself, and going to the library for lunch (flight)
I forgot to eat this morning and did not get enough sleep.	Hungry; tired	Weak; low energy; irritated	I can't think clearly or focus.	Snapping at everyone around me; criticizing everything (fight)
My mom yelled at me this morning.	Mad; angry	Fists clenched; jaw tense	Everyone hates me.	Trying to be perfect and please my teacher so they don't get mad (fawn)
My parents are getting divorced and arguing a lot.	Worried	Jumpy; racing thoughts	I hate my life.	Failing classes and missing homework (flight and freeze)
I have to give a presentation in front of the class tomorrow.	Anxious	Sweaty palms; stomach in knots	Everyone will laugh at me and make fun of me.	Talk to the teacher and tell them about my anxiety and ask if there is an alternative way to handle the presentation, such as recording it in advance (healthy response)

Emotion Meter

This tool is represented by a *tape measure* because just as a tape measure is used to determine the size of objects, paying attention to the size and intensity of one's emotions is an important skill that leads to developing inner self-awareness. Self-awareness includes the ability to identify the size/intensity of sensations and emotions in the moment. The size of the internal state of emotions can range from calm (no or low stress) to moderate stress to highly stressed and dysregulated. Understanding one's thoughts and the intensity of sensations and emotions that a student is experiencing inside the body is the next step in developing internal self-awareness to manage stress and adversity. A laminated thermometer can be a helpful visual to engage students in learning about the size of their emotions. The thermometer can be placed next to a feelings poster, allowing students to identify a feeling and then moving the arrow of the thermometer to indicate the size and intensity of their emotional state in that moment.

The visual image of a thermometer can be an effective way for students to check in and identify the level of emotional intensity of their internal states.[17]

Green (low; minimal stress, calm) represents "calm" and "regulated." In this state, students can engage in school, focus, learn, solve problems in healthy ways, and access their creative and critical thinking.

Orange (medium; moderate stress, more alert) means that "emotions are beginning to rise up inside of me" or "my emotions are moving from intense and overwhelming toward calm."

Red (high; significant stress, intense reaction) is the highest zone of intensity and means that "my emotions are heated up" and "my feelings are really big!" (Fight, Flight, Freeze, Fawn)

Some teachers add a Velcro arrow which students can move up and down the thermometer to represent the different levels of intensity of their emotions.

A simple thermometer can be laminated and posted for students to use, or they can have individual thermometers on their desks.

Instead of thermometers, older students can identify their emotions across a continuum ranging from 1 to 10:

Small: Green Zone (1–4)

Medium: Orange Zone (5–7)

Large: Red Zone (8–10)

Or early childhood teachers might use an arrow with the following images:

Small: Mouse

Medium: Cat

Large: Lion

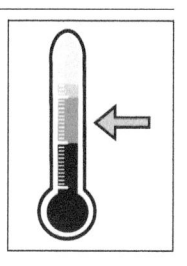

Chill Skills

This tool is represented by a *shovel* because planting in a garden requires discipline, patience, and effort. The shovel clears away dirt for new growth and symbolizes the importance of "growing the seeds" of emotional control and self-regulation so students can get better at managing stress and the intensity of big emotions. As students develop a foundation of self-awareness and listening to the signs of stress in their body, next they can strengthen and develop skills that help them calm their activated nervous systems. Once students learn the foundation of self-awareness skills—understanding their sensations, feelings, and thoughts and noticing their behaviors—it's crucial to teach them self-regulation and calming techniques.

Self-regulation strategies help them feel safer, calm their big emotions, and prevent reactive behaviors that can cause harm to themselves or others around them. In chapter 1, we introduced various pathways for regulating the nervous system: relational approaches, bottom-up methods (repetitive somato-sensory activities), top-down techniques (using thoughts to calm down), and intentional disconnection tactics (taking brain breaks). By introducing these pathways, students can manage stress responses more effectively. As they develop their emotional emergency tool kits of calming practices, they enhance their resilience against adversity and decrease their stress-related behaviors. Learning and practicing regulation strategies empower students to cultivate healthy social and emotional skills that will serve them well throughout life.

Breathing: The Breath Is the Remote Control for Self-Regulation

Breathing is often referred to as the remote control for self-regulation due to its immediate impact on our stress levels. As a bottom-up regulation strategy described in chapter 1 (four pathways to regulation), teaching students to use breathing techniques is a highly effective way to manage stress. Under stress, our sympathetic nervous system is activated, leading to physical reactions such as an accelerated heart rate, rapid breathing, and muscle tension. By consciously slowing our breathing, we engage the parasympathetic nervous system, which mitigates the stress response and brings about a state of calm. Techniques like diaphragmatic or belly breathing—taking slow, deep breaths through the nose, expanding the diaphragm, fully inflating the lungs, and then exhaling slowly through the mouth—can quickly send signals to the body to relax and decrease stress. Try the following breathing exercises that calm and regulate with your students.

> **Balloon Breathing (Early Childhood)**
>
> 1. Have the students sit comfortably with their backs straight and feet flat on the floor.
> 2. Instruct them to imagine that their belly is a balloon.
> 3. Ask them to take a slow, deep breath in through their nose, inflating their "balloon" belly as much as they can.
> 4. Have them exhale slowly through their mouth, deflating the "balloon" belly.
> 5. Repeat this process several times, encouraging them to focus on the sensation of their belly rising and falling with each breath.
>
> **4-7-8 Breathing (PreK–12)**
>
> 1. Instruct the students to sit comfortably with their backs straight, and their eyes closed if they wish.
> 2. Have them take a slow, deep breath in through their nose while counting to four.
> 3. Instruct them to hold their breath for a count of seven.
> 4. Ask them to exhale slowly and completely through their mouth, making a whooshing sound, while counting to eight.
> 5. Encourage them to repeat this cycle for a few rounds, focusing on the length of each breath and the sensation of relaxation that comes with each exhale.
>
> These breathing exercises can help students of different ages to calm their minds, reduce stress, and improve focus and concentration.

Learning "chill skills" or self-regulation is a very important part of the emotional emergency tool kit. Teachers can help students build this part of their tool kit by learning and practicing strategies that they can use to find regulation and calm so they can increase access to their prefrontal cortex to be able to reason, listen, and learn. Teachers can invite students to list the people, places, activities, objects, mantras, and daily rituals/routines that help them feel calmer and more regulated (see table 4.2). They can support students to brainstorm both individual strategies and group strategies where the classroom works together to identify their collective ideas of how they can regulate, as follows:

- **Classroom regulation poster.** Each student adds one thing that helps the body feel safer or calm and a classroom poster is created so students can visually be reminded of their own strategy or borrow one from another student.
- **Individual list.** Support students in creating a list of people, places, objects, activities, mantras, daily routines, or rituals that can regulate them when their stress response system is activated.
- **Regulation bin.** The classroom can collectively assemble or have the teacher create a regulation bin containing items that are designed to promote regulating the nervous system. For example, it could have fidget toys, coloring books, Rubik's cubes, Play-Doh, scented erasers, and laminated cards with quotes.

Practice to create a habit. Just like doing earthquake, tornado, or fire drills in school, practicing coping skills when students are calm (students learn and wire new habits better when calm than when dysregulated) helps them build habits. By promoting body awareness, fostering sensory and emotional literacy, and teaching ways to regulate emotions, educators can help students to develop resilience to manage everyday stress. With practice, students build strong habits that

TABLE 4.2 Classroom regulation poster: Things that help me chill in an emotional emergency

People/animals	Places	Activities
• Parents	• Nature	• Drawing
• Friends	• My room	• Doing a movement activity
• Neighbors	• The library	• Talking to someone
• Teachers	• A calmer area	• Listening to music
• Higher power	• Safe/reset space	• Shooting hoops
• Animals	• McDonald's	• Listening to music
• Memory of an ancestor	• Grandma's house	• Playing basketball with friends each day after school
Objects	**Mantras/quotes/prayers**	**Routines/rituals**
• Necklace that grandma gave me	• "This too shall pass."	• Meeting friends after school to play basketball
• Rock that is special	• "I can do hard things."	• Going to theater club after school every Tuesday
• Comfort object	• "One day at a time."	
• Fidget toys	• "Let it go."	• Having dinner with my family
• Weighted stuffed animal		• The daily school schedule

they can use during intense emotional moments. Being able to recognize their body's signals—whether calm or stressed—gives them more control in tough situations. This means that they can stop automatic stress reactions like fighting, fleeing, freezing, or fawning, and instead choose regulation strategies, leading to more coping behaviors and maximizing their capacity to listen, learn, and engage in school.

Cortex Captain

The first three tools highlighted in this discussion are designed to support students to develop the skills they need to handle everyday emotional emergencies. By building their capacity for self-awareness and regulation, students will have methods for navigating life's stressors. Just like a captain who commands a ship, students using these skills will have more control and ability to maintain a state of calm and regulation so they can engage their prefrontal cortex. We associate prefrontal cortex skills with a *gauge* because it provides precise measurements and adjustments to changing conditions, similar to what is required when the cortex is open and engaged for a student. A student who has access to the cortex can approach a problem or stressful event by carefully making informed decisions, doing complex problem-solving, paying sustained attention to detail, performing self-regulation, and utilizing the ability to adjust and be flexible in different circumstances. As captains of their cortex, students will have more ability to do the following:

- Listen and absorb academic content in school (listen and learn academics).
- Learn social, emotional, and resilience-building skills (restorative practices, positive behavioral intervention strategies, social-emotional learning, trauma-informed practices and strategies).
- Engage with social activities and peers at school (friendship and social skills).
- Discuss problems and solutions to stressful situations they encounter (complex problem-solving skills).
- Be receptive to reminders about classroom or school expectations and rules (follow rules and expectations).
- Maintain sustained focus and attention in class (focus and listen for extended periods).
- Have logical discussions to reflect on their behavior and consider more appropriate actions (enhance self-reflection and be open to take responsibility for actions and consequences of their behavior and choices).

The following vignette is about a middle school classroom teacher who is intentional about supporting children to build their emergency emotional tool kits.

Vignette: "Reset Your Body and Energy": Regulating in a Seventh/Eighth-Grade Math Class

> If you as their teacher are not going to give this student the security, the safety, the comfort, the happiness, the enjoyment of being in your classroom, you can't expect them to open up to your lessons, to be open to the academics.
> —Michael Lang, at Three River Charter School, Fort Bragg, California

Michael Lang is a junior high combined seventh- and eighth-grade math teacher who is making a real difference in the day-to-day lives of his students in a rural community. His commitment to creating a stress-reducing classroom is inspiring through the variety of strategies that he has implemented, such as morning movement activities, choice boards, and decompression spaces. Many of their students are experiencing homelessness, live in foster care, and/or have had many adverse childhood experiences. In addition to a focus on academics, Michael ensures that the whole child is seen, heard, and supported.

Michael prioritizes building relational connections with his students and cultivates a strong emotional support system for them at school. Here is what he says about the strategies that he uses:

> I begin each day with a morning activity that supports regulation and/or movement. It gives them a chance to start their day with something that's enjoyable, fun, playful and regulating. I've developed a Morning Movement and Regulation Choice Board, and I give my students nine different options in the morning to choose from. Some are movement based ("going for a walk with a friend"), some are calming-based strategies, or a journaling prompt. One example is our juggling scarves, and for body movement, they can take them out and practice. There are a wide variety of options to choose from.

MORNING MOVEMENT AND REGULATION CHOICE BOARD		
Please begin the day with your choice of the following regulating activities:		
Meditation/prayer/quiet time	Stretching	Math fun
Gardening	Reading	Walking
Journaling	Art video	Audio book

> I also have a lot of kids in my classroom affected by toxic stress or trauma, and big body movement is crucial for them. I want to have movement activities

throughout the day. And sometimes we do start the day as a group with a movement activity. The movement activities are just as important as the quiet activities that we do, such as journaling. On our visual regulation board, there's always something for everybody. When students get overwhelmed, I can say, "All right, just pick one of these practices that will help you reset and renew your body and energy." Here are some examples:

- **Breathing.** I can do number breathing with them, or I let them watch a video that walks them through it. Or, I have taught them techniques that they can implement themselves.
- **Stretching.** We have "just do basic stretching" as an option. Not quite yoga, but an opportunity to be with your body and let out energy with light, small movements.
- **Gardening.** We have a really cool garden outside, so I let the kids go outside, water some plants, or pick weeds, a very mindful activity.
- **Reading.** I have my audiobooks for readers and for kids who love books who aren't quite readers yet.
- **Walking** is always a big one because it's also a social activity. I let them walk and talk with a friend. It's cool to have friends that you don't get to see outside of school that you get to come in and start the day with.
- **Journaling.** I give them a prompt. For example, pick a mistake you made. What did you do wrong? How can we fix it? What can we do differently next time? What could you have done differently? Choose a moment in which you showed a strength or showed something you're able to do or a proud moment. Or write about somebody important in your life.
- **Art.** I provide a prompt such as draw a penguin, shark, planet, or a view of Earth, or choose your own. They love those!

The following are additional regulation practices at the school and in Michael's class:

- **Reset or decompression space.** I created a decompression space in my library. I put up these sheets to dim some of the lighting coming in. I've brought in an egg chair and some soft lights. In the decompression space, they can have a little stuffed animal. I've got a basket to put the used ones in so I can launder them to make sure they're cleaned between uses. And there is a curtain to give themselves privacy. If they can hide themselves, they feel more secure. So, one student at a time, but they get to close the curtain and get to be in that space by themselves. They have a five-minute hourglass timer. If they need five more, flip it again, but understanding that we're here to decompress and it doesn't take a crazy amount of time. You decompress and then come back to class. When students are using the calming area too much, I have a conversation with them privately: "You're in there a long time. I'm wondering what you need. We're here for education, so how can I support you to reregulate your body to come back to learn?" I think it's a conversation in the context of a trusting relationship.

- **Mistakes are mandatory.** One expectation in my class is, "Mistakes are mandatory always and forever." Anytime somebody makes a mistake in any subject, they are reminded that it is because they are not learning if they are not making mistakes. That goes for them and for teachers. "You have to try it, to take some risks and fail; we're here together to hold each other up and to wonder about it and to learn from it together." I tell my kids every day, "I make my mistakes all the time." It's a reinforcement that mistakes are mandatory: I'm making them; they're making them. We're all learning.
- **Red, yellow, and green cards.** At the end of the lesson, I use a feedback system with colored cards. They have red, yellow, and green cards that they can hold up. How did you understand/like this lesson? Am I teaching it in a way that you can understand? They hold a card up. I've had an entire lesson; forty minutes go by, and I see a fleet of red cards. So I say, "Well, that was on me. I messed something up because so many kids didn't understand that. I am going to stop and think tonight figuring out how I can improve, and we will try again tomorrow." I also ask if anyone has ideas for improvement. And I have continued to develop the system, and now I also have a blue card, which is "I need a break." "I want all my kids to feel comfortable asking for a three-minute break. I want all my kids to feel comfortable asking for a different seat. I want all my kids to feel comfortable asking for the supports and to feel safe to have a voice.

Michael has beautiful examples as an educator working to create a trauma-informed classroom. His story is a reminder that we can all make a difference and help our students feel safe and regulated, even in small ways. Here are some key highlights/takeaways from Michael, including stress-reducing strategies he uses:

- **Relational regulation.** Michael prioritizes building strong connections with his students, recognizing the challenges that they may face outside the classroom.
- **Voice, agency, and control.** Through the Morning Movement and Regulation Choice Board, Michael gives students the opportunity to make decisions about how they start their day. This practice instills a sense of agency and control, reinforcing the idea that their voices matter. In addition, the colored card feedback system at the end of lessons further empowers students to express their understanding and needs in the learning process.
- **Fun and play.** He incorporates games and fun activities into the learning environment to create an enjoyable atmosphere. By doing so, he ensures that students have opportunities to regulate their body so their cortex stays open for academic learning.
- **Making mistakes and a growth mindset.** The classroom environment that Michael creates promotes a culture where mistakes are not only accepted, but embraced as part of the learning process. By explicitly stating that mistakes are mandatory and sharing his own experiences of making mistakes, he cultivates a growth mindset among his students.
- **Decompression spaces.** Michael creates a calming space in the library for students to decompress, giving them a pathway to regulate their body when their stress response system is activated.
- **Big body movement.** Understanding the impact of big body movement, Michael integrates movement breaks into the routine, both in the morning and as group activities during the day. Whether it's playing disc golf or participating in a stretch and strength elective, these activities contribute to the overall well-being of students, helping them release energy and stay engaged in the learning process.
- **Listening to our bodies.** Michael incorporates activities on the visual regulation board that address both physical and emotional needs, promoting self-awareness and regulation.
- **Offering pathways to regulation.** Through the visual regulation board and various practices mentioned in this vignette, Michael provides students

with multiple pathways to regulation. This approach acknowledges the diversity of student needs and preferences, allowing each student to choose strategies that resonate with them. The collaborative nature of the stretch and strength elective further reinforces the importance of collective well-being.

In summary, Michael Lang's teaching strategies demonstrate a holistic and stress-reducing approach that addresses not only academic needs, but also the social, emotional, and physical well-being of his students.

CONCLUSION

Through intentional instruction in self-awareness and resilience skills, we guide our students toward more empathetic and humane ways of being in the world. This includes managing their stress and emotional triggers effectively without moving to fight, flight, freeze, or fawn strategies, which can lead to harm for themselves and others. By fostering strong connections at school, creating environments that facilitate nervous system regulation, and intentionally teaching students to develop their own emotional regulation tool kits, we are providing them with the essentials, maximizing their learning and engagement in school. This proactive approach benefits not just the students but the entire educational system: schools become safer and calmer, students are more regulated and therefore, more capable of learning and educators experience less stress, fewer dysregulated stress-related behaviors, allowing them to focus more effectively in school.

CASE STUDY 3

"My Daddy Was Killed by the Cops": The Importance of Listening, Observation, and Flexibility in Reducing Children's Stress

Melany Spiehs, a preK teacher in Omaha, Nebraska, tells a story of one of her students, Devon, and the relationally rich environment that she created to support him after he experienced a triggering event that left his stress response system activated in her classroom. She explains:

> Four-year-old Devon kept me on my toes. His intelligence, humor, and physical agility were astonishing. He had an intense imagination and a confidence rare for a child his age. As the only African American child in our class, I worried about Devon feeling accepted in our classroom community. Devon's family had recently moved across town from a predominantly African American neighborhood into another segregated community. Our school is nearly 90 percent Hispanic/Latino, and African American students make up less than 2 percent of our enrollment. As a white female educator in a classroom full of children of color, I learned that I need to consistently check my own biases and be vigilant about noticing biases in my students. Sure enough, during the second week of school, another student, Curtis, told Devon, "Sorry, you can't come over to my house 'cause my dad don't like Black people." I immediately said, "In our classroom, we welcome all children and value all skin colors." Later that day, I would contact both boys' families to let them know what happened.
>
> As a teacher, broaching the topics of race and racism are the most difficult conversations I ever have with families. Acknowledging that a child in my class

made this comment was painful. I will never forget the absence of shock or emotion on Devon's father's face—a likely reflection of the realities he faces daily as a Black man living in the United States. I promised him that we were addressing this issue in our classroom. I knew there was nothing I could say that would ever completely repair the harm that had been done. We spent the next several weeks in class reading books that celebrated diverse bodies, and we explored melanin by creating skin color paints that matched each child's skin tone.

A few weeks later, while playing on the playground, we heard a police siren, and Devon approached me and said, "My daddy was killed by the cops." Stunned, because his father had brought him to school that morning, I was unsure of how to respond. All I could do in the moment was offer him a hug and reassure him that he was safe. While talking with his mother that evening on the phone, she shared with me that his dad is a musician, and some of his lyrics address police brutality. She also shared that they had moved across town to try to escape the violence and increased police presence in their neighborhood.

In our curriculum, we were about to begin a car study, and each year at this time we invited a police officer and firefighter to bring their vehicles to show the children. Undoubtedly, I knew this might be triggering emotionally for Devon, and I worried about causing trauma or retraumatizing him. I certainly could not argue with the statistics about the disproportionate number of Black men dying at the hands of law enforcement.

One of my coworkers was married to a police officer and suggested that, before the police car visit, we invite him into class, out of uniform, to meet my students. After running the plan by Devon's parents, we invited the officer to come and eat breakfast with us, and he showed up one morning out of uniform. I intentionally saved a seat for the officer at Devon's table and seated myself next to Devon to monitor his emotional state. Casually, in conversation, I asked the man what his job was, and he explained to our table that he was a police officer. Devon looked right at him and said, "Then why don't you got a gun?" The officer explained that he was not working today but asked if he could bring his car by next week to show the class, and Devon agreed that would be okay.

The next week when we walked the class to the parking lot to see the vehicles, Devon immediately recognized the officer, exclaiming, "Hey, I know you!" and the officer responded, "Hey, Devon!" At that moment, I could see that both Devon and the police officer recognized the humanity in each other. Devon declined the invitation to climb through the police car with his peers, but he walked around the car while holding my hand.

Committing to being a trauma-responsive educator means not doing the same things every year just because "it's how we have always done things." We listen to and observe our students to identify possible triggers and provide an alternative path that feels safer and more humane. This path would not have been possible without the connections and relationships built with Devon's family and the community. The more bridges we build between families, schools, and communities, the more routes that lead to healing.

Devon's story reinforces the effectiveness of trauma responsiveness in the classroom. This scenario also highlights the need to be aware of the intergenerational nature of trauma. Using the RYSE framework, we examine this story across four distinct dimensions—individual and interpersonal, school and community, systemic, and historical—identifying levels of stress and trauma, as well as actions to support preschool-age children in building resilience.

INDIVIDUAL AND INTERPERSONAL FACTORS THAT CONTRIBUTE TO STRESS IN SCHOOLS OR STRENGTHEN STUDENTS' AND EDUCATORS' WELL-BEING

Toxic Stress and Trauma

On the individual and interpersonal levels, Devon was in a vulnerable period. At just four years of age, he was still experiencing significant brain growth and had an emerging sense of self and racial identity. He had recently moved to a new neighborhood and a new school. Devon was experiencing racial isolation as the only African American student in his class. He had also experienced racial bullying within the first two weeks in his new school environment. At this critical time, school could quickly become a source of toxic stress for him. Due to this, Devon needed to feel safe as he navigated the many new relationships within the school setting.

Reducing Stress, Fostering Resilience, and Promoting Healing and Well-Being

Many of the strategies that Melany used are hallmarks of a relationally rich educational environment. Building from the positive trusting relationship she had developed with Devon, she was very intentional to take actions that increased his felt sense of safety and belonging in her presence, and therefore buffered his stress in the classroom. They include the following:

- **Relational observation, attunement, and listening.** Children need to be presented with accurate information stated in an age-appropriate manner so they learn to understand inequality and learn how they can take actions to disrupt it.[1] Melany did not ignore the painful comment that Curtis made to Devon ("Sorry, you can't come over to my house 'cause my dad don't like Black people."), nor did she shame him for making it. Instead, she took this situation very seriously (see the box "Take Discussions of Racism Seriously with Young Children"), acknowledging what happened and immediately taking intentional actions. She recognized that talking about race and racism in a manner that emphasized what children and adults can do to address discrimination would help all her students to feel a sense of agency and belonging in her classroom. For children of color like Devon, these conversations can support their resilience, strength, psychological well-being, and a healthy sense of racial identity and self-esteem. Yet all students—and especially Curtis in this moment—would benefit from her guidance to help them learn about skin color/race and racism, through intentional instruction and open conversation. She took action to reinforce messages to all her students that affirmed their racial identities and her value for diversity, inclusion, and belonging in her classroom. She took time to create intentional activities through readings, books, and expressive arts that helped the children to learn about the beautiful skin colors of all the children in the classroom. She also reassured them that it was her responsibility to keep them safe at school.

- **Building relationships.** Melany knew that having the police officer come to her classroom in uniform, without any warning, might cause distress for young Devon. Instead, scaffolding the experience and supporting Devon to build a relationship with the officer created an opportunity for both the officer and Devon to make a genuine connection that could challenge societal implicit biases (e.g., all officers are dangerous and cause harm; all Black males are criminals).
- **Bridging the home-school connection.** Melany reached out immediately to both families to discuss Curtis's comment and the actions that she would take in the classroom in response. It would have been easy to ignore the comment and avoid these painful discussions, but instead she addressed it directly with both families, reinforcing her value and commitment to create a learning environment where all students are valued and respected.
- **Creating inclusive classroom environments.** This classroom emphasized the importance that all students experience a sense of affirmation and belonging. Bringing in books that helped the students to see positive

images of children of all skin colors helped to disrupt implicit bias and to promote healthy racial identities and positive narratives about racial diversity.

> **Take Discussions of Racism Seriously with Young Children**
>
> Many adults mistakenly assume that young children are incapable of harboring prejudices or engaging in behaviors that marginalize their peers based on social identity categories. However, this is unfounded. Ignoring instances of discrimination in children's language or interactions only perpetuates the development of prejudice.[2] Therefore, it is crucial to initiate discussions about race, racism, privilege, and inequality during early childhood. This developmental state is when feelings of shame, fear, anxiety, and bias initially take root.[3] The following are suggestions for addressing negative racial statements that young children make:[4]
>
> - **Ask them in a nonjudgmental tone, "What makes you say that?"** Try not to jump to conclusions. Listen to children, validate their feelings, and strive to understand what lies underneath their statements. Teachers can then build from what the children say to address generalizations or talk about an idea that hurts.
> - **Read books that introduce children to diverse people and characters and talk about race, racism, and social justice topics.** Ask questions while reading to help children develop empathy for the characters who experience racism or other forms of prejudice/bias (e.g., "How do you think Jesse feels when they talk about him that way/when they say he can't be the leader because he has dark skin?").
> - **State very clearly and consistently that it is wrong to treat another person (whether adult or child) differently because of race.** Children need to hear this message reinforced by the adults around them during their early childhood years, when they are developing foundational beliefs about diversity.
> - **Make a rule that it's never OK to tease, reject, or be unfair to someone for any reason, including because of their identity.**

Derman-Sparks and colleagues provide several examples of age-appropriate language that adults can use in these discussions:

> Sometimes people are treated badly because of the color of their skin or where their family came from, or how they talk, or because they are experiencing homelessness or because they have a disability. That is never okay. . . . If someone is mean or unfair to you or to someone else, you can do something. You can help turn unfair into fair. You can tell people to stop! You can explain that unfairness hurts. You can be a friend to someone. . . . You can ask a grownup to help you.[5]

SCHOOL AND COMMUNITY FACTORS THAT CONTRIBUTE TO STRESS IN SCHOOLS OR STRENGTHEN STUDENTS' AND EDUCATORS' WELL-BEING

Toxic Stress and Trauma

Devon may have been experiencing stressors within the school setting and within the larger community. With his recent move, Devon was experiencing racial isolation. He was the only African American student in his class, and the school and larger community primarily consisted of Latino children and families. Devon may have been experiencing loneliness and uncertainty. In addition, Devon's mother disclosed that his family moved from their previous neighborhood due to community violence and heavy police presence. This indicates that up until recently, Devon had been subjected to the toxic stress associated with living in communities with high rates of violence.

Reducing Stress, Fostering Resilience, and Promoting Healing and Well-Being

Partnering with the community to promote healing. Due to Devon having recently moved and experiencing racial isolation, it was important that Devon's teacher, Melany, was intentional in creating a sense of community for Devon. Here are some actions she could take to promote healing through community:

- **Facilitating relationships and creating community.** Melany had already been intentional about forming relationships with Devon's parents. To help Devon's family acclimate to the neighborhood, Melany could use her relationships in the community to connect Devon's family with other families in the community with shared racial/cultural backgrounds or shared interests like music. Melany should be sure to educate Devon's family about the community, its history, and the people who live in it to raise their cultural awareness. She also could intentionally connect Devon's parents with the parents of his classmates and explicitly ask the other parents to extend a warm welcome to Devon's family.

- **Creating a sense of belonging in the classroom.** Based on Devon and Curtis's interaction, Melany could facilitate a collective sense of belonging in the classroom by encouraging open dialogue about race, culture, and community among her students. This can be accomplished by allowing the students to be seen as the experts about their cultural practices, holidays, and traditions, and giving all the students the ability to teach each other about their families and backgrounds. This would give them an opportunity to acknowledge their similarities and differences.

SYSTEMIC FACTORS THAT CONTRIBUTE TO STRESS IN SCHOOLS OR STRENGTHEN STUDENTS' AND EDUCATORS' WELL-BEING

Toxic Stress and Trauma

As highlighted in previous chapters, throughout history, systems and policies have subjugated communities of color. Racial bias is a significant driver of inequitable treatment of children and families of color in the education sector. When teachers, administrators, and other school personnel operate as if racial bias does not exist, individual children and families are held responsible and treated in a punitive manner as they try to navigate oppressive systems. This is evident in the hyperfocus on the behavior of children of color and the judgments that many parents face if their children struggle academically, behaviorally, or socially in school settings. When schools do not actively seek to address racial bias, students and parents of color are left feeling isolated, ashamed, fearful, and distrustful. This can lead to an increase in maladaptive behaviors from both students and families and can also greatly increase the amount of stress that children and families of color experience and make it more likely that the school setting will traumatize or retraumatize them. This was evident in Devon's experience of racial bullying shortly after he arrived at his new school. Furthermore, the pain of this incident was intergenerational, as evidenced by Devon's father's reaction when he was notified of Devon's experience. Healing this level of trauma requires a systemic approach to relationship building, policy reform, and confronting ongoing systemic inequities.

Reducing Stress, Fostering Resilience, and Promoting Healing and Well-Being

At the systems level, institutional racism has led to racial segregation, overpolicing, and housing discrimination. These issues are a source of toxic stress for families and communities of color. This has also created neighborhoods and schools that experience higher levels of violence and underinvestment and lack diversity. These systemic factors and the impact that they have on the environment can create significant stress for children and families. Supporting systemic level change might look like this:

- **Engaging in power sharing and giving voice to children and families.** The formation and maintenance of active, engaged, and diverse parent and student councils and committees are essential to ensuring equitable school environments. Parent and student voices should be considered and included in the creation and ongoing examination of school practices, policies, and procedures.
- **Providing ongoing training and development for educators.** Racial bias is extremely common. Encourage or mandate school personnel to engage in racial bias assessments. Ensure that *all* school personnel receive high-quality professional development and training in racial bias and bias mitigation and the mechanisms and impact of racism. Provide school personnel with best practices to combat racism and other exclusionary practices in the school setting.
- **Prioritizing equity by engaging in restorative and healing-centered practices.** Historically, children of color have been treated inequitably when it comes to discipline and school punishment. Moving forward, to build trust, it is imperative that schools intentionally engage in restorative and healing-centered practices to repair the intergenerational impact of racial bias on families of color.
- **Facilitating family and community involvement.** Create and fully fund auxiliary positions dedicated to ensuring family and community involvement. These positions must act as bridges between the school and the children, families, and communities that it serves. They should also advocate for families and communities in a culturally responsive manner.

HISTORICAL FACTORS THAT CONTRIBUTE TO STRESS IN SCHOOLS OR STRENGTHEN STUDENTS' AND EDUCATORS' WELL-BEING

Toxic Stress and Trauma

The scenario in this case study highlights the importance of school personnel understanding historical trauma as it pertains to the students and communities that they serve. Historically, the relationship between law enforcement and communities of color, particularly African American and Latino communities, is one of distrust.[6] This stems from violent racial discrimination throughout the history of law enforcement in our nation. Police have historically enforced both overt and covert racist policies and engaged in informal racist practices and procedures (e.g., racial profiling). This is an example of institutional racism within our legal system that has led to profound historical trauma defined as multigenerational trauma experienced by a specific cultural, racial, or ethnic group.[7] As generations of people have shared negative experiences and encounters with law enforcement (e.g., police brutality, unarmed police shootings, and "driving while Black"), they engage in the process of racial socialization of their children and other children in their communities to prepare them for encounters with law enforcement in an attempt to ensure their survival.[8]

REFLECTION/DISCUSSION QUESTIONS

- As an educator, how do you address racial bias and racial microaggressions (RMAs) in your classroom or sphere of influence?
- As an educator, how do you address racial bias and RMAs with colleagues?
- How do you address racial bias when you see it in the outcomes of campuswide or districtwide policies?

CHAPTER 5

Rethinking Discipline and Classroom Management

*B*efore I realized the profound impact of stress and trauma on our students, my primary focus used to be ensuring student compliance. I had not grasped that students that are quiet, compliant, or those who exhibit challenging behaviors might actually be feeling unsafe. An incident involving a student at the school I led marked the beginning of my paradigm shift. The student, Jasmine, was dysregulated and exhibiting disruptive behavior by throwing items in the classroom. Previously, my approach would have demanded compliance, potentially resorting to punitive practices such as seclusion or restraint. However, my evolving understanding of stress prompted a change in my response. Standing by the classroom door, I established eye contact with Jasmine and gently acknowledged their potential frustration. I conveyed, "I am here when you are ready to talk." Despite Jasmine's initial continued struggle, a pivotal moment emerged when they began to regulate a bit. Moving closer, I sat on the floor at the front of the room, reiterating my availability to assist in resolving the issue, whatever it might be. After some time, Jasmine chose to sit near me in a chair, expressing their frustration at being looked at by a classmate when they were upset—a typical response from students enduring stress and trauma. After some time, my calm state started to co-regulate Jasmine, and they began to de-escalate. As we continued the conversation, we formulated a solution and next steps that included trying to pinpoint the causes of their distress and then taking some deep breaths together. Once they were calm, they started to clean up the mess they made. I chose to help Jasmine clean because they had started cleaning up independently. This transformative experience highlights the significant change made in my approach: rather *than focusing on compliance, it's crucial to first establish a genuine connection and employ calming strategies. Once the student is in a regulated state, we can then address accountability and compliance.*

—M. P.

In this story, Principal Portell illustrates his transformation—transitioning from a sole focus on compliance to a holistic approach centered on students' well-being and emotional regulation. He shines a light on the important and pivotal shift highlighted throughout this chapter—as stress levels in schools rise, we have seen a shift toward considering the "whole student"—recognizing that while schools are academic institutions, they also have a responsibility to prioritize students' social-emotional health and stress reduction, so they have the maximum capacity to learn. Students' stress-related behaviors are communicating a story that shares the same plotline: *they are dysregulated and/or don't perceive that they are safe.* When adults respond to such behaviors with punishment, blame, shaming, criticism, bribery, or exclusionary discipline, they only exacerbate the students' stress and escalate their nervous systems even more in the direction of "high alert." This not only reinforces their view of the world as dangerous, but also intensifies their stress response.

Educators—including teachers, administrators, and district leaders—must shift away from historical patterns of responding to challenging and dysregulated behavior with punitive strategies. Instead, we need to adopt methods grounded in understanding the neurobiology of stress, trauma, and regulation. In today's educational environments, given how many students are entering our schools and classrooms with activated nervous systems on high alert, educators need to begin seeing themselves as navigators of their students' nervous systems. To truly succeed in academics and reduce stress-related behavioral issues, schools must prioritize reducing stress, ensuring safety, and helping both students and adults regulate their nervous systems.

In this chapter, we discuss:

- The many aspects of safety in schools that support nervous system regulation.
- Effective and ineffective responses to students' fight, flight, freeze, and fawn behaviors.
- The use of restorative practices.
- Interrupting reactivity and creating a pause with a self-regulation tool.

IMPROVING SAFETY IN SCHOOLS: UNDERSTANDING THE IMPORTANCE OF REGULATED NERVOUS SYSTEMS

Human beings cannot learn, teach, or focus their attention on anything requiring their cortex unless they feel safe and are regulated.

Essential to the reduction of stress in schools is creating environments that lead students and staff to experience real safety (*being* safe), while also leaving them with a felt sense of safety (*feeling* safe). Schools need policies, procedures, and practices that establish real safety. However, students and adults also have a critical need to *feel* safe (felt safety). Establishing safety in schools requires that educators attend to the multiple dimensions as outlined here (see figure 5.1).[1]

- **Physical safety—"I feel safe."** Students and educators have physical safety in environments where they do not face risks or threats from any type of physical harm. Physical safety in schools might look like a clean, well-lit campus in good repair, filled with comfortable and functioning equipment and furniture in every classroom, restrooms with working locks providing necessary privacy, the presence of a security guard, and a robust system for campus entry, as well as a system for reporting instances of bullying.

FIGURE 5.1　Safety in schools has many dimensions

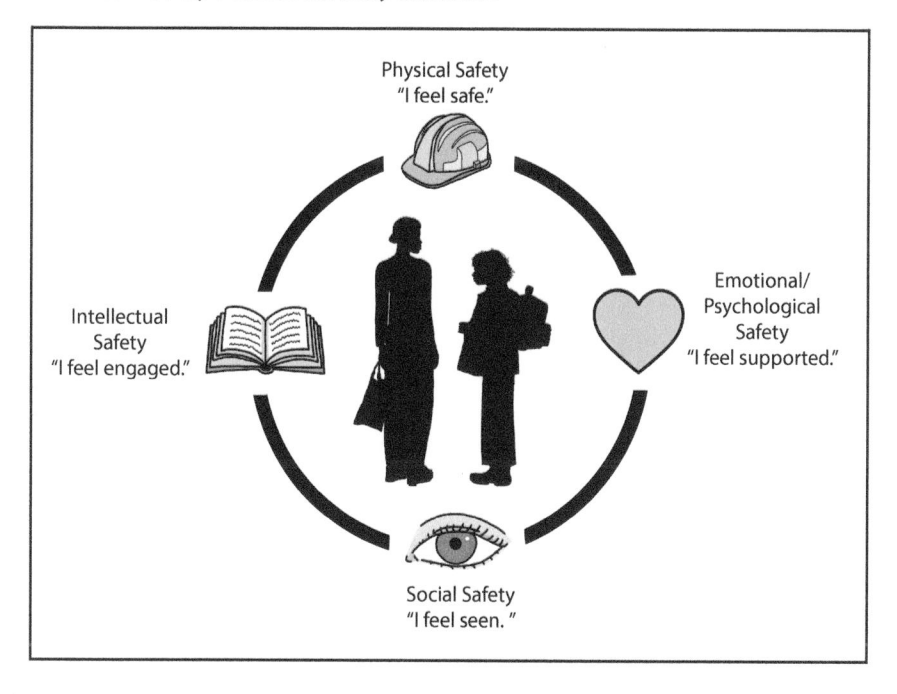

- Physical Safety — "I feel safe."
- Intellectual Safety — "I feel engaged."
- Emotional/Psychological Safety — "I feel supported."
- Social Safety — "I feel seen."

- **Emotional/psychological safety—"I feel supported."** Students and educators have emotional/psychological safety in school environments that recognize the signs of psychological stressors, communicate clear expectations about the importance of being a safe school, and actively work to prevent and/or disrupt any form of psychological harm for students or adults (e.g., bullying, shaming, harassment, discrimination, and gaslighting). Psychological safety and emotional safety are strengthened in schools that actively promote and foster a culture based on values of antiracism/antioppression, fairness, respect, kindness, and support for inclusion, diversity, and belonging.
- **Social safety—"I feel seen."** Students and educators have social safety when they experience a sense of belonging in the school setting. This results from perceptions that students are respected for their authentic selves—they don't have to hide parts of who they are—they are truly "seen" within the school setting. For educators, this could be the security of knowing that school administrators recognize their strengths and contributions or that they have developed trusting relationships with one or more colleagues in the school or district to whom they talk. Experiencing opportunities to have one's ideas and feedback shared *and acted upon* by school and district leaders is another form of social safety, by supporting staff and students to feel seen and heard, which increases perceptions of safety.
- **Intellectual safety—"I feel engaged."** We have intellectual safety when there is access to our cortex to think logically, analyze and solve problems, explore new perspectives, engage in academic learning, and have sustained focal attention. As discussed throughout the book, people can't have intellectual safety when they are dysregulated. When adults or children feel stressed, there is reduced access to the cortex (used for thinking, reasoning, listening, and engaging). Feeling safe and regulated opens the cortex and allows children to learn and educators to engage in their jobs without the risk of burnout.

REDUCING STRESS AND INCREASING REGULATION AS PATHWAYS TO LEARNING AND ACCOUNTABILITY

We learned in chapter 1 that when students or educators are faced with a threat—real or perceived—their stress response system (nervous system) activates and their internal state changes, often causing stress-induced dysregulation. *The more distress and fear they experience, the further they shift from calm to states of alarm and fear. States of alarm and fear shut down access to cortical thinking, reasoning, and learning capabilities.* The myth that an empathic, whole-child, brain-based approach to classroom management and discipline in schools is antithetical to accountability is easily debunked once we clarify the true aim of accountability: to cultivate an environment where students develop the skills necessary to become responsible, respectful, and well-adjusted individuals. Accountability extends beyond merely imposing consequences; it involves guiding students to comprehend and assume responsibility for their actions. The long-standing belief within our educational system that punitive measures are essential for altering children's behavior conflicts with an understanding of neurological functioning, especially state-dependent learning. As discussed in chapter 1, students can reflect on and modify their behavior only when they feel safe, understood, and regulated, not when they perceive a threat. Genuine accountability ensures that students have opportunities to utilize their cortex. By creating such opportunities, educators enable students to rectify their mistakes and genuinely learn from their experiences.

If we expect students to reflect on their behavior, understand the consequences of their choices, and adopt new, more responsible behaviors that are in line with the school's mission and core principles and that ensure their own and others' safety, then it is imperative for them to have functional access to the cortex. When adults react to students' stress-induced behaviors by yelling, punishing, shaming, blaming, or isolating them, they only serve to further dysregulate them and impede their access to higher-level brain functions (see figure 5.2).

Educators might think that they need to know the background of students who display dysregulated behavior before they can assist them. Some believe that they cannot help students because of what is happening at home or outside of school. However, it is not necessary for educators to know the history or even the "why" behind the behavior in the moment of dysregulation to help students re-regulate their nervous system. In addition, students are subject to different expectations at school than at home (e.g., at home, they might be allowed to talk back to adults, but at school, they can learn that respectful behavior with adults is expected). What is needed is to recognize that a student may be missing the skill set to engage in the expected behavior, and therefore needs to be taught

FIGURE 5.2 How approaches to discipline and classroom management affect states of the nervous system

The steps from bottom to top: Calm, Alert, Alarm, Fear, Terror.

Regulation (Optimal Zone of Regulation): Trusting Relationships, Trauma-Informed Practices, Predictable Environments, Social Emotional Learning, Restorative Practices, PBIS*

Dysregulation (Fight Flight Fawn Freeze): Lack of Trust in Relationships, Harsh and Punitive Discipline Practices, Detention, Suspension, and Expulsion, Zero-Tolerance Policies

*Positive Behavioral Interventions and Supports

rather than punished; and adults can recognize the signs that the student is in fight, flight, freeze, or fawn mode—indicative of a nervous system signaling increased levels of stress and/or a lack of safety.

Understanding how the brain functions provides us with a clear choice in our approach to student behavior:

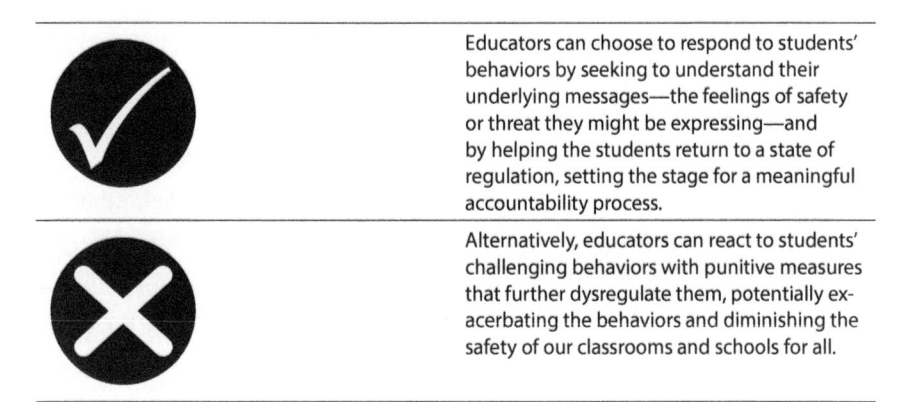

✓	Educators can choose to respond to students' behaviors by seeking to understand their underlying messages—the feelings of safety or threat they might be expressing—and by helping the students return to a state of regulation, setting the stage for a meaningful accountability process.
✗	Alternatively, educators can react to students' challenging behaviors with punitive measures that further dysregulate them, potentially exacerbating the behaviors and diminishing the safety of our classrooms and schools for all.

RESPONSES TO STUDENTS' CHALLENGING AND DYSREGULATED BEHAVIOR THAT EITHER ESCALATE TENSION OR FOSTER CALM AND SAFETY

What follows are illustrative cases of students exhibiting stress-related behaviors. Accompanying these examples, we outline proactive steps that adults can take to help students regulate their emotions initially and subsequently move to an accountability process. Conversely, we also discuss actions that might further dysregulate students, hindering the possibility of any constructive accountability and mindset or behavioral change from occurring.

Brock, Age Ten, Elementary School ("Fight" Stress-Induced Behavior)

Brock frequently exhibits "fight" stress responses, like getting into fights with other students, talking back to teachers, and having difficulty staying on task in school and completing his assignments. He disrupts lessons with outbursts such as, "This is stupid! Why do we even need to learn this?"

- **Actions that would exacerbate Brock's stress and dysregulation.** If Brock's math teacher, Emily, threatens to contact his parents during his peak moments of dysregulation, like warning him in front of the class, "Brock, do I need to tell your parents you're talking back again?," this is sure to intensify his stress and further dysregulate his behavior.
- **Actions that reduce Brock's stress and improve his regulation.** Instead of saying that she will call his parents when he talks back, Emily waits until after class and says: "Brock, do you have some time to chat now or later today?" At that time, they talk about his frustration in class and difficulty focusing. "I care about you and your learning but more importantly how you feel. I notice that at times, you make comments like today in the middle of a lesson, when you said, 'This is stupid! Why do we even need to learn this?' I just want to understand and learn how you feel and what is happening for you when you make a comment like that." The teacher provides a safe place for Brock to talk about his feelings. She discovers that Brock sometimes has a hard time focusing, and when he does not understand or like a subject, he talks back or blurts inappropriate comments as a way of deflecting when he does not follow the class lecture, is lost, or is not interested. Emily works with Brock to identify tools that he can use to support his focus or when he feels frustrated. They also talk about ways

for him to identify when he is not understanding a lesson and how he can use a visual cue to ask for his teacher's support (e.g., placing the Rubik's cube fidget at the top corner of the desk). They agree that when Emily sees that visual cue, she can come over and provide individual support to Brock to help scaffold his learning. The teacher and Brock also identify some additional after-school tutoring opportunities for Brock to get more support for learning the math content that is giving him the most difficulty in class.

- **The stress-reducing strategies that Emily used to support Brock include the following:**
  - **Relational safety.** Emily establishes trust, listens to how Brock feels, shows genuine concern rather than threatening him by saying, "You are in trouble if . . ." Her actions calm his nervous system, allowing him more access to his cortex so he can think and reason with her about strategies that might help him, or even to name how he feels.
  - **Agency and choice.** Brock is given autonomy to choose a time for discussion, reinforcing his sense of control, which can improve willingness to engage.
  - **Visual cues.** When he feels frustrated, the use of the Rubik's cube is Brock's way of communicating that he feels lost or is confused. Feeling seen and heard, and yet not shamed in front of class, will be regulating for Brock. He can access support during office hours or during a break in the lecture, the teacher can provide individualized guidance.
  - **Focus strategies.** Brock and Emily made an agreement about what he could do when his brain feels overloaded and he needs help to refocus. They agreed that he can use his Rubik's cube, doodle on blank paper, or raise his hand to use the restroom to take a mini-break. The teacher suggested a swivel chair, as the movement could help him focus, but Brock decided he did not like that idea.
  - **Academic support.** Together, Emily and Brock identify extra tutoring to bolster his comprehension of the subjects that challenge him.
- **Achieving resolution and accountability.** Resolution is achieved when Brock uses agreed-upon signals and strategies to manage his stress. This approach respects his neurological needs, encourages him, and supports his development of self-regulation and engagement in his learning process.

Emily's support validates Brock's fears, stressors, and efforts to learn and disrupts his stress-induced behaviors. These strategies empower him to take responsibility for his actions and learning, therefore fostering accountability for his behavior and educational progress at school.

In the case of Brock, the school was able to uncover the underlying meaning of the behavior, but in this next vignette, the source of stress is uncertain. Even so, all the adults in the student's life can still find ways to support her and help reduce her stress responses.

Shelby, Age Twelve, Middle School ("Flight" Stress-Induced Behavior)

Shelby is telling her mom that she can't go to school. This new behavior started about a month ago, after a sleepover at her friend's house. Something happened at the sleepover, but Shelby has not felt comfortable sharing details with her parents, and she refuses to talk to an adult or any counselor about the experience. Since the sleepover, Shelby finds any excuse not to attend school. She tells her parents that she is sick or anxious and resists her parents' efforts to encourage her to go to school. Mom emailed Shelby's teacher to explain the situation and request assignments that Shelby can complete at home. Mom has been honest that she is unsure what happened that may have caused this new behavior and led her daughter to go from loving school to avoiding it to the degree that she now asks regularly if she can be homeschooled.

- **Actions that would exacerbate Shelby's stress and dysregulated behavior.** Mom calls the school and leaves a message for the principal and school counselor. After a week goes by, she still has not received a response from anyone at the school. Mom finally reaches the front desk staff member, who sends an urgent message to Shelby's school counselor, Gerry. He returns the call but starts the conversation with a very direct and harsh tone, saying, "I have only five minutes until my next parent meeting." After Shelby's mom shares what is going on with Shelby, Gerry responds, "Did something happen at home that may have caused her stress?" The call is cut short due to the counselor's time constraints, so the issues are not explored in depth.
- **Actions that reduce Shelby's stress and improve her regulation.** The school handbook offers parents multiple pathways to communicate with the school. There is an online messaging system that parents can use to

communicate directly with the teacher. Parents can call the front desk at the school, they can send a message to a teacher or the school counselor, and finally, there is an app where parents can communicate with teachers, coding the message green (nonurgent; respond within seven days), orange (moderate; connect in forty-eight hours), or red (urgent; respond within twenty-four hours). Gerry receives a red message from Shelby's mom and calls her back within twenty-four hours, showing concern and compassion by listening intently to all of her concerns about Shelby. "Shelby is such a great kid, I hear you have some concerns about her recent behavior. Tell me more about what you are observing with her." Gerry asked the mom for permission to talk to all her teachers to see if they observe any changes in Shelby, and he suggested that they set another time in two days to connect again to share information on what they are both observing and to strategize how they could support Shelby both at school and at home. When Gerry and the mom reconnected, they discovered that the teachers are not observing any unusual or new behavioral concerns from Shelby. The counselor said, "That can happen; often, a child wants to fit in and tries hard to hold it together at school. That does not mean that internally they are not struggling, and she may feel more comfortable at home and showing you that by saying she does not want to go to school."

- **The stress-reducing strategies used to support Shelby included the following:**
  - **Staying calm to provide relational co-regulation.** Gerry conveys a calm tone and concern for what the parent was sharing.
  - **Counselor's relational empathy.** Gerry expresses genuine interest and concern and responds with empathy and curiosity.
  - **School responsiveness.** The counselor responds in a timely manner to mom's call.
  - **Counselor carves out ample time to talk.** Gerry calls back when he has ample time to talk and is not rushed.
  - **Co-creating next steps.** Gerry and Shelby's mom come up with a communication plan and a date to reconnect.
  - **Seeking consent.** Gerry asks permission to talk to other teachers.
  - **Include parent(s) as experts.** Gerry believes mom even though the teachers were not seeing behavioral concerns with Shelby.

- **Connect to resources.** Gerry offers to see Shelby to help her talk through her feelings, and he also makes two referrals outside of school for counseling for her.
- **Achieving resolution and accountability.** Providing support to the family can reduce parents' stress, which in turn can help them to be more regulated for their children at home. A more regulated parent with access to resources provided by the school can provide Shelby with supports inside and outside the home. Her teachers and counselors can keep an eye out for any warning signals out of the norm for Shelby, which gives her immediate family a sense of relief and collective support.

Stress-related behavior can manifest in physical and somatic symptoms for many students. Instead of dysregulated or challenging behavior, in the next vignette, Abdullah shows signs of distress, with frequent bouts of physical ailments.

Abdullah, Age Sixteen, High School ("Freeze" Stress-Induced Behavior)

Abdullah has frequently reported feeling unwell over the past month, requesting visits to the nurse's office two to three times a week with complaints of stomachaches. In class, he often appears to be daydreaming, not engaging with the class lectures. His distress escalated following several bullying incidents in the lunchroom, where groups of students mocked his clothing, accent, and the food that he brings to school. For example, when Abdullah enters the lunchroom, there are a few kids who point, laugh, and make comments that are hurtful, like "raghead" or "Al-Qaeda," or they ask him, "Where is your gun? Are you going to hijack us?"

Abdullah's teacher, Roxanne, had noticed his increasing detachment in class but hadn't fully grasped the extent of the bullying he was experiencing. Although she saw some of the interactions in the lunchroom, she initially hesitated to act, thinking Abdullah's smiles indicated he wasn't deeply affected. However, as his requests to visit the nurse and signs of distress continued to escalate, Roxanne began to recognize that Abdullah needed more support.

- **Actions that would exacerbate Abdullah's stress and dysregulated behavior.** Lunchroom monitors, who are parent volunteers, do not intervene in these bullying episodes because they are not consistent and change frequently, and neither are they trained in school safety procedures, such as how to respond to and report school bullying. They tend to ignore these comments made to Abdullah because he appears to be unaffected emotionally (e.g., he smiles, laughs, and does not show visual signs of distress in his body language) and because he has not reported any concerns to the lunch duty staff. In addition, because the volunteer monitor changes every few days, there is diffuse responsibility, and the thinking is, "Someone else will report it," "This is beyond my role as a volunteer," or "Kids will be kids."

- **Stress-reducing strategies that could be used to support Abdullah include the following:**

    Teacher actions:

- Roxanne, Abdullah's teacher, understands that she is a source of relational safety and regulation for students. She does not ignore bullying; instead, she responds swiftly, upholding the school's policies on campus safety by reporting it immediately to the administrator responsible for initiating an urgent plan of action. She checks in with Abdullah to see how he is feeling and to let him know that the bullying behaviors he is experiencing are unacceptable and that she will be reporting these incidents to the dean or assistant principal in writing, including the names of all students involved. She contacts Abdullah several times over the next few days to see if things have improved and follows up with administration for closure.
- She remains calm to avoid contributing to a tense atmosphere.
- To create a safe environment, Roxanne asks the involved students to speak with the school counselor or principal.
- Roxanne and other adults avoid public confrontation (i.e., they do not question the students in front of everyone in the lunchroom) and avoid language that would imply punishment, like "You are in trouble."

    Schoolwide actions:

- The school develops a code of conduct that explicitly states a mission to maintain emotional and psychological safety. They also have a Student Bill of Rights, created in collaboration with students.
- Annual teacher and student anti-bullying training is provided to communicate expectations and procedures related to bullying in the school and to ensure that everyone recognizes their responsibility to uphold a safe school culture.

- The school implements a confidential reporting system for teachers, parents, and students who observe instances of bullying on campus.
- The school creates a school safety task force and an annual safety summit (with student panels and professional panels) to learn about increasing safety at school.

Counselor/principal actions:

- Once the students are in the office, they are interviewed privately and individually as to what was said and what happened. These interviews inform formal documentation, and all evidence is reviewed to create a plan of action.
- **Achieving resolution and accountability.** Achieving resolution and accountability could involve several carefully considered actions, including the following:
  - Students are told that retaliation outside the interview/investigation is not acceptable and will not be tolerated.
  - Students are also told that regardless of the outcome, the students, with the support of adults, will be able to find a solution that includes and is aligned with the school values of not harming others, themselves, or things around them.
  - Students should be made aware of how bullying affects others and to take responsibility for their behavior by completing an assignment such as researching bullying and its effects on students and giving a presentation. Responsibility should also include sharing their behavior with family members and caregivers.
  - Students must work to restore the relationship and/or make restitution by engaging in a restorative dialogue if Abdullah is open to doing so.

Compliance and perfection can be stress-related goals, and although students may not be acting out with disruptive behaviors, they have the same high levels of stress. In the next vignette, Eva experiences an activation of her stress response system, which she communicates through fawning behaviors.

Eva, Age Eleven, Elementary School ("Fawn" Stress-Induced Behavior)

Eva presents as the perfect student. She never causes disruptions and tends to fly under the radar of her teachers. She is always scanning her teachers' voice tone, facial expressions, and body language and adjusts her behavior accordingly. Eva defaults to pleasing and perfectionism, which comes from a place of feeling unsafe, and even terror, relationally. She never disagrees and has trouble saying no when she is asked to do something that she does not want to do. If she makes a mistake in class, she apologizes profusely and starts to bite her nails or twist her hair. She is sensitive to criticism, and if she perceives that her teachers are frustrated or disappointed, she tries to stay after class to talk to them to see how she can improve. Sharon, one of Eva's teachers, once called on her, and she froze and became unresponsive. Eva had a hard time answering because she was worried she would not give the answer that was most popular or that was approved by the teacher.

- **Actions that would exacerbate Eva's stress and dysregulated behavior.** Fawning happens for Eva because she has learned through her primary relationships that safety is gained by becoming helpful, acting compliant, and not causing more tension for her parents, who are extremely volatile. Unexpectedly calling on Eva for her opinion and pressuring her for a response, as well as unstructured group work, could worsen her stress. If Sharon calls on Eva unexpectedly and asks her opinion about a particular issue being discussed, and when Eva sits quietly without responding, she walks over to her and pressures her, saying, "Come on, Eva, don't be scared to have an opinion," Eva's stress is likely to skyrocket. Or, if the teacher creates teams in class and provides an assignment for a group project to complete in two weeks without providing expectations or group norms for their work together, Eva is likely to take on more work than everyone else. If someone in the group has a differing opinion from her own, she will frequently apologize profusely and say it was her mistake and will fix it immediately (even though she disagrees or knows that it is not her mistake). She has difficulty identifying her own ideas and opinions and will wait to hear what the majority thinks, and then agree. During the day, Eva's stress increases, and she begins to have painful stomachaches. She frequently asks to go to the school nurse, who calls home asking that Eva be picked up for the day.
- **Actions that could reduce Eva's stress and improve regulation.** Sharon is interested in asking the students their opinion about a particular issue that they are discussing in class. The teacher uses an app, poses questions, and confidentially gathers the four responses of the class in aggregate form.

She announces the percentage of each response from the class. Then the teacher asks each student to pull out a piece of paper and write down why they gave their response, stating they will turn this in and it will be shared only with the teacher. At the end of class, Sharon carefully constructs teams based on what she knows about students' strengths, needs, and preferences. In addition, she asks students to name a few people whom they would like to work with, assuring them that she will try to group them with at least one person from their form. She reviews group expectations, norms, and documentation of contributions in writing with a rubric she distributes to the class. Sharon engages students in activities that are fun and playful. She uses soft and warm tones of voice and humor throughout the class to make students laugh, have fun, and to ease the overall stress levels of the students. When her students arrive to class each day, she has a unique and personalized way of greeting them when they arrive.

- **The stress-reducing strategies used to support Eva included the following:**
  - **Personalized interaction.** The teacher reads the individual cues of Eva and recognizes her overcompliance and people-pleasing behavior are defenses against her stress response system feeling threatened. It would be easy to ignore her distress, given that Eva is so compliant. Sharon individualizes her relational strategies (offering alternative ways to participate) in a way that Eva can tolerate without moving outside the Optimal Zone of Regulation.
  - **Voice tone, facial expressions, and body language.** Using soft tones, nonverbal body cues, and calm facial expressions are powerful ways to send a message to the brain and body of a student like Eva that the adult is a safe and regulated person, and she can borrow the teacher's calm to regulate her own nervous system in times of stress. The teacher getting down to Eva's eye level and offering an opportunity to share an answer personally with her is providing a safe pathway for Eva to take the risk of sharing her unique perspective in the presence of a caring adult.
  - **Agency and control.** Calling on Eva first and asking her to voice her opinion increases her stress level. Instead, the teacher can offer her an option to participate and raise her hand when she is ready. She can also call on Eva in a way that gives her a choice, asking, "Is there anything you want to add, Eva?" The teacher can privately ask Eva what her

thoughts are, which might increase her levels of safety to share an opinion, reflection, or thought about an issue. Alternatively, giving students a choice to privately write down their thoughts or opinions might also be a way to help Eva feel safe to identify and articulate her individual perspective. After students write down their opinions individually and privately, having them pair-share might increase Eva's ability to slowly feel more comfortable sharing in a smaller two-person team. After she writes down her ideas, she can choose what to share with her assigned partner. Some teachers use an app to gather aggregate opinions in a confidential and private way, which is another strategy to give their students agency, choice, and voice.

- **Setting group norms and expectations.** When assigning a project, Sharon has a rubric that each student will fill out, identifying who will take responsibility for what parts of the project. The teacher also communicates listening strategies so when the small group meets during class, no single student will dominate the conversation or take over with strong opinions. Instead, there is a procedure to ensure that every voice is heard in the group. There are also norms that guide students to feel safe in expressing differing opinions and to have challenging conversations, as well as clear steps to resolve conflict and land on final solutions. The norms encourage students to value differing opinions as a means of learning and growth. Sharon also has a procedure for communication when students are not contributing to the project, so that one or two students do not take on most of the work. Finally, throughout the day, Sharon encourages risk taking and not only talks about how mistakes are inherent to the learning process, but also models for students how she responds in a healthy manner to her own mistakes to help students feel safe to take risks in her classroom.
- **Achieving resolution and accountability.** To facilitate accountability, Sharon ensures that Eva's contributions are recognized and valued. Through establishing group norms, Sharon has naturally incorporated boundaries, expectations, and rules that help students like Eva with fawn-related behaviors to feel safe. Her modeling of healthy responses to mistakes allows Eva to understand that perfection is not expected, creating a safer learning space for Eva's learning and growth.

Getting into fights, perfectionism, a sudden refusal to attend school, and curious and puzzling stomachaches are all signals from students telling us about how they feel and what they need from adults to feel safe. When we take time to wonder about, and attempt to understand, the meaning behind a specific dysregulated behavior, we give voice to students whose behavior is communicating a story—through fight, flight, freeze, or fawn stress behaviors—that they feel threatened, emotionally escalated, and/or unsafe. We have two choices:

- React in ways that increases their dysregulation and state-dependent regression;
- Or, respond in ways that guide them back to regulation so they can think, talk, reflect, repair and learn.

In all the positive versions of these scenarios, teachers and school staff understood that they need to engage in co-regulating behaviors and create the experiences that students need in order to decrease their brain's perception of threat so they can calm their activated stress response systems and return to their Optimal Zone of Regulation. Educators understood that without calming students' overwhelmed nervous systems, they could not move toward problem-solving and resolution, ensuring that they were able to feel safe and ensure the safety of others. By responding with empathy, understanding, and intentional interventions, the educators were able to guide the students back to a regulated state where the outcomes would be learning, growth, and accountability.

Reflection/Discussion Questions

- Do you have an example of a time when you looked past a student's dysregulated behavior and wondered what the challenging behavior was communicating about the student's feelings or needs?
- Do you have a story of moving away from punitive actions (e.g., shaming, blaming, reward systems, exclusionary practices, and harsh discipline) and toward using strategies that promote nervous system regulation before engaging in a conversation that involves problem-solving (taking accountability for one's actions and finding solutions)?
- How will you use what you have learned from this book so far to shift or grow your practices?

FROM DISCIPLINE TO DIALOGUE: RESTORATIVE PRACTICES AS A FOUNDATION FOR ENHANCING SCHOOL CONNECTION AND SAFETY

Restorative practices, often referred to as "community circles" or simply "circles" in educational settings, are equity-focused approaches for improving school climate nationwide. Much of the methodology behind restorative practices is rooted in Indigenous traditions of justice and peacemaking. The sacred practice of the circle stems from many tribes' processes of sharing ideas, addressing issues, and making community decisions. Recognizing that decisions affect every tribe member, each person, regardless of age or status, has an equal seat at the table. Here, everyone's voice can be heard and valued.[2]

Public schools originally introduced restorative processes as alternatives to prevalent exclusionary discipline methods, such as suspensions, expulsions, and detention. These practices are grounded in the understanding that humans are inherently social and require strong, meaningful relationships to flourish. Exclusionary discipline can undermine the relational foundations that are crucial for nurturing healthy educational environments. Moreover, restorative practices address criticisms that punitive discipline fails to affect the vital social and emotional skills that students need for productive problem-solving and conflict resolution. Restorative circles offer a disciplinary and restorative approach that bolsters students' agency and learning of prosocial behavior. Instead of punitive actions like detention, where minimal learning occurs, restorative practices shift the emphasis toward students acknowledging their actions, taking responsibility for violations of school or classroom norms, collaborating on solutions, and collectively repairing any harm done. When practiced consistently, the circle process is a transformative method for fostering empathy and meaningful connections. Rather than reinforcing isolation, students, teachers, and staff can co-create an environment marked by warmth, camaraderie, and strong relationships. Envision a scenario where students and educators gather in a welcoming circle to share lived experiences and the accompanying spectrum of emotions.

Restorative practice is a continuum of practices that are essential for creating safe and regulated school environments.[3] They include both preventative and responsive practices. Preventive practices—such as classroom and community building exercises and curricula designed to enhance social-emotional skills, in addition to teaching the language of restorative practices—equip students with the ability to prevent conflict and dysregulated behavior that could be harmful to themselves or others. Responsive practices—including relational conversation norms, peer mediation, restorative groups, and formal community conferences and healing circles—address and mend issues in ways that restore relationships and prioritize healing, safety, and fairness.[4]

Questions to Guide Restorative Conversations

Here are examples of questions that can guide restorative conversations.[5]

- **Questions for the person responsible for the rupture or harm:**
  - What happened?
  - What were you thinking or feeling at the time?
  - Who has been affected by your actions, and how?
  - What have you thought about since this incident?
  - What actions are needed to make things right?
- **Questions for the person who experienced the rupture or harm:**
  - How have you been feeling since the incident?
  - What were your thoughts when you realized what had occurred?
  - What impact has this incident had on you or others?
  - What has been the most challenging aspect for you?
  - What do you feel is necessary to make things right?

Restorative practices expert Joe Brummer explains the transformative power of restorative circles.[6] He explains:

> What I've found in my work across the country is that kids don't want to miss circle time. When implemented consistently, tardiness goes down. Absenteeism goes down. This is because kids love it. If you want a healthy relational ecology in the building, restorative practices, such as circles, must be implemented. Not only are restorative practices responsive, they are also a set of preventative practices that allow students to be involved in defining school values such as respect. Circles, restorative chats, and respect agreements are tools we should use to create schools that don't have a need for punitive practices such as detention because you have fewer kids causing harm. On the responsive side, when harm has been done, restorative practices allow us to strengthen relationships through the process of rupture and repair.

> For example, in a fifth-grade classroom, the kids were lining up to go to lunch. One kid was a little too eager to be first in line and ended up pushing a

classmate to the ground. The classmate was a new kid who had just migrated from Ukraine and did not speak English. A conflict followed, and I was called to the classroom. Upon my arrival, it became apparent that the student from Ukraine believed I was "the authorities," there to take him away. The language barrier and the trauma of migrating from a war zone prevented the child from understanding the other child's attempt to apologize and my intentions to address the conflict. We were eventually able to engage in a restorative chat after locating a sixth-grader who was fluent in Ukrainian to interpret. Through restorative practices, not only was the conflict resolved, but the student from Ukraine was able to make his first friend in his new school. That's the beauty of circles. Relationships develop through rupture and repair. Punitive practices only focus on the infraction and often fail to address harm. Restorative practices focus on the harm to relationships. Traditional punitive practices focus all efforts on teaching the child who broke a rule a lesson through suffering, and everyone else involved is left out of the picture. The repair never happens, and harm is rarely addressed.

The benefits of restorative practices and the use of circles are extensive. They enhance communication skills, refine problem-solving abilities, and bolster students' social-emotional and conflict resolution skills.[7] When integrated into daily experiences, research indicates that restorative practices help students build trusting relationships and develop conflict resolution and collaborative problem-solving abilities. Moreover, these transformative community circles can positively affect the entire school community.[8] By promoting teamwork and instilling a culture of mutual respect, they contribute positively to the broader school environment. The growing evidence base shows that restorative practices are linked with fewer disciplinary incidents, improved satisfaction ratings from students and adults, and positive impacts on student academic achievement.[9] Understanding restorative practices and their documented benefits is crucial for educators and administrators dedicated to alleviating stress in schools and cultivating safe, well-regulated, and positive school cultures.

The use of restorative practices and circles requires educators to be well regulated and adept at recognizing stress responses in themselves, as well as coworkers and students. It is imperative that all educators and school personnel have the tools to help them identify their own stress triggers and restore their own state of calm. Next, we introduce the S.T.O.P. tool, which can be used to build self-awareness and disrupt reactivity.

The S.T.O.P. Tool: Interrupting Reactivity and Creating a Pause

The S.T.O.P tool helps people learn to pause and build self-awareness about their internal states and stress-related behaviors. With this awareness, they can then disrupt their reactivity and instead respond more effectively in their interactions with others.

Each letter in S.T.O.P. stands for an action that we can take to help use self-awareness, to create an intentional pause in order to disrupt reactivity and allow us to respond in healthy ways during stressful situations. When we pause, it allows time for the cortex to engage to increase the capacity to listen, problem-solve, consider different perspectives and to respond with empathy.

The *S* stands for *STOPPING* for less than a minute, putting the brakes on a current situation and momentarily reflecting. In cultivating a pause for a moment, we can prevent a default, knee-jerk reaction from our reactive hindbrain, especially when we are triggered with big emotions.

The *T* stands for *TAKING a deep grounding breath*. Breathing is an important method of regulating stress. With the IN breath, we stimulate our sympathetic nervous system, which creates an energy charge in our body (an accelerator). In contrast, with a long and slow OUT breath, we stimulate the parasympathetic nervous system, promoting calm and a relaxation response. Taking one deep breath in through the nose for three seconds and a longer exhale through the mouth for five to seven seconds can be a fast-acting way to step on the brakes of anxious thoughts, dysregulated behaviors, or stress-related reactions from the hind/survival parts of the brain.

The *O* is *OBSERVING the messages that the brain and body are sending you*. We can all build self-awareness about our internal state by noticing our **sensations** (racing heart, clenched fists, headache, tense shoulders, grinding teeth, back pain, or stomachache), **thoughts** (I want to yell; nothing goes my way; everyone dislikes me), **feelings** (mad, sad, happy, worried) and **behaviors** (calm, harmful reactions).

> The *P* is for *PROCEED with more intentionality rather than reactivity.* With intentionality and cortex access, adults and children can respond with logical reasoning, problem-solving, and self-regulated behavior.
>
> The S.T.O.P. tool can be a visual reminder or mental image to assist in learning the steps to cultivate a pause and to disrupt reactivity that could be harmful to those around you.

Vignette: "After Practicing with the S.T.O.P. Tool, Maya Remembered to Pause"

Thirteen-year-old Maya found herself caught in a whirlwind of emotions. The smallest of triggers often set off a cascade of reactions, transforming her into a storm of impulsive actions. It was her teacher, Tony, who taught Maya the power of using the S.T.O.P. tool. One day, a comment from a classmate triggered her emotionally. Maya typically yelled at this other student, coming back at her with a hurtful comment. However, after practicing using the S.T.O.P. tool with Tony, she remembered to pause.

In the midst of the hallway chaos, she *S* (stopped), closed her eyes briefly, and mentally hit the brakes on her instinct to retaliate. This momentary reflection prevented a knee-jerk reaction that could have escalated the situation.

T (taking) a deep grounding breath and inhaling slowly through her nose for three seconds, she felt her nervous system calming slightly. As she exhaled through her mouth for a longer count of five to seven seconds, Maya felt a subtle shift, like stepping on the breaks of her racing thoughts and desire to react by causing harm back to the other student.

With her mind in a calmer state, Maya proceeded to the third step, *O* (observe internal emotions and sensations), where she was aware of the tension in her shoulders and her clenched fists, physical manifestations of her big emotions. Thoughts of anger and frustration swirled in her mind, and Maya noticed them.

Finally, Maya *P* (proceeded) with more intentionality rather than reactivity. With the cortex engaged, she could respond with logical reasoning and self-regulated behavior. Instead of firing back, she chose to walk away.

As Maya practiced the S.T.O.P. tool with her class, she honed her ability to interrupt reactivity and cultivate a pause to respond versus reacting. The visual reminder of S.T.O.P. became a mental image that guided her through emotional challenges of middle school. With increased self-awareness, Maya disrupted her default harsh reactions and learned to respond more effectively in her interactions with others. The S.T.O.P. tool became her compass, helping her navigate the stormy seas of adolescence with more resilience.

The next vignette highlights how educators can also use the S.T.O.P. tool to interrupt their reactivity and build their empathy with students—especially when they present with stress-induced behaviors. In this case, a high school government teacher uses the S.T.O.P. tool to interrupt his reactivity with an anxious student.

Vignette: "I Am Sorry, I Can't Make an Exception for You"

Donald Carter is a high school government teacher in New Hampshire. As part of his class assignments, he requires his students to speak in front of the class about a bill and to role-play advocating for it in the Senate. One student, Gemma, comes up to Mr. Carter after class, teary. She says that she has too much anxiety to present in front of everyone. His first response to her is, "I am sorry, but all kids are required to present, and I can't make an individual exception for you." He is short with Gemma, dismissive of her feelings, and is even working on his laptop while talking with her. Gemma's response is, "Fine, I will take a zero on this assignment," and she walks away rapidly, arms crossed and barely able to hold in her tears.

Mr. Carter had just attended professional development training on the S.T.O.P. tool. After Gemma left his class dysregulated, he tries to use it for himself.

Mr. Carter stops (*S*), alone in his classroom, and decides to take a brief pause and reflect on what had just happened.

T (take a breath or grounder to regulate). He takes a deep breath, scans through the nature photos on his phone from his recent hiking trip; an activity that is very calming. After a few moments, he feels a bit more present in the moment.

O (observe what the body is telling him he might be feeling). Mr. Carter is feeling overwhelmed with too many papers to grade, requirements with deadlines from the school district, and parent night coming up that week. Also, he personally is going through a rough time financially as the single dad of two teen boys. He has just received a bill in the mail for his two sons to pay for their high school sports uniforms, and he knows that he cannot afford that cost, let alone the groceries needed to feed two growing boys. Taking a moment to notice his thoughts, Mr. Carter discovers all the worried thoughts about his life and the tension these thoughts are creating in his neck (slight soreness).

The next step is *P* (proceed with regulation and more intentional responses). That afternoon, once Mr. Carter had calmed a bit, he calls the school counselor to reflect more deeply on the interaction. He wonders with the counselor what advice she might have for this situation, and then he pauses and takes time to listen to new ideas. As a result of this conversation with the counselor, the next day, Mr. Carter asks Gemma if she would be willing to stay after class and revisit their initial conversation. Their conversation unfolds as follows:

Mr. Carter: Thank you for taking some time to meet again after school to continue our conversation. I am sorry I was dismissive initially. I want to learn more about this project and how you feel about it.

Gemma: I have so much anxiety at the thought of speaking in front of others. So much that I would rather get a zero and risk failing the class.

Mr. Carter: Thank you for sharing that with me, and I am sorry that this project is causing so much stress for you. I wonder if you can think of any other way to complete the project but still achieve the same learning goals.

Gemma: When I present with PowerPoint slides, I don't have as much anxiety. I feel like if I get too stressed, I have a place to find more words that I otherwise lose when my anxiety increases. Would it be possible to stand in front of everyone with cue cards or a projected PowerPoint?

Mr. Carter: I really appreciate hearing some strategies we can consider together so you can still learn, present, and meet the assignment requirements. Can I take a day to think more about it, and you take some time as well, and then tomorrow, after school, let's finalize our decision together. How does that sound to you?

Gemma: That sounds good. I appreciate you listening and taking time to find a solution with me.

Mr. Carter did several things that were reducing Gemma's stress and helping her feel safe and regulated at school:

- **Pausing and slowing down.** The first thing was to walk away and find space between the stressful event and the associated reactions. In slowing

down and pausing, his nervous system shifted into a calmer state, which allowed him to access his cortex to think and reason more clearly.
- **Reflecting.** The second thing he did to acquire additional calm was to find a trusted colleague to talk things through. Adding a reflection with his pause allowed him time to gain additional perspective. He was able to disrupt his reactivity and rigid reaction and replace it with one that allowed more flexibility and an individualized solution. Pausing allowed time for his brain to move from a reactive and stressed state to engaging the prefrontal cortex where he could think, reason, and come to a solution with his student.
- **Model repair and restoration.** When adults make mistakes or have regrets in their interactions, they can always make repairs. When they model for students saying, "I am sorry," "I wish I would have handled it differently," or "Let's start over and try again," they teach them that it is OK to be vulnerable, to make mistakes, to give ourselves grace, and actively try to repair our relationships.
- **Relational regulation: Mirror neurons and co-regulation.** Mr. Carter went to a trusted colleague, the school counselor, to find a safe place and person to regulate his own nervous system. He then used his calm nervous system to co-regulate his distressed student when he entered this second conversation with Gemma. Through his regulated state, he created a safe space so that Gemma could borrow his calm to regulate her nervous system. Stress is contagious, but so is calm.

Both Gemma and Mr. Carter were experiencing stressors that were affecting their behavior. As a result, Mr. Carter was initially dismissive in his interaction with Gemma, not taking time to learn why she was feeling so stressed by his assignment. Gemma, who entered the conversation with a predisposition to be highly stressed, was further dysregulated by her teacher's reaction to her concerns. This story highlights how, in taking time to slow down, teachers can choose responses to students' stress-induced behaviors that are regulating and support students to feel seen, heard, regulated, and safer.

The S.T.O.P. tool is one of many methods for supporting educators and students in learning and embodying the habits of self-awareness, nervous system regulation, and strengthening their ability to share their calm with others (i.e., co-regulation). Because calm is contagious, tools such as this one provide us with the opportunity to decrease stress and increase calm, safety, and regulation in our schools. The more calmness, safety, and regulation is present, the more learning we can achieve together.

CONCLUSION

This chapter marks a clarion call to move away from punitive strategies toward compassionate and relational approaches to discipline and classroom management within our schools. Understanding the critical role of nervous system regulation is key to fostering a safe environment, which is fundamental for effective teaching and deep learning. We encourage you to unapologetically disrupt the traditional disciplinary systems that cause harm. There is an urgency to embrace humane and compassionate approaches, including restorative practices, that alleviate the weight of the invisible backpacks of stress and trauma carried by students and educators alike in our schools today. As you move forward, we invite you to reflect on the stories and strategies shared in this chapter, allowing them to inform and transform your approach. We will never reduce stress in our schools by continuing to use exclusionary and harsh practices. Every act of understanding, empathy, co-regulating, and strengthening students' social-emotional capacities will fortify their sense of safety and belonging, transforming our schools into more than just learning spaces. With these investments, our schools will become environments where healing, growth, and flourishing are possible for students and adults.

CASE STUDY 4

"I Know Byron's Life Is Better Because We Decided to Love Him Instead of Expel Him"

The collective trauma of the COVID-19 pandemic was one of the driving forces behind this book. The pandemic affected everyone, but it had an especially profound impact on communities and populations already coping with the stress of racism, discrimination, and poverty. So how do educators ensure individual accountability during a collectively traumatic experience? One of the coauthors, Dr. Tyisha Noise, shares a story from the front lines as a middle school leader that highlights the impact of COVID. She illustrates how educators and administrators can be trauma-informed while maintaining accountability in school settings. Her story focuses on an experience that took place as students returned to the classroom in the aftermath of the COVID-19 lockdowns:

> I met Byron during my tenure as principal in an urban middle school in South Los Angeles. This was a school in the neighborhood where I grew up. A lot of the students had been in school together for a long time and had longstanding relationships.
>
> Byron was a little chipmunk of a sixth-grader when the COVID pandemic started, but by the time he returned to school in eighth grade, he was the size of a grown man. Byron was a leader with charisma, a sparkle that caught the attention of adults and peers. He was athletic, boisterous, and could hold the attention of his peers without trying.
>
> When the students returned to school, conditions were different. They had missed a year and a half of school and lost daily opportunities to practice their

social skills. During COVID, the school day was shortened, and students got used to thirty or forty-five minutes of class, logging in and out at will. Yet, when they returned to campus, we had block schedules of eighty minutes, which was extremely hard. Students couldn't focus or sit still for that length of time. They were out of the habit of being in the same space with so many other people and tolerating all of the different little things that come with being a middle schooler.

The opportunity to choose to love Byron presented itself after a truly intense incident. One day he was in English class, talking to another student, Marcus, who said something sarcastic to him about his grandmother. Byron had an immediate fight reaction. He jumped up, knocked Marcus out of his chair, and landed on top of him, punching him right in the face repeatedly. He pushed off the teacher who was trying to break them up. There was blood; it was intense. I remember sitting across from him after it happened and trying to help him regulate, but it was tough to get him to breathe. Looking in his eyes, I saw a lost little boy. He looked confused, embarrassed, and flustered. I was trying to figure out what triggered him and led him to attack another student as he did. For a while, he needed to walk around my office before he could talk. I offered him water, and I just listened. At first, he was raging and rambling, but I let him talk until he talked himself down. He said that the other student said something about his grandma, he saw red, and that was all he could remember.

He had so many emotions, but as he began to calm, his first question was, "Oh my God, I'm so sorry. Is Marcus OK? Can I go now and apologize?" I said, "We need to take some beats and give everybody a minute. We're going to focus on you calming down. Let's get some water, some food, and let's just calm down. This is a big deal. Just saying, 'I'm sorry' isn't going to cut it. What we need to talk about is how we make sure you aren't this angry again in a classroom." Byron knew that he needed to do something to fix the situation. And I knew we had a lot of "fixing" to do.

When I met with the admin team, including our school counselor, dean, and assistant dean, I asked them to tell me about Byron and here is what they told me:

Byron lost his grandma during COVID. She was the grounding of his life: his safe place, his favorite person, his structure. Byron and his mom were not nearly as close as he and his grandma. His mom was severely grieving the loss of her mother, and she couldn't hold her own grief and his at the same time. And so, in many cases, she was just trying to find places to put him and give him things to do. On top of everything, he was also losing his home due to family infighting over the property. He was thirteen. It was a lot to manage at thirteen. When Byron returned to school after COVID, he was depressed, grieving, and miserable. He was raw and easily triggered. And our team had a choice. We knew he and his mom needed help. We knew that expulsion or forced transfer was not going to serve him. We also knew that we would have to repair a lot of relationships to move forward together.

Later in the day, we had an emergency meeting with the staff. This had happened in a classroom filled with kids and a teacher. What could we do for the teacher? What could we do for the other students who saw this happen? As a principal, I explained to my staff that our response was an administration decision, and that I knew that in most schools, this incident would get Byron expelled, but I also knew that expulsion was not going to help him. Mr. Bryant, the English teacher whose classroom was the location of the incident, had been a teacher for twenty-five years—he had actually come out of retirement to help after COVID. He stated, "I don't want you to expel him. I know he didn't do it on purpose." He shifted the attitudes of every other teacher in the room. He said, "I want to keep working with Byron. I don't think putting him out is going to help, but I think we can. I think *I* can." The staff agreed to bring Byron back to school, but they were terrified about how to keep everyone safe. What could we do? We decided to sit and process through his story. Was he triggered? Suffering from depression? We don't talk enough about how boys, especially boys of color, are socialized to externalize any feelings of sadness or anger. When people see boys who fight all the time as angry and aggressive, I see them as sad and in despair, and possibly depressed or anxious or both. We realized that Byron did not have any mental health support after his grandmother's death.

Together we created a plan that ensured everyone's safety, including a daily behavior monitoring sheet he carried from class to class, individual and group counseling, an offering of services for his mom, mentorship with Mr. Bryant, and a "break pass" system that allowed him to visit one of his preferred adults when he began to feel agitated and escalated. Byron had a restorative conference with Mr. Bryant. Then, after some long talks with the other student (who was very forgiving) and his family, Byron was able to have a restorative dialogue and take responsibility for his actions with the student who he harmed. He also took responsibility with his classmates, using a community circle as a vehicle for students to express how they felt when it happened and what they needed from him to feel safe. The implementation was rocky at first. We had a few more uncomfortable (but nonviolent) incidents throughout the school year, but we watched him begin to heal, to grow, and the young man we believed he was inside began to emerge. In fact, by the end of the year, he was a graduation speaker and discussed how much our school had helped him.

The following year, after Byron had gone to high school, he returned for a visit. He gave me a big hug and said, "When I was here, I was mad at you all the time because I felt like you were always on me. You didn't let me slide with anything. Now I understand everything you were trying to teach me about what it was going to take to survive in high school and to be good. Thank you for what you did for me!" My eyes fill with tears every time I think about him.

Byron's visit reminded me of the power of having a team of people who are willing to wrap around a child when they are at their absolute worst. Byron was at the worst moment in his life during these experiences. He felt like his life was falling apart. For us to be able to see past his aggression, past the impulsivity of being thirteen, and for him to have that moment where he thanked us was everything. Stories like Byron's are why we work so hard to create environments that reduce stress. They are why we work so hard to teach educators to co-regulate kids and to co-regulate each other so that we can reduce stress in our schools. When a student can't regulate because their life literally feels like a tornado or a hurricane, we can be the calm that allows them to find, or to build and develop, their best selves. *I know Byron's life is better because we decided to love him instead of expel him.* We've got a shot at creating a lot more opportunities for kids to be loved in schools instead of pushed out. Let's love them into being their best selves! Let's pull them in instead of pushing them out.

Byron's story highlights the importance of being healing-centered and engaging in restorative practices. It reinforces the necessity of recognizing the collective and systemic nature of trauma, particularly the collective trauma of the COVID pandemic, while also holding people accountable for harming others. Using the RYSE framework, this story is examined across different dimensions—individual and interpersonal, school and community, and systemic—identifying levels of stress and trauma and proposing actions to support school-age children to take accountability in a trauma-informed manner.

INDIVIDUAL AND INTERPERSONAL FACTORS THAT CONTRIBUTE TO STRESS IN SCHOOLS OR STRENGTHEN STUDENTS' AND EDUCATORS' WELL-BEING

Toxic Stress and Trauma

Byron was significantly affected by the collective trauma of the COVID-19 pandemic, compounded by his own grief and loss, as well as living with a parent likely suffering from depression due to her own grief. It is important to remember that at least 204,000 children and youth in the United States lost parents and other in-home caregivers to COVID-19—more than 1 in every 360 youth.[1]

This loss was compounded by considerable anxiety within the family system due to a battle over the family home and financial challenges. The lack of a robust support system significantly affected Byron, his mother, and the school community.

Reducing Stress, Fostering Resilience, and Promoting Healing and Well-Being

At a personal level, supporting Byron involved addressing biases and fostering empathy and understanding. With 85 percent of the teaching staff at the school being white and Byron being a young Black boy, it was crucial to engage in anti-bias conversations. Statements like "He is so violent" were reframed to recognize Byron's behavior as a stress-induced trauma response. Bias can cloud the way that adults interpret children's behavior. African American children frequently experience a specific form of bias labeled "adultification," leading to inaccurate assumptions that they are older and more mature than they are.[2] Adultification can also lead to expectations that are not age appropriate and can result in harsher punishment, including exclusion from the learning environment, which can be traumatizing for these children and their families.[3]

SCHOOL AND COMMUNITY FACTORS THAT CONTRIBUTE TO STRESS IN SCHOOLS OR STRENGTHEN STUDENTS' AND EDUCATORS' WELL-BEING

Toxic Stress and Trauma

Byron's story is emblematic of the heightened anxiety and collective trauma experienced by many students and families during the postpandemic period. Low-income and poor people, as well as people of color, were the ones most affected by the pandemic, not just medically but also socioemotionally, mentally, and financially.[4] Schools, underprepared to meet the increased emotional and mental health needs of their students and educators, faced significant challenges. To manage Byron and many other students' needs, the school hired a dean who was trained as a therapist and knowledgeable about crisis management. The dean collaborated with an assistant dean familiar to the students, a school counselor who was a former special educator with important insights into students' academic and social-emotional needs, and a mental health consultant who could facilitate student groups and support students who could not be accommodated by the school counselor's caseload. The school staff also partnered with the Los

Angeles County Department of Mental Health to provide after-hours and off-campus services for students and their families. Principal Noise described herself as "a mental health octopus," having her hands everywhere and reaching for services to support kids in any way she could. These measures were essential to prevent an already stressed and underserved system from imploding.

Reducing Stress, Fostering Resilience, and Promoting Healing and Well-Being

Supporting Byron at the school and community level involved several key actions:

- Providing support to Marcus and his family and answering their questions while protecting Byron's privacy.
- Providing Byron with an opportunity to make amends at school through restorative conversations with Marcus and Mr. Bryant, the teacher involved in the incident. The focus on relationships throughout the school allowed a process of relational restoration to take place over time.
- Offering Byron counseling to manage his emotional responses, emphasizing the importance of self-regulation for his own and others' safety, and encouraging Byron to seek support from trusted adults within the school whenever he felt overwhelmed. Principal Noise explained to him:

    > Byron, not being able to regulate your temper is going to cost you the things you love the most. You don't need to be under control for me. I need you to be under control for you—for your own safety. As a young Black man, the world is not forgiving when you make a mistake. Trayvon Martin was walking home when he was murdered in the street with a hoodie and an Arizona and some Skittles in his pocket. If you are upset, grab your stuff and go see Ms. Z, the school counselor. If she is unavailable, myself as the principal, the dean, or the assistant dean, will meet with you. An adult who cares for you is going to make themselves available. You can learn these skills.

- Holding circles with students to process the incident, ensuring them of their safety and the school's measures to maintain their safety.
- Training educators and administrators in de-escalation strategies and restorative practices.
- Providing mental health supports for students *and* educators who often experience significant impacts from ongoing work with trauma-impacted kids.

SYSTEMIC FACTORS THAT CONTRIBUTE TO STRESS IN SCHOOLS OR STRENGTHEN STUDENTS' AND EDUCATORS' WELL-BEING

Toxic Stress and Trauma

Byron's school, located in a historically underserved community, faced significant systemic challenges. As the school's demographics shifted toward more socioeconomically disadvantaged students, its financial resources decreased. There was a lack of adequate security and resources on campus, including lack of fencing around the campus or funding for a security guard. Each night, unhoused individuals slept on the school lunch tables, and some carried weapons for their own protection. Dr. Noise was responsible for arriving early and securing the campus. In addition, the staff needed to navigate complex COVID-19 protocols without any district support, placing enormous strain on the school's single administrator. These systemic issues highlight how increased pressure on already stressed and underresourced systems can lead to adverse outcomes.

Reducing Stress, Fostering Resilience, and Promoting Healing and Well-Being

Supporting systemic-level change could look like this:

- Ensuring dedicated support for restorative practices in all schools.
- Avoiding situations where a school operates with only one administrator, as it's unsustainable and unhealthy.
- Hiring staff from the local community who share a deep understanding of the community and cultural context, providing different levels of understanding and support for students during difficult times.
- Securing adequate funding to provide necessary resources and services, including comprehensive training in trauma-informed practices for educators, especially in underserved, historically trauma-impacted communities.
- Creating partnerships with local universities and offering scholarships to increase the number of students who enter school counseling or trauma counseling programs for children and youth.

By applying these and other systemic-level strategies, schools can better support students like Byron, promoting healing and resilience within their communities while addressing the broader systemic challenges that exacerbate stress and trauma.

REFLECTION/DISCUSSION QUESTIONS

- Have you ever chosen an unpopular path to support a student and yielded a positive outcome from it?
- Have you ever wanted help for a student on your campus and had no idea whom to turn to?
- How often do you celebrate small wins with students, whether as an individual or collectively as a staff?

CONCLUSION

Stress in schools across the country has led to a reckoning—a demand to shift the paradigm of how we understand the purpose of schools and the roles and responsibilities of educators. This paradigm shift reminds us that we are raising future leaders, decision-makers, and citizens through our daily work. Moreover, to successfully develop safe, healthy, happy, bright, regulated, and resilient students, we must embrace the responsibility and privilege of being navigators of our own nervous systems and those of others. The burgeoning international movement advocating for trauma-responsive and brain-based practices assures us that change is possible without waiting for policy or funding to catch up with the science. We can begin to shift our practices through our daily interactions and ways of being.

Educator training has long focused on methodology, content knowledge, lesson planning, and classroom management. However, we have often overlooked teaching educators about becoming self-aware, recognizing our stress triggers, and identifying self and collective care needs to function optimally as nervous system navigators in the classroom. This missing piece of the puzzle is reflected in our current historically high rates of teacher attrition. The outdated belief that students and teachers can leave their stress and trauma at the schoolhouse door has been disproven. We now know that our brilliant brains and nervous systems are not actually capable of doing this. We now understand that everyone in the school community carries their full range of experiences, including stress and trauma, with them throughout the day in our school buildings. Acknowledging this, we must pivot to create systems and supports that allow educators to engage in the vibrant and dynamic culture of schools each day in ways that cultivate calm, highly regulated, and safe environments benefiting everyone involved.

We cannot continue to ask teachers, staff, and administrators to pour from empty cups, as this risks overwhelming their nervous systems and creating a relentless cycle of burnout and harm for them as well as for students. If we want better outcomes for students, we must also provide better support for educators.

By creating relationally rich environments and implementing restorative practices and community circles and many of the other practices described throughout this book, we can increase feelings of safety and belonging in educators, who can then infuse the same into their practices and the lives of students. We must recognize the human limitations of educators, support their health and well-being, and stop shaming them if and when they struggle in this challenging world. We need to give educators opportunities to get to know themselves and their needs, provide them with tools and professional learning or coaching to meet these needs, and invite the messiness that change brings. As educators blaze this trail, we can reassure them that they are not alone. Others have made these shifts in their practices, and their school communities are all the better for it.

Creating environments that strengthen our educators' and students' nervous system regulation begins with individual efforts but requires the entire school community to advance the work. Schools, districts, and regional education agencies must allocate funds and personnel to reduce workloads and bolster support for implementing trauma-responsive, healing-centered, and restorative practices. Systems that perpetuate stress, racism, discrimination, marginalization, and other dysregulating experiences and practices need to be dismantled. Policies must evolve and barriers must be overcome if we are to meet the needs of all educators and students. If we know that calm is contagious, so are its benefits, and no one at any school site, district, or system can deny the need for supports that yield well-regulated and high-functioning adults who are at their very best at serving children each and every day.

As we rethink the purposes, methods, and practices for discipline and classroom management to align with our understanding of neurobiology and stress response systems, we invite you to join us by first finding and engaging in your own regulation and self-awareness practices. Become a beacon of regulation and calm in the environment where you work and live. Explore the tools and practices in this book, experiencing the benefits of promoting calm, regulation, and safety. Reflect on the case studies and ideas presented and consider your role and positive influence for change in your classroom, school, or organization. Commit to learning, growing, and expanding your practice to lead with the truth about neurobiological responses to stress and their impact on the wellness, safety, and success of students and educators. Be the change that our students, staff, and educators are asking for.

As you use this text in your practices—whether in your classroom, team, committee, or department—our aim is to support systems changes that lead to a significant reduction of stress in our schools by creating environments that promote relational regulation and emotional and environmental safety. We hope that the skills, tools, and ideas that we have provided will inspire a new day in schools as we work together to embrace new perspectives, forge innovative pathways, and expand the use of concrete methods to reduce stress in schools. The teachers and schools featured in this book are the evidence that this paradigm shift is already happening across the nation every day. We invite you to join this movement and be part of the change that our students and educators urgently need.

Notes

Introduction

1. Sean Darling-Hammond, *Fostering Belonging, Transforming Schools: The Impact of Restorative Practices*, Learning Policy Institute Report (Palo Alto, CA: Learning Policy Institute, 2023), https://doi.org/10.54300/169.703.
2. Elizabeth D. Steiner et al., *Teacher and Principal Well-Being Is an Essential Step for Rebuilding Schools: Findings from the State of the American Teacher and State of the American Principal Surveys*, RR-A1108-4 (Santa Monica, CA: RAND Corporation, 2022), https://www.rand.org/pubs/research_reports/RRA1108-4.html.
3. Sue B. Whiting et al., "Stress and Learning in Pupils: Neuroscience Evidence and Its Relevance for Teachers," *Mind, Brain, and Education* 15, no. 2 (2021): 177–88, https://doi.org/10.1111/mbe.12282.
4. Jeffrey S. Ashby et al., "The Relationship of COVID-19 Traumatic Stress, Cumulative Trauma, and Race to Posttraumatic Stress Disorder Symptoms," *Journal of Community Psychology* 50, no. 6, Special Issue: COVID-19 and Vulnerable Populations Volume/Section 1 (August 2022): 2597–2610, https://doi.org/10.1002/jcop.22762.
5. American Psychological Association, 2022, *Stress in America 2022: Concerned for the Future, Beset by Inflation*, accessed May 18, 2024, https://www.apa.org/news/press/releases/stress/2022/concerned-future-inflation.
6. Doug Donovan, "U.S. Officially Surpasses 1 Million COVID-19 Deaths," Johns Hopkins University of Medicine, last modified May 2022, https://coronavirus.jhu.edu/from-our-experts/u-s-officially-surpasses-1-million-covid-19-deaths#:~:text=Experts%20say%20the%20tragic%20milestone,vaccinations%20could%20have%20prevented%20fatalities; Tori DeAngelis, "Thousands of Kids Lost Loved Ones to the Pandemic: Psychologists Are Teaching Them How to Grieve, and Then Thrive," *American Psychological Association* 53, no. 7 (2022): 69, https://www.apa.org/monitor/2022/10/kids-covid-grief.
7. Anne Branigin, "10 Anti-LGBTQ Laws Just Went into Effect: They All Target Schools," *Washington Post*, July 8, 2022, https://www.washingtonpost.com/nation/2022/07/08/anti-lgbtq-education-laws-in-effect/; Federal Bureau of Investigation, "Hate Crime Statistics 2020," August 30, 2021, https://www.fbi.gov/news/press-releases/fbi-releases-2020-hate-crime-statistics; Shailly Gupta Barnes, "The Economic Impact of Housing Insecurity in the United States, 2022," Washington Center for Equitable Growth, December 8, 2022, https://equitablegrowth.org/the-economic-impact-of-housing-insecurity-in-the-united-states/; Joe Hernandez, "Hate Crimes Reach the Highest Level in More than a Decade," NPR, September 1, 2021, https://www.npr.org/2021/08/31/1032932257/hate-crimes-reach-the-highest-level-in-more-than-a-decade; *The State of the Nation's Housing 2022* (Cambridge, MA: Joint Center for Housing Studies of Harvard University, 2022), https://www.jchs.harvard.edu/state-nations-housing-2022; Roudabeh Kishi and Sam Jones, "Fact Sheet: Anti-LGBT+ Mobilization on the Rise in the United States," ACLED, June 16, 2022, https://acleddata

.com/2022/06/16/fact-sheet-anti-lgbt-mobilization-is-on-the-rise-in-the-united-states; US Department of Justice, "2021 Hate Crime Statistics," March 15, 2024, https://www.justice.gov/hatecrimes/hate-crime-statistics; Elaine Waxman et al., "Food Insecurity Trended Upward in Midst of High Inflation and Fewer Supports," Urban Institute, September 2022, https://www.rwjf.org/en/insights/our-research/2022/09/food-insecurity-trended-upward-in-midst-of-high-inflation-and-fewer-supports.

8. Donna St. George, "School Shootings Rose to Highest Number in 20 Years, Federal Data Says," *Washington Post*, June 28, 2022, https://www.washingtonpost.com/education/2022/06/28/school-shootings-crime-report/; Véronique Irwin et al., "Report on Indicators of School Crime and Safety: 2021," Institute of Education Sciences, National Center for Education Statistics, June 2022, https://nces.ed.gov/pubsearch/pubsinfo.asp?pubid=2022092; Naaz Modan, "2023 School Shootings Outpace Record High from 2022," *K-12Dive*, November 10, 2023, https://www.k12dive.com/news/2023-school-shootings-outpace-2022-record-high/698809/.

9. American Immigration Council, "U.S. Citizen Children Impacted by Immigration Enforcement," June 24, 2021, https://www.americanimmigrationcouncil.org/research/us-citizen-children-impacted-immigration-enforcement; American Medical Association, "Issue Brief: National Snapshot of Overdose Epidemic," American Medical Association Advocacy Resource Center, updated June 2024, www.ama-assn.org/system/files/issue-brief-national-snapshot-overdose-epidemic.pdf; Centers for Disease Control and Prevention, "U.S. Overdose Deaths in 2021 Increased Half as Much as in 2020—But Are Still up 15%," May 11, 2022, https://www.cdc.gov/nchs/pressroom/nchs_press_releases/2022/202205.htm; National Centers for Environmental Information (NCEI), National Oceanic and Atmospheric Administration, "U.S. Billion-Dollar Weather and Climate Disasters," 2024, https://www.ncei.noaa.gov/access/billions/; Anne Elizabeth Sidamon-Eristoff et al., "Trauma Exposure and Mental Health Outcomes among Central American and Mexican Children Held in Immigration Detention at the United States–Mexico Border," *Developmental Psychobiology* 64, no.1 (December 30, 2021), https://doi.org/10.1002/dev.22227.

10. Elizabeth D. Steiner et al., *Teacher and Principal Well-Being Is an Essential Step for Rebuilding Schools: Findings from the State of the American Teacher and State of the American Principal Surveys*, ERIC Research Report, RR-A1108-04 (Washington, DC: Institute of Education Sciences, 2022).

11. Steiner et al., *Teacher and Principal Well-Being*.

12. EdWeek Research Center, *1st Annual Merrimack College Teacher Survey: 2022 Results*, Merrimack's Winston School of Education and Social Policy, June 2, 2022.

13. National Center for Education Statistics, "More Than 80 Percent of U.S. Public Schools Report Pandemic Has Negatively Impacted Student Behavior and Socio-Emotional Development," July 6, 2022, https://nces.ed.gov/whatsnew/press_releases/07_06_2022.asp; Tamsin Newlove-Delgado et al., "Annual Research Review: The Impact of COVID-19 on Psychopathology in Children and Young People Worldwide: Systematic Review of Studies with Pre- and Within-Pandemic Data," *Journal of Child Psychology and Psychiatry* 64, no. 4 (April 2023): 611–40, https://doi.org/10.1111/jcpp.13716; Lauraine Langreo, "How Many Teachers Have Been Assaulted by Students or Parents? We Asked Educators," *Education Week*, August 9, 2022, https://www.edweek.org/leadership/how-many-teachers-have-been-assaulted-by-students-or-parents-we-asked-educators/2022/08.

14. National Center for Education Statistics, "More Than 80 Percent of U.S. Public Schools Report Pandemic Has Negatively Impacted Student Behavior and Socio-Emotional Development"; Institute of Education Sciences, "School Pulse Panel," 2022, https://ies.ed.gov/schoolsurvey/spp/.
15. Bruce Perry, "Emotional Contagion," Neurosequential Network Stress & Trauma Series, March 30, 2020, YouTube video, https://www.youtube.com/watch?v=96evhMPcY2Y.
16. Bruce D. Perry et al., "Childhood Trauma, the Neurobiology of Adaptation, and 'Use-Dependent' Development of the Brain: How 'States' Become 'Traits,'" *Infant Mental Health Journal* 16, no. 4 (Winter 1995): 271–91, https://doi.org/10.1002/1097-0355(199524)16:4<271::AID-IMHJ2280160404>3.0.CO;2-B; Bruce Perry, "Understanding Regulation," Neurosequential Network Stress & Trauma Series, April 3, 2020, YouTube video, https://youtu.be/L3qIYGwmHYY.
17. Peggy McIntosh, "White Privilege and Male Privilege: A Personal Account of Coming to See Correspondence Through Work in Women's Studies," 1988, https://www.collegeart.org/pdf/diversity/white-privilege-and-male-privilege.pdf.
18. Urie Bronfenbrenner, "Ecological Models of Human Development," in *International Encyclopedia of Education*, 2nd ed., ed. T. N. Postlethwaite and Torsten Husen (Oxford: Pergamon, 1994), 37–43.
19. RYSE Center, https://rysecenter.org.
20. Vincent T. Cunliffe, "The Epigenetic Impacts of Social Stress: How Does Social Adversity Become Biologically Embedded?," *Epigenomics* 8, no. 12 (2016): 1653–69, https://doi.org/10.2217/epi-2016-0075.
21. Linnea Evans et al., "How Are Social Determinants of Health Integrated into Epigenetic Research? A Systematic Review," *Social Science & Medicine* 273 (March 2021): 113738, https://doi.org/10.1016/j.socscimed.2021.113738.
22. "Infographic: Epigenetics and Child Development: How Children's Experiences Affect Their Genes," Center on the Developing Child, Harvard University, https://developingchild.harvard.edu/resources/what-is-epigenetics-and-how-does-it-relate-to-child-development/.
23. Arline T. Geronimus et al., "'Weathering' and Age Patterns of Allostatic Load Scores among Blacks and Whites in the United States," *American Journal of Public Health* 96, no. 5 (May 2006): 826–33, https://doi.org/10.2105/AJPH.2004.060749.
24. Michelle A. Chen et al., "Immune and Epigenetic Pathways Linking Childhood Adversity and Health across the Lifespan," *Frontiers in Psychology* 12 (November 26, 2021): 788351, https://doi.org/10.3389/fpsyg.2021.788351.
25. Cunliffe, "The Epigenetic Impacts"; Evans et al. "How Are Social Determinants of Health Integrated?"
26. Vincent J. Felitti et al., "Relationship of Childhood Abuse and Household Dysfunction to Many of the Leading Causes of Death in Adults: The Adverse Childhood Experiences (ACE) Study," *American Journal of Preventive Medicine* 56, no. 6 (June 2019): 774–86, https://doi.org/10.1016/j.amepre.2019.04.001; Geronimus et al. "'Weathering' and Age Patterns."
27. World Health Organization and the United Nations Office of the High Commissioner for Human Rights, *Mental Health, Human Rights and Legislation: Guidance and Practice* (Geneva, Switzerland: World Health Organization and the United Nations Office of the High Commissioner for Human Rights, 2023), https://iris.who.int/bitstream/handle/10665/373126/9789240080737-eng.pdf?sequence=1.

28. Andrew S. Winston, "Scientific Racism and North American Psychology," in *Oxford Research Encyclopedia of Psychology* (May 29, 2020), https://oxfordre.com/psychology/view/10.1093/acrefore/9780190236557.001.0001/acrefore-9780190236557-e-516; Melanie Bertrand and Julie Marsh, "How Data-Driven Reform Can Drive Deficit Thinking," *Phi Delta Kappan* 102, no. 8 (April 26, 2021): 35–39, https://doi.org/10.1177/00317217211013936.
29. Jaime La Charite et al., "Specific Domains of Positive Childhood Experiences (PCEs) Associated with Improved Adult Health: A Nationally Representative Study," *SSM–Population Health* 24 (December 2023): 101558, https://doi.org/10.1016/j.ssmph.2023.101558.
30. Christina Bethell et al., "Positive Childhood Experiences and Adult Mental and Relational Health in a Statewide Sample: Associations across Adverse Childhood Experiences Levels," *JAMA Pediatrics* 173, no. 11 (September 9, 2019): e193007, https://doi.org/10.1001/jamapediatrics.2019.3007.
31. Ronald Gardner and Tammy Stephens-Pisecco, "Fostering Childhood Resilience: A Call to Educators," *Preventing School Failure: Alternative Education for Children and Youth* 63, no. 3 (2019): 195–202, https://www.tandfonline.com/doi/full/10.1080/1045988X.2018.1561408.
32. Mary A. Sciaraffa, Paula D. Zeanah, and Charles H. Zeanah, "Understanding and Promoting Resilience in the Context of Adverse Childhood Experiences," *Early Childhood Education Journal* 46 (2018): 343–53, https://doi.org/10.1007/s10643-017-0869-3.
33. Lucinda M. Sisk and Dylan G. Gee, "Stress and Adolescence: Vulnerability and Opportunity During a Sensitive Window of Development," *Current Opinion in Psychology* 44 (April 2022): 286–92, https://doi.org/10.1016/j.copsyc.2021.10.005.
34. Blair Paley and Natassia J. Hajal, "Conceptualizing Emotion Regulation and Coregulation as Family-Level Phenomena," *Clinical Child and Family Psychology Review* 25 (2022): 19–42, https://doi.org/10.1007/s10567-022-00378-4.
35. Qi Wang, "Cultural Pathways and Outcomes of Autobiographical Memory Development," *Child Development Perspectives* 15, no. 3 (September 2021): 196–202, https://doi.org/10.1111/cdep.12423.
36. Joyce S. Dorado et al., "Healthy Environments and Response to Trauma in Schools (HEARTS): A Whole-School, Multi-Level, Prevention and Intervention Program for Creating Trauma-Informed, Safe and Supportive Schools," *School Mental Health: A Multidisciplinary Research and Practice Journal* 8, no. 1 (March 2016): 163–76, https://doi.org/10.1007/s12310-016-9177-0.
37. World Health Organization and the United Nations Office of the High Commissioner for Human Rights, *Mental Health, Human Rights and Legislation*.
38. María Del Carmen Salazar, "A Humanizing Pedagogy: Reinventing the Principles and Practice of Education as a Journey toward Liberation," *Review of Research in Education* 37, no. 1 (March 1, 2013): 121–48, https://doi.org/10.3102/0091732X12464032.
39. Linda Darling-Hammond and Channa Cook-Harvey, *Educating the Whole Child: Improving School Climate to Support Student Success* (Palo Alto, CA: Learning Policy Institute, September 7, 2018), https://learningpolicyinstitute.org/product/educating-whole-child-report.
40. Tracey Benson and Sarah Fiarman, *Unconscious Bias in Schools: A Developmental Approach to Exploring Race and Racism* (Cambridge, MA: Harvard Education Press, 2019).
41. Shawn Ginwright, "Healing Centered," Keynote Address, SRI Summer Virtual Meeting 2020, August 13, 2020, YouTube video, https://www.youtube.com/watch?v=kPNJkr2hdQQ.

Chapter 1
1. Wen Li and Andreas Keil, "Sensing Fear: Fast and Precise Threat Evaluation in Human Sensory Cortex," *Trends in Cognitive Sciences* 27, no. 10 (October 2023): 341–52.
2. David W. Willis et al., *Early Relational Health National Survey: What We're Learning from the Field* (Washington, DC: Center for the Study of Social Policy, 2022), 10.
3. Mine Conkbayir, *Early Childhood and Neuroscience: Theory, Research and Implications for Practice* (London: Bloomsbury Academic, 2017).
4. Clancy Blair and Adele Diamond, "Biological Processes in Prevention and Intervention: The Promotion of Self-Regulation as a Means of Preventing School Failure," *Developmental Psychopathology* 20, no. 3 (2008): 899–911.
5. Blair and Diamond, "Biological Processes in Prevention and Intervention."
6. James M. Shine et al., "The Dynamics of Functional Brain Networks: Integrated Network States during Cognitive Task Performance," *Neuron* 92, no. 2 (2016): 544–54, https://doi.org/10.1016/j.neuron.2016.09.018.
7. Bruce D. Perry, "Fear and Learning: Trauma-Related Factors in the Adult Education Process," *New Directions for Adult and Continuing Education* 110, no. 2006 (2006): 22, https://doi.org/10.1002/ace.215; Bruce D. Perry and Richard Pollard, "Homeostasis, Stress, Trauma, and Adaptation: A Neurodevelopmental View of Childhood Trauma," *Child and Adolescent Psychiatric Clinics of North America* 7, no. 1 (1998): 33–51, PMID: 9894078.
8. Harvard University Center on the Developing Child, "Toxic Stress," https://developingchild.harvard.edu/science/key-concepts/toxic-stress/.
9. Bruce D. Perry et al., "The Impact of Neglect, Trauma, and Maltreatment on Neurodevelopment: Implications for Juvenile Justice Practice, Programs, and Policy," *The Wiley Blackwell Handbook of Forensic Neuroscience, Volumes I and II*, ed. Anthony R. Beech et al. (Hoboken, NJ: Wiley, 2018), 813–35.
10. Perry et al., "The Impact of Neglect, Trauma, and Maltreatment on Neurodevelopment," 822.
11. Perry et al., "The Impact of Neglect, Trauma, and Maltreatment on Neurodevelopment," 822.
12. Bruce D. Perry, "Understanding State-Dependent Brain Functioning," *Neurosequential Network Stress and Trauma Series*, Episode 2, March 26, 2020, YouTube video, https://youtu.be/PZg1dlskBLA.
13. Perry, "Understanding State-Dependent Brain Functioning"; Perry, "Fear and Learning," 22.
14. Perry, "Understanding State-Dependent Brain Functioning."
15. Perry et al., "The Impact of Neglect, Trauma, and Maltreatment on Neurodevelopment," 822.
16. Perry et al., "The Impact of Neglect, Trauma, and Maltreatment on Neurodevelopment," 822; Perry, "Understanding State Dependent Functioning."
17. Bruce D. Perry et al., "Childhood Trauma, the Neurobiology of Adaptation, and 'Use-Dependent' Development of the Brain: How 'States' Become 'Traits,'" *Infant Mental Health Journal* 16, no. 4 (Winter 1995): 271–91, https://doi.org/10.1002/1097-0355(199524)16:4<271::AID-IMHJ2280160404>3.0.CO;2-B.
18. Perry et al., "Childhood Trauma, the Neurobiology of Adaptation, and 'Use-Dependent' Development of the Brain."
19. Louis Cozolino, *The Neuroscience of Human Relationships: Attachment and the Developing Social Brain, Norton Series on Interpersonal Neurobiology* (New York: W. W. Norton, 2014).

20. Diane S. Kaplan, Ruth X. Liu, and Howard B. Kaplan, "School Related Stress in Early Adolescence and Academic Performance Three Years Later: The Conditional Influence of Self Expectations," *School Psychology of Education: An International Journal* 8, no. 1 (March 2005): 3–17, https://doi.org/10.1007/s11218-004-3129-5; Maureen E. Kenny et al., "Sources of Support and Psychological Distress among Academically Successful Inner-City Youth," *Adolescence* 37, no. 145 (Spring 2002): 161–82, PMID: 12003288; Michael Windle and Rebecca C. Windle, "Coping Strategies, Drinking Motives, and Stressful Life Events among Middle Adolescents: Associations with Emotional and Behavioral Problems and with Academic Functioning," *Journal of Abnormal Psychology* 105, no. 4 (November 1996): 551–60, https://doi.org/10.1037//0021-843x.105.4.551.
21. Eva Oberle and Kimberly A. Schonert-Reichl, "Stress Contagion in the Classroom? The Link between Classroom Teacher Burnout and Morning Cortisol in Elementary School Students," *Social Science & Medicine* 159 (June 2016): 30–37, https://pubmed.ncbi.nlm.nih.gov/27156042.
22. Patricia A. Jennings and Mark T. Greenberg, "The Prosocial Classroom: Teacher Social and Emotional Competence in Relation to Student and Classroom Outcomes," *Review of Educational Research* 79, no. 1 (March 1, 2009): 491–525, https://doi.org/10.3102/0034654308325693.
23. Jennings and Greenberg, "The Prosocial Classroom"; Robert J. Marzano, Jana S. Marzano, and Deborah J. Pickering, *Classroom Management That Works: Research-Based Strategies for Every Teacher* (Alexandria, VA: ASCD, 2003); David Osher et al., "A Comprehensive Approach to Promoting Social, Emotional, and Academic Growth in Contemporary Schools," in *Best Practices in School Psychology V, Volume Four,* ed. Alex Thomas and James Grimes (Bethesda, MD: National Association of School Psychologists, 2008), 1263–78.
24. Oberle and Schonert-Reichl, "Stress Contagion in the Classroom?"
25. Perry, "Understanding State-Dependent Brain Functioning."
26. Bruce D. Perry and Maia Szalavitz, *Born for Love: Why Empathy Is Essential—and Endangered* (New York: HarperCollins, 2011).
27. Oprah Winfrey and Bruce Perry, *What Happened to You? Conversations on Trauma, Resilience, and Healing* (London: Macmillan, 2021).
28. Christine R. Ludy-Dobson and Bruce D. Perry, "The Role of Healthy Relational Interactions in Buffering the Impact of Childhood Trauma," in *Working with Children to Heal Interpersonal Trauma: The Power of Play*, ed. Eliana Gil (New York: Guilford, 2010), 26–43.
29. Bruce D. Perry, "Understanding Regulation," *Neurosequential Network Stress & Trauma Series,* April 3, 2020, YouTube video, https://youtu.be/L3qIYGwmHYY.
30. Perry, "Understanding Regulation."
31. Perry, "Understanding Regulation."
32. Perry, "Understanding Regulation."

Chapter 2

1. Bessel A. van der Kolk, *The Body Keeps the Score: Brain, Mind, and Body in the Healing of Trauma* (New York: Penguin, 2014).
2. van der Kolk, *The Body Keeps the Score.*
3. Vincent J. Felitti and Robert F. Anda, "The Relationship of Adverse Childhood Experiences to Adult Health, Well-Being, Social Function, and Health Care," in *The Impact of Early Life*

Trauma on Health and Disease: The Hidden Epidemic, ed. Ruth A. Lanius, Eric Vermetten, and Clare Pain (Cambridge: Cambridge University Press, 2011), 77–85.
4. Arline T. Geronimus, *Weathering: The Extraordinary Stress of Ordinary Life in an Unjust Society* (New York: Little, Brown Spark, 2023).
5. Debra Durado, "To Improve Attendance, We Must Build Connection, Understanding, and Community," EdSource, August 14, 2023, https://edsource.org/2023/to-improve-attendance-we-must-build-connection-understanding-and-community/695625.
6. Thomas Dee, "Higher Chronic Absenteeism Threatens Academic Recovery from the COVID-19 Pandemic," *Proceedings of the National Academy of Sciences* 121, no. 3 (2024): e2312249121, https://doi.org/10.1073/pnas.2312249121.
7. Jeannie Myung and Heather J. Hough, "Why Aren't Students Showing up for School? Understanding the Complexity behind Rising Rates of Chronic Absenteeism," *Policy Analysis for California Education*, November 17, 2023, https://edpolicyinca.org/newsroom/why-arent-students-showing-school.
8. Myung and Hough, "Why Aren't Students Showing up for School?"
9. Myung and Hough, "Why Aren't Students Showing up for School?"
10. Centers for Disease Control and Prevention, *Youth Risk Behavior Survey Data Summary & Trends Report: 2011–2021*, https://www.cdc.gov/healthyyouth/data/yrbs/pdf/YRBS_Data-Summary-Trends_Report2023_508.pdf.
11. Maddy Reinert, Theresa Nguyen, and Danielle Fritze, Mental Health America, *The State of Mental Health in America 2023* (Alexandria, VA: Mental Health America, October 2022), https://mhanational.org/sites/default/files/2023-State-of-Mental-Health-in-America-Report.pdf.
12. Myung and Hough, "Why Aren't Students Showing up for School?"
13. Bruce D. Perry, "Understanding State-Dependent Brain Functioning," https://youtu.be/PZg1dlskBLA.
14. Perry, "Understanding State-Dependent Brain Functioning."
15. Perry, "Understanding State-Dependent Brain Functioning."
16. Adapted from Myung and Hough, "Why Aren't Students Showing up for School?"

Case Study 1

1. Trigger warning: The content in this vignette is sensitive and addresses the topic of sexual abuse. Although statistics reported across studies vary somewhat, research confirms that about 1 in 4 girls and 1 in 20 boys under eighteen years of age in the United States experience child sexual abuse (Centers for Disease Control and Prevention, "About Child Sexual Abuse," Child Abuse and Neglect Prevention, accessed September 5, 2024, https://www.cdc.gov/child-abuse-neglect/about/about-child-sexual-abuse.html#:~:text=Quick%20facts%20and%20stats&text=Although%20estimates%20vary%20across%20studies,States%20experience%20child%20sexual%20abuse). If you or someone you know is experiencing or has experienced sexual violence, please reach out for help if you need support. You are not alone.
   - National Sexual Assault Hotline: 1-800-656-HOPE (4673)
   - Rape, Abuse & Incest National Network (RAINN): www.rainn.org
   - National Domestic Violence Hotline: 1-800-799-7233
2. Second Step, "Child Protection in Schools: A Four-Part Solution," 2014, https://www.cfchildren.org/wp-content/uploads/programs/docs/child-protection-in-school.pdf.

Chapter 3

1. Ricky Robertson, "Leading for Resilience," featuring Mathew Portell, MEd, *Trauma and Resilience Podcast*, Episode 104, May 30, 2023, National Educators Association (NEA), https://podcasts.apple.com/us/podcast/episode-104-leading-for-resilience-with-mathew-portell-med/id1686970131?i=1000614606568 (emphasis added).
2. Bruce D. Perry, "Episode #47," *Trauma Informed Educators Network Podcast*, YouTube video, streamed live June 3, 2021, https://www.youtube.com/watch?v=3ZQHJ1nHhqs.
3. Michael P. Leiter and Christina Maslach, "To Curb Burnout, Design Jobs to Better Match Employees' Needs," *Harvard Business Review*, March 17, 2023, https://hbr.org/2023/03/to-curb-burnout-design-jobs-to-better-match-employees-needs.
4. Stephanie Marken and Sangeeta Agrawal, "K–12 Workers Have Highest Burnout Rate in U.S.," Gallup, June 13, 2022, https://news.gallup.com/poll/393500/workers-highest-burnout-rate.aspx.
5. Brandon Busteed, "To Fix U.S. Education, Free Our Teachers," *Forbes*, February 23, 2024, https://www.forbes.com/sites/brandonbusteed/2024/02/23/to-fix-us-education-free-our-teachers/?sh=34f121817a87.
6. Leiter and Maslach, "To Curb Burnout, Design Jobs to Better Match Employees' Needs."
7. Leiter and Maslach, "To Curb Burnout, Design Jobs to Better Match Employees' Needs"; Christina Maslach and Michael P. Leiter, *The Burnout Challenge: Managing People's Relationships with Their Jobs* (Cambridge, MA: Harvard University Press, 2022).
8. Bruce D. Perry, "Understanding Regulation," *Neurosequential Network Stress & Trauma Series*, April 3, 2020, https://youtu.be/L3qIYGwmHYY.
9. Kathryn Parker Boudett and Elizabeth A. City, *Meeting Wise: Making the Most of Collaborative Time for Educators* (Cambridge, MA: Harvard Education Press, 2014).
10. Perry, "Understanding Regulation."
11. Alex Shevrin Venet, "Role-Clarity and Boundaries for Trauma-Informed Teachers," *Educational Considerations* 44, no. 2 (2019): https://doi.org/10.4148/0146-9282.2175.
12. Michelle C. Brooten-Brooks, "How to Set Healthy Boundaries with Anyone: A Guide to Setting Limits with Parents, Partners, Friends, and Co-Workers," *Verywell Health*, September 14, 2023, https://www.verywellhealth.com/setting-boundaries-5208802.
13. Trigger warning: The following content discusses experiences of a particular form of microaggression titled "microassaults." Please prioritize your well-being when deciding whether to read this section. Despite the misleading prefix, microassaults are far from "micro" in impact and can have substantial and enduring effects on those who experience them. These subtle acts of hostility can accumulate over time, leading to a significant emotional and psychological toll and challenging those who experience them by challenging their sense of safety, belonging, and mental health. For those on the receiving end, these experiences can erode confidence, inflict emotional wounds, and perpetuate a sense of isolation. They contribute to a climate of exclusion and can significantly affect an individual's ability to thrive and engage with their school environment. The term "micro" is intended to signal the subtle and often everyday nature of these encounters. Derald Wing Sue et al., "Racial Microaggressions in Everyday Life: Implications for Clinical Practice," *American Psychologist* 62, no. 4 (May/June 2007): 271–86, https://doi.org/10.1037/0003-066X.62.4.271.
14. Leiter and Maslach, "To Curb Burnout, Design Jobs to Better Match Employees' Needs."

Case Study 2

1. Lisa Nishii, *Diversity and Inclusion at Work*, eCornell Course, Cornell University, 2022.

Chapter 4

1. Bruce Perry and Maia Szalavitz, *Born for Love: Why Empathy Is Essential—and Endangered* (New York: Harper, 2011).
2. Alex Shevrin Venet, "Role-Clarity and Boundaries for Trauma-Informed Teachers," *Educational Considerations* 44, no. 2 (2019), https://files.eric.ed.gov/fulltext/EJ1206249.pdf.
3. Bruce D. Perry, "Understanding Regulation," *Neurosequential Network Stress & Trauma Series*, April 3, 2020, https://youtu.be/L3qIYGwmHYY.
4. Oprah Winfrey and Bruce Perry, *What Happened to You? Conversations on Trauma, Resilience, and Healing* (London: Bluebird/Macmillan, 2021).
5. Bruce D. Perry et al., "Childhood Trauma, the Neurobiology of Adaptation, and 'Use-Dependent' Development of the Brain: How 'States' Become 'Traits,'" *Infant Mental Health Journal* 16, no. 4 (Winter 1995): 271–91, https://doi.org/10.1002/1097-0355(199524)16:4<271::AID-IMHJ2280160404>3.0.CO;2-B.
6. Trigger warning: The following content discusses experiences of microaggressions. Please prioritize your well-being when deciding whether to read this section. As introduced in chapter 3, despite the misleading prefix, microaggressions are far from "micro" in impact and can have substantial and enduring effects on those who experience them.
7. Rui Fu et al., "Racial Microaggressions and Anti-Racism: A Review of the Literature with Implications for School-Based Interventions and School Psychologists," *School Psychology Review* 53, no. 1 (2024): 1–16, https://doi.org/10.1080/2372966X.2022.2128601.
8. Fu et al., "Racial Microaggressions and Anti-Racism," 1; Derald Wing Sue et al., "Racial Microaggressions in Everyday Life: Implications for Clinical Practice," *American Psychologist* 62, no. 4 (May/June 2007): 271–86, https://doi.org/10.1037/0003-066X.62.4.271.
9. Fu et al., "Racial Microaggressions and Anti-Racism."
10. Sue et al., "Racial Microaggressions in Everyday Life."
11. Sue et al., "Racial Microaggressions in Everyday Life."
12. Sue et al., "Racial Microaggressions in Everyday Life."
13. Recent research highlights the pervasive impact of RMAs in K–12 educational settings, underscoring a pressing need for school-based interventions and awareness among school psychologists and educators. Fu et al. (2024) provide a comprehensive review of the literature surrounding the prevalence of RMAs and their detrimental effects on minoritized students, including heightened psychological distress and adverse academic outcomes. Annahita Ball's research emphasizes that microaggressions are common yet harmful acts of racism that occur in schools and can perpetuate institutional racism. Cerda-Smith et al. evaluated a schoolwide antiracist curriculum intervention and found that the program did not increase stress among students, suggesting the value of implementing such educational reforms to combat racism effectively. Literature is expanding to describe how teachers can mitigate the impacts of racial and language microaggressions through preventive strategies and educational reforms that promote equity. These studies highlight the urgent need for systematic approaches to reduce microaggressions and support racial equity in schools. They emphasize the role of educators, school curricula, and research-informed interventions to create safer and more supportive learning environments for all students.
14. Fu et al., "Racial Microaggressions and Anti-Racism."
15. Derald Wing Sue et al., "Disarming Racial Microaggressions: Microintervention Strategies for Targets, White Allies, and Bystanders," *American Psychologist* 74, no. 1 (2019): 134, http://dx.doi.org/10.1037/amp0000296.

16. Fu et al., "Racial Microaggressions and Anti-Racism."
17. Teachers can find a free and downloadable thermometer at https://www.optimalbrain integration.com/freeresources.

Case Study 3

1. Lawrence Hirschfeld, "Children's Developing Conceptions of Race," in *Handbook of Race, Racism, and the Developing Child*, ed. Stephen M. Quintana and Clark McKown (Malden, MA: Wiley, 2008), 37–54; Dominique Parris, Victor J. St. John, and Jessica Bartlett, "Resources to Support Children's Well-Being amid Anti-Black Racism, Racial Violence and Trauma," *Child Trends*, June 23, 2020, https://www.childtrends.org/publications/resources-to-support-childrens-emotional-well-being-amid-anti-black-racism-racial-violence-and-trauma; Erin N. Winkler, "Children Are Not Colorblind: How Young Children Learn Race," *PACE* 3, no. 3 (2009): 1–8.
2. Frances E. Aboud, "A Social-Cognitive Developmental Theory of Prejudice," in *Handbook of Race, Racism, and the Developing Child*, ed. Stephen M. Quintana and Clark McKown (Malden, MA: Wiley, 2008), 55–71; Hirschfeld, "Children's Developing Conceptions of Race"; Debra Van Ausdale and Joe R. Feagin, *The First R: How Young Children Learn Race and Racism* (Lanham, MD: Rowman & Littlefield, 2001); Winkler, "Children Are Not Colorblind."
3. Parris, St. John, and Bartlett, "Resources to Support Children's Well-Being."
4. Marianne Celano, Marietta Collins, and Ann Hazzard, "8 Tips for Talking to Your Child about Racial Justice," 2018, EmbraceRace, https://www.embracerace.org/resources/young-kids-racial-injustice.
5. Louise Derman-Sparks, Julie Olsen-Edwards, and Catherine M. Goins, *Anti-Bias Education for Young Children and Ourselves*, 2nd ed. (Washington, DC: National Association for the Education of Young Children, 2020), 18.
6. Rafael Outland, "Why Black and Brown Youth Fear and Distrust Police: An Exploration of Youth Killed by Police in the US (2016/2017), Implications for Counselors and Service Providers," *Open Journal of Social Sciences* 9, no. 4 (April 2021): 222–40, https://doi.org/10.4236/jss.2021.94017.
7. Administration for Children & Families, "What Is Historical Trauma?," accessed May 4, 2024, https://www.acf.hhs.gov/trauma-toolkit/trauma-concept.
8. Outland, "Why Black and Brown Youth Fear and Distrust Police."

Chapter 5

1. Julie Nicholson et al., *Trauma-Responsive Family Engagement in Early Childhood: Practices for Equity and Resilience* (New York: Routledge, 2021).
2. Ted Wachtel, *Defining Restorative* (Bethlehem, PA: International Institute for Restorative Practices, 2016).
3. Wachtel, *Defining Restorative*.
4. Wachtel, *Defining Restorative*.
5. Wachtel, *Defining Restorative*.
6. Joe Brummer, Margaret Thorsborne, and Lori Desautels, *Becoming a Trauma-Informed Restorative Educator: Practical Skills to Change Culture and Behavior* (Philadelphia: Jessica Kingsley, 2024).
7. Keith Hickman, *Creating Cultural Change in Education: Implementation Science and Capital Human Theory* (Bethlehem, PA: International Institute for Restorative Practices, 2022).

8. Catherine H. Augustine et al., *Restorative Practices Help Reduce Student Suspensions* (Santa Monica, CA: RAND, 2018), https://www.rand/org/pubs/research_briefs/RB10051.html.
9. Augustine et al., *Restorative Practices Help Reduce Student Suspensions*.

Case Study 4

1. Tori DeAngelis, "Thousands of Kids Lost Loved Ones to the Pandemic. Psychologists Are Teaching Them How to Grieve, and Then Thrive," *American Psychological Association* 53, no. 7 (October 1, 2022; updated April 21, 2023): 69, https://www.apa.org/monitor/2022/10/kids-covid-grief.
2. Early Education Division, California Department of Education, *Creating Equitable Early Learning Environments for Young Boys of Color: Disrupting Disproportionate Outcomes*, 2022, https://www.cde.ca.gov/sp/cd/re/documents/boysofcolor.pdf.
3. Tyisha Noise, *Adverse Childhood Experiences and Leadership in Urban Public Schools*, Doctoral dissertation, Azusa Pacific University (ProQuest Dissertations Publishing, 2019), Publication No. 13885736.
4. Yaphet Getachew et al., *Beyond the Case Count: The Wide-Ranging Disparities of COVID-19 in the United States, Survey Brief* (New York: The Commonwealth Fund, September 2020), https://www.commonwealthfund.org/sites/default/files/2020-09/Getachew_beyond_case_count_COVID_disparities_sb_v2.pdf.

Acknowledgments

Thank you to the students, teachers, staff, and families of Fall-Hamilton Elementary for your dedication and support. Your enthusiasm and commitment make our community exceptional. Special thanks to Metro Nashville Public Schools for their invaluable support and resources. Together, you all inspire and uplift, making this book possible. Your collective efforts and unwavering belief in the power of education are deeply appreciated.

—M. P.

I want to give thanks to my mother, Virginia Talley, for making me who I am today, and to my husband, Jurnell, for your sacrifice and support. Lastly, I want to thank the RYSE Center for giving voice to and honoring our youth and our ancestors.

—I. C.

I would like to thank God for the challenging circumstances and amazing opportunities which have converged to bring me to this moment. I would like to extend my gratitude to every single family I have served throughout my career and to thank my family who has been there every step of the way.

—T. N.

Thank you to the teachers and administrators who shared their collective wisdom in our book. We thank *you* and all the teachers across the globe for giving every child a voice and for being brain architects. You are the North Star holding the light to healing and building resilience for the future of our planet Earth.

—J. K.

I am profoundly grateful to David, Hannah, Isabella, and Anasofia, whose love and unwavering support have been my foundation throughout every book project. You make everything possible. Special thanks to Alice Blecker, a thought partner, educator, and artist whose beautiful illustrations elevate our work. Thank you to Harvard Education Press for inviting us to undertake this important project. And sincere appreciation to our editor, Shannon Davis, for your faith in our vision, your wise input, and for making the process so enjoyable. Finally, I honor the influence of bel hooks, who inspires me daily to bring love into my teaching and leadership. The type of love that challenges and changes us. More than a feeling, love as actions for justice.

—J. N.

About the Authors

Mathew Portell, MEd, leverages his multifaceted background as an educator, administrator, podcaster, writer, and international speaker to influence global education as a trailblazer and champion of trauma-informed practices. Serving as the principal of Fall-Hamilton Elementary in Nashville, Tennessee, Portell harnessed the latest neuroscience findings to revolutionize the institution into an exemplary model for trauma-informed education worldwide. In 2017, Edutopia conducted a comprehensive case study on Portell's school, producing an eight-minute documentary that garnered millions of views, propelling Portell to international recognition. His fervor and expertise have established him as a highly sought-after keynote speaker and facilitator on a global scale, with engagements across the United Kingdom, Australia, New Zealand, and numerous other countries. In addition, Portell is the visionary behind the Trauma Informed Educators Network, a global community of over 33,000 practitioners, which he supports through a biweekly podcast and an annual conference. Notably, he has been honored with several accolades, including the 2021 Elementary Principal of the Year for Metro Nashville Public Schools, catering to nearly 90,000 students. Portell is an alumnus of Tennessee State University, where he earned his BA and MEd. He further enriched his credentials by completing his administrative licensure at Trevecca University and obtaining trauma and resilience certifications one and two from Florida State University.

Ingrid L. Cockhren, MEd, utilizes her understanding of stress, trauma, and human development to transform her research and knowledge into trauma-informed and healing-centered community, workplace, and organizational solutions. Cockhren's academic journey, which spans a BS in psychology from Tennessee State University and an MEd in child studies from Vanderbilt University's Peabody College, is just the beginning of her extensive expertise. She specializes in positive and adverse childhood experiences (PACEs), collective and historical trauma, brain development, and developmental psychology.

Her career spans two decades and includes roles in juvenile justice, family counseling, early childhood education, professional development and training, and community education. She is a thought-provoking keynote speaker, an adjunct psychology professor at Tennessee State University, and the former CEO of PACEs Connection, an international social network dedicated to raising awareness of trauma and resilience. Over the last decade, Cockhren's consulting services have made a tangible difference for her clients and affiliates. Through Cockhren Consulting, she has coached leaders and executives and advised hospitals, colleges, PreK–12 schools, nonprofits, and other institutions. Cockhren is not just a professional, but an advocate for women and children and a community change agent. She sits on several boards for organizations that heal women, children, and communities.

Tyisha J. Noise, EdD, has approximately twenty-four years of experience supporting, nurturing, and creating success in underserved populations from coast to coast in both nonprofit and educational settings. This includes teaching most grades K–12 and early college, with specific and extensive expertise in special education. Dr. Noise has experience as both a teacher and administrator in the middle and high school contexts. She has extensive experience building systems to support best practices implementation and has been a passionate coach of teachers and leaders in academic content as well as special education, athletics, and leadership. Dr. Noise is an equity warrior currently leading work at the county level with a focus on creating equity for underserved student populations. Her current major projects include piloting culturally responsive afterschool programming and leading anti-bias work. Her primary research has been focused on how trauma-informed schools and leaders can cultivate better outcomes for students in underserved communities. Her personal passion project is creating faith-based content and products to uplift, encourage, and inform young children and their families through her company, HeavenSent Kids.

Julie Kurtz, MS, LMFT, is a renowned author and national speaker specializing in trauma and resilience, particularly within educational settings spanning from early childhood to twelfth grade. As the founder and executive director of the Center for Optimal Brain Integration, she is deeply committed to amplifying the voices of individuals who have experienced toxic or traumatic stress, striving to empower both children and adults. Kurtz's expertise shines through her coauthored works, which include groundbreaking titles such as *Trauma-Informed Practices for Early Childhood Educators*, *Culturally Responsive Self-Care Practices for Early Childhood Educators*, and *Trauma-Informed Practices for Early Childhood Leaders*. These resources provide invaluable guidance for educators and organizations seeking to foster healing, resilience, and equity within their communities. In addition to her contributions to professional literature, Kurtz is the creative force behind award-winning children's books like *Understanding My Brain: Becoming Human(E)!* These engaging works offer young children ages four to ten insight into their own brain, behavior, and emotional experiences, promoting understanding and self-awareness from an early age. Her dedication to supporting children's emotional well-being extends to innovative projects like Trigger Stop: Sensory and Emotional Check-In, an app designed to help children ages three to eight navigate their emotions and sensations. Outside of her professional work, Kurtz finds her greatest joy in her family, cherishing moments spent with her grandchild. Through her multifaceted work and personal connections, she continues to make a profound impact on the lives of children, educators, and communities alike, inspiring hope, healing, and resilience.

Julie Nicholson, PhD, MBA, is a champion for children, with over twenty years of leadership in direct service, higher education, and the nonprofit sector. As a professor of practice at Mills College in Oakland for seventeen years, she directed several innovative programs, including the Leadership Program in Early Childhood, a Joint MBA/MA Educational Leadership Program, and the Center for Global Play Research. In addition, she served as the research director for the Mills Teacher Scholars (now Lead by Learning). Her community-engaged scholarship and her teaching, research, and publications focus on social justice and equity in early childhood. She has specific expertise in bridging early childhood with public education, implementing trauma-responsive practices, and promoting equity in early education. She is coeditor of one book and coauthor of thirteen others, including *Principals as Early Learning Leaders: Effectively Supporting Our Youngest Learners* (Teachers College Press, 2022) and *Supporting Young Children to Cope, Build Resilience and Heal from Trauma Through Play: A Practical Guide* (Routledge, 2023). She regularly gives keynote speeches and provides professional development, coaching, and mentoring to schools, districts, organizations, and leadership teams both in the United States and internationally. Currently, she is vice president for implementation and impact at the Children's Funding Project, a nonprofit social impact organization that helps communities, states, and Native nations expand equitable opportunities for children and youth through strategic public financing.

Index

4-7-8 breathing, 159

abuse. *See* child abuse; sexual abuse
academic learning, 70, 146, 165, 180
academic support, 184
actions
    counselor/principal, 189
    school, 188–89, 208
    teacher, 188
Administration for Children & Families, 175
adrenal glands, 33
adrenaline, 33, 51
adults
    nervous system regulation, 41–48, 89–117
    nonparent, 14
    relationships and connections, 91–94
    stress de-escalation of, 110–17
    See also discipline/classroom management; school environments
adverse childhood experiences (ACEs), 9, 13. *See also* positive childhood experiences (PCEs)
agency
    choice, 184
    control, 55, 101–2, 191–92
    voice, 132–33, 165
agenda, 102, 106–7. *See also* brain
alarm state, 36
alert state, 36
American Psychological Association, 2
amygdala, 28
antiracism programs, 153

anxiety, 2, 52, 75, 119–20, 137, 148–49, 171, 199–200, 207.
    See also depression; mental health; stress
art, 85, 163

balloon breathing, 159
Becks Anxiety Inventory, 120
Becks Depression Inventory, 120
behaviors, 49–79
    bodies response and, 51–53
    brain functioning and, 34–37
    challenging/dysregulated, 183–93
    fight/flight/freeze/fawn, 57–59, 64–74, 183–93
    harmful, 108
    internal states and, 53–57
    is communication, 38–41
    microaggression, 149–54
    microassaults, 106, 150
    microinsults, 149
    state-dependent regression and, 67–74
being clear, 108
being direct, 108
being responsive, 108–9
belly breathing, 158
belonging feelings, 14–15
"Be Well Rooms," 89, 125–26
big body movement, 49, 162, 165
bilingual advocate, 85
bioecological model, 7–8
blood pressure, 28, 33, 120, 123
body detective, 156

233

The Body Keeps the Score: Brain, Mind, and Body in the Healing of Trauma (van der Kolk), 51
bottom-up pathway, 43–44, 47, 133, 158
brain
  amygdala, 28
  basics, 27–30
  bottom regulation of, 133
  functioning and behavior, 34–37, 181–82
  hindbrain, 27–28
  integration, 29–30
  limbic system, 28
  memory, 29
  mirror neurons, 39–40, 127, 134, 201
  neurochemicals in, 33–34
  prefrontal cortex, 28–29
  regulation breaks, 46
  self-regulation, 29
  sensory cortex, 28
  See also nervous system regulation; regulation pathways
breathing. *See specific breathing*
Bronfenbrenner, Urie, 7–8
Brummer, Joe, 195–96
bullying issues, 11, 45, 62, 115–16, 152–54, 187–89
burnout, 94–110
  chronic stressors to, 96–97
  and cortisol levels, 41
  K–12 employees, 95
  mitigation, 97–110
  preventing, 109–10
  roots of, 94–97
  signs of, 120
  See also educators/education

Calm Down Time (Toddler) Listening to My Body (Garcia), 142
calming activities, 140, 146
calming corners, 142–48
calm state, 36

caregivers, 15–16, 122, 189, 206–7
case studies
  children's stress, 167–75
  co-regulation, 134–37
  COVID-19 pandemic, 203–10
  educators' health, 119–24
  fair school environment, 106–9
  ill system preparation, 81–88
  microaggression, 150–52
  relational regulation, 132–34
  reset and calming spaces, 143–45
  staff member, 115–17
  state-dependent regression, 70–74
  S.T.O.P. tool, 198–202
  tool kit regulation, 162–66
Center on the Developing Child, 30
check-ins, 43, 91–92. *See also* peer check-ins
child abuse, 86
child protection, 87
chill skills, 157–60, 157–61. *See also* skills
chronic absenteeism, 59–60
chronic stress, 10, 33, 53, 68, 96–97
classroom management. *See* discipline/classroom management
classroom regulation poster, 160
clubs/interest groups/gathering places, 129–30
co-creating next steps, 186
collaborative efforts, 153
communication, 15, 38–41, 54, 68, 100, 186, 196
community
  circles and classroom meetings, 128
  creating, 172–73
  family and, 174
  lack of supportive, 97
  LGBTQIA+, 3, 62, 104, 131
  school and, 10–11, 84–86, 122–23, 172–73, 207–8
  traditions, 16–17
competence/mastery feelings, 63–64
compromised safety, 73

conflicts, 14–15, 97, 104–5, 194–95
connections. *See* informal connections; organic connections; relationships/connections; structured connections
coping skills, 146–47. *See also* skills
co-regulation, 134–37, 186, 201
Cornell University, 121
cortex, 135–36, 161–66. *See also* brain; prefrontal cortex; sensory cortex
cortisol, 33, 41, 51
counselor/principal actions, 189
COVID-19 pandemic, 2, 59, 104, 203–10
creativity and reflection, 68–69, 72

decompression spaces, 163–65. *See also* calming corners; reset spaces
deep breathing, 44, 99, 134–36, 158–59, 199
de-escalation, 110–17
DEI. *See* diversity, equity, and inclusion (DEI)
depression, 2, 52, 61, 75, 120, 131, 149, 205–6
Derman-Sparks, Louise, 172
discipline/classroom management, 177–202, 212
　dysregulated behaviors, 183–93
　learning/accountability, pathways to, 180–82
　punitive practices, 193–96
　restorative practices, 194–202
　safety improvement for, 179–80
district leadership, 124
diversity, equity, and inclusion (DEI), 12, 121
dysregulation, 6–7, 37–40, 51, 70, 71–72, 78, 111–12, 135–36, 143–48, 157, 178, 180–83, 185, 187–93. *See also* regulation

early childhood, 23, 129, 138, 159, 171
earthquakes, 6, 31, 154, 160

educators/education
　acknowledged/respected, 77–78
　advice for, 17–19
　agency and control, 101–2
　campaign, 86
　conflicts, 104–5
　effort recognition of, 102–3
　as emergency responders, 4–5
　as facilitators of, 127–37
　fair, 105–9
　fight/flight/freeze/fawn behaviors, 64–74
　health of, 119–24
　healthy stress response systems, 32–33
　humanizing, 20
　ill system of, 81–88
　jobs of, 78
　K–12, 95
　mental health support for, 103–4
　as navigators, 41–48
　needs of, 74–79
　neurobiology in, 27–30
　physiological needs, 75–76
　professional development of, 78, 147–48, 174
　racial justice, 20
　reset spaces for, 142–48
　in RMAs detecting, 152–54
　safety perceptions of, 76–77
　sense of belonging, 77
　systems, 5–7
　trauma-informed practice, 19, 87
　voices, ideas, and feedback, 56–57
　whole child, 20
　See also workload; workplace
effort recognition, 102–3
elementary school, 22, 41, 106, 129, 138, 183–85, 189–93. *See also* school
emergency responders, 4–5, 154–62
emotional/psychological safety, 180
emotion meter, 157

endorphins, 34
engaging/learning conditions, 64
executive function skills, 29.
    See also skills
exhaustion, 41, 68, 96

fairness improvement, 105–9
family and community
    involvement, 174
fawn behaviors, 59, 66–67, 189–93.
    See also behaviors
fear state, 36–37
federal funding, 87
"feel-good chemicals." *See* endorphins
fight behaviors, 57–58, 65, 183–85.
    See also behaviors
"fight-or-flight" hormone.
    See adrenaline
financial counseling, 148
flight behaviors, 58, 65, 185–87.
    See also behaviors
focus strategies, 184
freeze behaviors, 58, 66, 187–89.
    See also behaviors
friends support, 14

gardening, 163
genetic expression, 9–10
Ginwright, Shawn, 21
glimmer sharing, 140
group norms and expectations, 192
growth mindset, 165

Harvard University, 30
healing, 7–13, 83–87. *See also* stress;
    trauma/resilience/healing
healing-centered practices, 12, 21, 174,
    206, 212
healthy and unhealthy levels, 30–33
healthy professional boundaries,
    100–101
healthy stress response systems, 32–33
heightened reactivity, 67–68, 72

Highs and Lows. *See* Roses and Thorns
high school, 14–15, 38–39, 94, 129,
    139, 150–52, 187–89, 205–6.
    See also school
hindbrain, 27–28, 57, 197. *See also*
    brain
historical and structural factors,
    12–13, 175
holistic learning, 2
homeostasis, 30
home-school connection, 170
hormones. *See* neurochemicals
humanizing education, 20
human needs, 74, 79, 96–97, 110

ill system preparation, 81–88
impulsive decisions, 69–70, 73
inclusive classroom environments,
    170–71
individual and interpersonal factors,
    9–10, 82–84, 121–22, 169–72,
    206–7
individualized education plan (IEP),
    82, 132
informal connections, 93
institutional racism, 174–75
insufficient recognition, 97
intellectual safety, 180
intentional disengagement pathway,
    46–47
internal states
    alarm, 36
    alert, 36
    calm, 36
    emotion meter for, 157
    factors affecting, 53–57
    fear, 36–37
    isolation, 55–57
    of nervous system, 34–37
    personal control, 55
    terror, 37
    uncertainty/unpredictability, 54–55
    unfamiliarity, 53–54

invisible backpacks, 6–7
isolation, 55–57

jobs, 3, 75–78, 96–97, 101–2,
    168, 180
journaling, 163

K–12 educators, 95
know the "why," 17

lack of fairness, 97
leadership. *See* district leadership;
    school
learning, 2–5, 30, 63, 122, 156–59,
    192–94, 212
  academic, 70, 146, 165, 180
  and accountability, 180–82
  conditions, 64
  educators' behaviors, 64–74
  holistic, 2
  humanizing, 20
  journey, 18
  peer, 12, 14
  students' behaviors, 57–59
Leiter, Michael, 95–96, 109
letting go, 102
levels of stress. *See* positive stress;
    tolerable stress;
    toxic stress
LGBTQIA+ community, 3, 62,
    104, 131
limbic system, 28
listening to bodies, 165
loss of care and belonging, 73
Lynwood Elementary School, 147

mandatory mistakes, 164
Mariposa Restorative Room, 147–48
Maslach, Christina, 95–96, 109
meeting fatigue, 99
mental health, 3, 11, 19–20, 86. *See also*
    anxiety; burnout; depression;
    stress; trauma

microaggressions, 108–9,
    149–54
  defined, 149
  RMAs, 149, 152–54
  subcategories of, 149–50
microassaults, 150
microinsults, 149
micro-interventions, 153
microinvalidations, 149–50
middle school, 47, 98, 129, 139,
    185–87, 203–4.
    See also school
mirror neurons, 39–40, 127, 134, 201.
    See also brain
mistakes, 165
model repair and restoration, 201
Morning Movement and Regulation
    Choice Board, 162, 165
movement activities, 163
My Moods. My Choices, 143

natural disaster. *See* earthquakes;
    tornado
nervous system regulation, 6, 17–18,
    41–48
  adults, 41–48, 89–117
  in discipline/classroom management,
    180–82
  importance of, 179–80
  internal states of, 34–37
  mirror neurons, 39–40
  PNS, 51
  SNS, 51
  students, 41–48, 125–66
  See also regulation pathways; school
    environments
neurobiology, 25–48
  basics of, 27–30
  neurochemicals, 33–34
  stress levels, 30–33
  See also brain; stress
neurochemicals, 33–34
neuroscience, 17–18

nonjudgmental tone, 171
nonparent adults, 14
norepinephrine (noradrenaline), 33, 51

Oberle, Eva, 39–40, 40–41
opportunities, 18, 63, 83–85, 99–100, 127, 146–47, 180–81, 212
Optimal Zone of Regulation, 36, 112–14, 140, 191, 193
organic connections, 93
Ortega, Juan, 71–73
oxytocin, 33, 93

paradigm shift, 5–7, 143, 211
parasympathetic nervous system (PNS), 51
parent(s), 15, 71–73, 153, 172–73, 186, 206–7
partnering on tasks, 98
patience, 133
pausing, 135, 200–201
PD. *See* professional development (PD)
peer check-ins, 129
peer learning, 12, 14
Pence, Robin, 143–45, 147
perceived control, 97
Perry, Bruce D., 4, 32, 34, 42, 46, 67, 91, 136
personal control, 55
personalized interaction, 191
physical safety, 179
physical symptoms, 51–53, 72, 187
physiological needs, 60–62, 75–76
playing games, 140
playing music or singing, 140
PNS. *See* parasympathetic nervous system (PNS)
positive childhood experiences (PCEs), 13–17, 42
  caregivers, 15–16
  community traditions, 16–17
  feelings of belonging, 14–15
  friends support, 14

nonparent adults, 14
safety/protection, 15
positive stress, 30–31
power sharing, 174
predictable schedules, 137–39, 137–42
  changing of, 142
  in elementary school, 138
  in middle and high school, 139
  in preK–kindergarten, 138
  routine, 139–40
  in seventh-grade class, 141–42
  tips for, 140
  transitions, 139–40
  See also school environments
preforgiveness, 18
prefrontal cortex, 28–29
preK–12 school, 3, 8, 21
preK–kindergarten, 138
present focus, 69, 72
preventive practices, 194–95
proactive educators, 109–10
problem-solving, 6, 29–30, 63, 70–71, 110, 135–36, 161, 196–98
professional development (PD), 21, 72–73, 78, 103, 105, 147–48, 174, 199
professional esteem and effectiveness, 73–74

questions. *See* reflection/discussion questions

racial–ethnic socialization, 153
racial justice education, 20
racial microaggressions (RMAs), 149, 152–54. *See also* microaggressions
racism
  discussions of, 171–72
  as form of trauma, 20
  institutional, 174–75
  scientific, 12–13
  systemic, 11–12

reading, 163
red, yellow, and green cards, 164
referrals, 147
reflection/discussion questions, 19, 37, 87–88, 101, 110, 117, 124, 153–54, 175, 193, 210
   de-escalation, 110–12
   reframing/engaging cortex, 114–15
   regulation, 112–14
regulation
   bin, 160
   bottom-of-the-brain, 133
   breaks, 99
   breathing for self, 158–59
   classroom, 160
   co-regulation, 134–37
   dysregulation vs., 35, 111–12
   Optimal Zone of, 36, 112–14, 140, 191, 193
   practices, 163–64
   strategies for relations, 132–33
regulation pathways, 41–48, 165–66
   bottom-up, 43–44
   intentional disengagement, 46
   to learning/accountability, 180–82
   relational, 42–43, 46–48
   top-down, 44–45
relational co-regulation, 135
relational empathy, 186
relational observation, attunement, and listening, 169–70
relational regulation, 42–43, 46–48, 133, 165, 201
relational safety, 184
relationships/connections
   adults, 91–94
   building, 170
   check-ins for, 91–92
   clubs/interest groups/gathering places, 129–30
   community circles and classroom meetings, 128
   co-regulation, 134–37

   facilitating, 172–73
   home-school, 170
   informal, 93
   organic, 93
   patience for, 133
   peer check-ins, 129
   regulating strategies for, 132–33
   remembering, 93–94
   smart start for, 127–28
   storytelling circles, 92–93
   structured, 91
   students, 127–37
relaxing, mindful, calming activity, 140
remembering concept, 93–94
reset spaces, 142–48, 163–64
   benefits of, 146–47
   Mariposa Restorative Room, 147–48
   materials in, 142–43
   students to, 145–46
   See also calming corners
resilience, 7–13, 83–87. *See also* stress; trauma/resilience/healing
resistance to change, 69–70
resolution and accountability, 184–85, 187, 189, 192
resources connection, 187
responsive practices, 108–9, 194–95
restorative practices, 174, 194–202
   circles and, 194–96
   healing-centered and, 12, 174, 206, 212
   questions to, 195
   responsive/preventive, 194–95
   S.T.O.P tool, 197–98
   whole child education, 20
RMAs. *See* racial microaggressions (RMAs)
Roses and Thorns, 130
RYSE model, 7–13, 82, 120, 169
   historical and structural, 12–13, 175
   individual and interpersonal, 9–10, 82–84, 121–22, 169–72, 206–7

RYSE model (*continued*)
  school and community, 10–11,
      84–86, 122–23, 172–73,
      207–8
  systemic, 11–12, 86–88, 123–24,
      173–74, 209–10

safety
  compromised, 73
  emotional/psychological, 180
  intellectual, 180
  perceptions, 62, 76–77
  physical, 179
  and protection, 15
  relational, 184
  school environment, 179–80
  social, 180
Schonert-Reichl, Kimberly, 41
school
  actions, 188–89
  and community factors, 10–11,
      84–86, 122–23, 172–73,
      207–8
  counselor, 16, 49, 98, 185–86, 207–8
  elementary, 129, 138, 183–85,
      189–93
  leadership, 120–21
  middle, 129, 139, 185–87
  principal, 147
  responsiveness, 186
school environments, 89, 212–13
  for adults, 89–117
  burnout mitigation in, 94–110
  calming corners/reset zones/regulating
      spaces, 142–48
  microaggressions in, 149–54
  predictable schedules for, 137–42
  relationships/connections in, 91–94,
      127–37
  safety improvement in, 179–80
  stress de-escalation in, 110–17
  for students, 125–66
  See also restorative practices

school stress
  COVID-19 pandemic, 2, 59, 104,
      203–10
  discipline/classroom management for,
      177–202, 212
  environments for, 89–117, 125–66
  policies and practices for, 12, 78
  RYSE model, 7–13
  safe and confidential ways for, 56
  signs of, 30, 35–36, 57, 67,
      158, 180
  social epigenetics and, 9–10
  state-dependent regression in, 67–74
  urgency to reduce, 2–5
  See also educators/education; stress;
      students
scientific racism, 12–13
seeking consent, 186
self-awareness, 6, 18, 29, 37, 70–71,
      135–36, 146–47, 196–97
self-regulation, 18, 29, 94, 136,
      158–59, 184, 208
sense of belonging, 14–15, 62–63, 73,
      77, 173
sensory cortex, 28
serotonin, 34
sexual abuse, 31, 82–83, 86, 115
short regulation breaks, 99
skills
  chill, 157–60, 157–61
  coping, 146–47
  executive function, 29
  social emotional, 5–6, 29, 63, 147,
      148, 158, 194
  teach, 18
slowing down, 200–201
smart start, 127–28
SNS. *See* sympathetic nervous system
      (SNS)
social emotional skills, 5–6, 29, 63,
      147, 148, 158, 194
social epigenetics, 9–10
social justice, 171

social safety, 180
soliciting feedback, 102
staff member, 18, 115–17
staff wellness lounges, 104
state-dependent regression, 67–74
   creativity and reflection, 68–69
   exhaustion, 68
   heightened reactivity, 67–68
   impulsive decisions, 69–70
   present focus, 68–69
   resistance to change, 70
   vigilance and misinterpretation, 68
stopping, taking, observing, proceed (S.T.O.P) tool, 197–99, 201
storytelling circles, 92–93
stress
   bodies response to, 51–53
   contagious, 39–41
   COVID-19 pandemic, 2, 59, 104, 203–10
   defined, 30
   emergency responders of, 154–66
   introduction, 1–23
   is contagious, 39–41
   levels of, 30–33
   neurobiology of, 25–48
   positive, 30–31
   reducing strategies, 165–66, 184–89, 191–93
   response system, 4, 31–34
   tolerable, 31
   tool kit, 154–62
   toxic, 31–32
   trauma/resilience/healing, 7–13, 83–87, 122–24, 169–74, 207–10
stretching, 163
structured connections, 91
students
   bullying issues of, 115–16, 152–54, 187–89
   challenging/dysregulated behaviors of, 183–93

competence/mastery feelings, 63–64
co-regulation of, 136–37
engaging/learning conditions, 64
fight/flight/freeze/fawn behaviors, 57–59
invisible backpacks, 6–7
navigators of, 41–48
needs for, 59–64
nervous system regulation, 41–48, 125–66
physiological need of, 60–62
referrals for, 147
relationships and connection, 127–37
response to emergency, 154–66
safety perceptions, 62
self-awareness, 6, 18, 29, 70–71, 135, 146
sense of belonging, 62–63
states of behavior, 35–37
S.T.O.P. tool for, 197–99, 201
threats and punishments for, 5
using reset/calm spaces, 145–46
See also burnout; predictable schedules; RYSE model; school environments
supportive community, 97
sympathetic nervous system (SNS), 51
systemic factors, 11–12, 86–88, 123–24, 173–74, 209–10
systemic racism, 11–12

teacher actions, 188
teach skills, 18. *See also* skills
terror state, 37
thermometer, 157
Thumbs Up and Thumbs Down. *See* Roses and Thorns
TikTok, 132–33
tolerable stress, 31
tool kit, 154–56, 154–62
   body detective, 156
   chill skills, 157–61

cortex captain, 161–62
emotional emergency, 155
emotion meter, 157
top-down pathway, 44–45, 46–47
tornado, 6, 31, 154, 160, 206
toxic stress, 9–13, 31–32, 82–87
transitions, 139–40
trauma-informed practice, 19, 87
trauma/resilience/healing, 7–13, 83–87, 122–24, 169–74, 207–10
trauma-responsive practice, 19–20, 63, 168, 211–12
traumatic stress. *See* toxic stress
turning lights, 140

uncertainty/unpredictability, 54–55
Understanding My Brain, Becoming Humane, 142
unfamiliarity, 53–54
unsustainable workload, 96

vigilance and misinterpretation, 68, 72
visual and auditory aids, 140
visual cues, 184

visual schedules, 137–38. *See also* predictable schedules
voice, agency, and control, 102, 165, 174
voices, ideas, and feedback, 56–57
voice tone/facial expressions/body language, 191

walking, 163
whole child education, 20
workload, 97–100
  healthy professional boundaries and, 100–101
  meeting fatigue, 99
  opportunities to reflect, 99–100
  partnering on tasks, 98
  short regulation breaks, 99
  See also educators/education
workplace, 105–6
  and basic human needs, 96–97
  conflicts in, 104–5
  fairness improvement in, 105–9
  unfairness in, 105–6
  See also educators/education